26.34

Jon Sutherland
Diane Sutherland
Edited by: Doris Patterson

BUSINESS AND ADMINISTRATION

NVQ Level 3

HODDER
EDUCATION
AN HACHETTE UK COMPANY

Orders: please contact Bookpoint Ltd, 130 Milton Park, Abingdon, Oxon OX14 4SB. Telephone: (44) 01235 827720.
Fax: (44) 01235 400454. Lines are open from 9.00 – 5.00, Monday to Saturday, with a 24 hour message answering service.
You can also order through our website www.hoddereducation.co.uk

If you have any comments to make about this, or any of our other titles, please send them to educationenquiries@hodder.co.uk

British Library Cataloguing in Publication Data
A catalogue record for this title is available from the British Library

ISBN: 978 1 444 144 222

Impression number   10 9 8 7 6 5 4 3 2 1
Year   2016, 2015, 2014, 2013, 2012, 2011

Hachette UK's policy is to use papers that are natural, renewable and recyclable products and made from wood grown in sustainable forests. The logging and manufacturing processes are expected to conform to the environmental regulations of the country of origin.

Cover photo from © Moment / Culture / Photolibrary.com.
Typeset by Fakenham Prepress Solutions, Fakenham, Norfolk NR21 8NN
Illustrations by © Richard Duszczak
Printed in Italy for Hodder Education, An Hachette UK Company, 338 Euston Road, London NW1 3BH by LEGO

Contents

Introduction

The *Level 3 Certificate in Business and Administration* is aimed at individuals who have experience of office-based skills. Learners can choose from a range of optional units. The units aim to show the ability to negotiate, supervise, manage and contribute to the running of an office. There is a wide range of units and the qualification is competence-based.

The Level 3 NVQ Certificate is part of a broader range of qualifications, all of which have been accredited onto the Qualifications and Credit Framework (QCF). The awarding body is Oxford Cambridge and RSA Examinations (OCR). The qualification has also been endorsed by the Council for Administration (CfA).

In order to achieve a Level 3 Certificate in Business and Administration students need to complete a total of 30 credits. At least 20 of these credits must be from Level 3 units. This book offers not only the four mandatory units but also six of the most popular optional units. There is a broader range of optional units available. This book is aimed specifically at Certificate candidates but could also be used by those working towards the Level 3 Diploma in Business and Administration, which requires an additional 7 credits to complete.

You will need to complete 13 credits from the mandatory units, 11 credits from the Group B optional units and a minimum of 6 others from either Group B or Group C optional units.

Not all of the units are worth the same number of credits. The mandatory units are:

- 301 – Manage own performance in a business environment (3 credits)
- 302 – Evaluate and improve own performance in a business environment (3 credits)
- 303 – Work in a business environment (4 credits)
- 309 – Communicate in a business environment (3 credits).

The optional units contained in this book have proved to be the most popular:

- 305 – Work with other people in a business environment (4 credits)
- 312 – Design and produce documents in a business environment (4 credits)
- 318 – Analyse and report data (6 credits)
- 322 – Plan and organise meetings (5 credits)
- 328 – Deliver, monitor and evaluate customer service to internal customers (3 credits)

- 329 – Deliver, monitor and evaluate customer service to external customers (3 credits).

Probably unlike anything you have done before, assessors will visit you in your working environment and make a judgement as to whether or not you have met the requirements for a unit. They will confirm this by signing an evidence record sheet that shows that the assessment process for the unit has been completed. They will agree with you about the best source of evidence for each unit. They will discuss with you the best way to assess you and also confirm the times, dates and places that any assessments will happen. The methods of assessment need to be valid, reliable, safe and suitable to you. In the vast majority of cases, the evidence that you present for optional units will provide the evidence needed for the mandatory units.

One of the key features of this book is that it identifies the typical type of evidence that you will need for each part of every unit covered. In some cases particular learning outcomes or assessment criteria may not be part of your normal working duties. However, real work situations are the best way to gather evidence and your assessor will be able to guide you in ways in which to gather evidence, even in situations where certain areas are not part of your normal work.

This book aims to cater primarily for candidates who are in part-time or full-time work. It provides guidance on the types of evidence and an explanation of all the assessment criteria and learning outcomes. The book can also be used as a guide for realistic working environments for full-time students carrying out a series of tasks in a model office or during work experience.

Features of the book

This book has four main goals:

- To explain what the learning outcomes mean and what you have to show that you can do or understand to help you meet the assessment criteria.

- To check that you actually understand what is involved by providing you with a range of suggestions as to how you could gather information for evidence.

- To provide you with suggestions as to how you could generate enough evidence for the assessment criteria.

- To explain exactly what type of evidence the assessor is looking for and whether there are any specific things that you should include.

The book systematically covers each learning outcome and each assessment criterion. Sometimes it is better to consider a number of assessment criteria or learning outcomes together. You will find clear headings for each learning outcome and each assessment criterion. Each of the chapters covering a unit gives you the following:

- a basic introduction which describes the purpose of the unit

- the assessment requirements which explain the scope of the unit and the main areas you will be covering

- a complete coverage of each learning outcome and each assessment criterion

- a gathering information feature that aims to point you in the right direction in terms of questions to ask, points to consider and evidence that you could begin to assemble

- a clear indication of what evidence the assessor is expecting to see for each of the assessment criteria.

The book has the following additional features:

What is Evidence ?

This feature appears at the end of each unit and lists typical evidence as recommended by OCR. Your assessor will be able to give you guidance on the appropriateness of evidence that you may have readily to hand. The assessor may also suggest how you can generate acceptable evidence. The assessor will also to able to give you guidance on particular evidence and how it can be used to cover more than one learning outcome.

Each unit consists of a number of learning outcomes. Usually, there are a number of Knowledge based learning outcomes at the beginning of each unit. These are marked in the Assessment Requirements section with the letter K. The remaining learning outcomes of the unit are Performance based and are marked with the letter P.

Gathering information

The Gathering information boxes are designed to help you think about your job role and the possible evidence you might be able to present. These often contain advice or a series of questions to ask yourself to give you an insight into the type of evidence that you can gather to show your assessor.

Give it a go

Give it a go boxes are designed so that you can try out tasks particularly if they are not part of your normal workload. If you do this sort of work on a regualr basis, they can be used as a guide to the type of evidence that you might need to present to the assessor. They are designed as practical sets of tasks and can also be used as portfolio evidence to show your ability to complete a series of activities relevant to the assessment criteria.

Assessment – how it works

Your centre will carry out an initial assessment, identifying any competences and knowledge that you already have. It will then focus on the gaps. This is an ideal way of helping you to understand how you need to go about collecting evidence. It will also identify a strategy in evidence collection that is acceptable to the assessor.

Your assessor will plan your assessments with you to help you find the best source of evidence for you to use and the best way of assessing you as an individual. The assessor will also confirm with you when and where any assessments will take place.

The assessors will make all the necessary assessment decisions. You will need to produce evidence to demonstrate competence when meeting all the assessment criteria. This will be planned alongside the assessor. As we have seen, the methods of collecting evidence have to be:

- Valid – evidence needs to measure your knowledge or skills. You need to know what is required of you and the evidence that you produce needs to do the job of meeting the assessment criteria.

- Reliable – simply it needs to show that you consistently meet the criteria because you may be assessed by different people in different places. It also needs to be your own work.

- Safe and manageable – it should not put any unnecessary demands on you or the organisation that you work for.

- Suitable – so the majority of the evidence that you collect is part of your normal working week. Collecting evidence should not involve carrying out too many tasks on a one-off basis.

Only approved and qualified assessors will examine your evidence. Evidence generally falls into three different categories:

- It can be an observation by an assessor on how you actually carried out a process.

- It can be a work product, such as a document.

- It can be an observation by a witness or a statement that confirms you show competence in a particular area of work.

It is a good idea to look at typical ways of collecting evidence. This is summarised in Table 1.

Table 1

What evidence?	Who is allowed to do it?	What does it mean?
Observation	Assessor	The assessor records their observation of you carrying out a task.
Questioning	Assessor	The assessor asks you questions to test your knowledge of facts, procedures, principle, theories and processes.
Professional discussion	Assessor	This is an in-depth discussion that allows you to present evidence of competence, skills, knowledge and understanding.
Witness testimony	Work colleagues/assessor	This can be a written or verbal statement, where a work colleague provides a list of skills and competences that they have witnessed you performing in the workplace.
Personal statements	Yourself/witness/assessor	You give an account of what you did, backed up by evidence or witnesses, such as log books or diaries. These need to be countersigned.
Performance evidence	Yourself	Some physical proof that you can do something, such as a document or a video. It can also be an assessor's observation of you working or a witness statement.

All the evidence that you collect and submit to the assessor needs to meet the requirements of the assessment criteria. This means there is a wide variety of evidence that you can produce:

- Assessor's observation of workplace activities – the assessor provides information based on their observations.

- Products – these are reports, letters, memos, printouts, emails, etc.

- Expert witnesses – these are identified and trained by the centre and are used to help fill any gaps in the competence of assessors. They also handle evidence that may be confidential or sensitive.

- Witness testimony – statements indicating how you carry out your job. Witnesses must direct the information in their testimonies to describing what the candidate did.

- Candidate reports – verbal or written reports that describe activities and processes, such as a work diary.

- Reflective accounts – an account written by you of how you carried out part of your job and including a record of events that happened.

- Recognition of prior learning or achievement – this will be determined by the assessor, who will look at what you have studied in the past, or have achieved already. They will match these to the assessment criteria.

- Professional discussions – structured and planned in-depth discussions to support observation or products.

- Verbal or written questions – these are used to fill in gaps only where knowledge is not obvious.

- Projects – extended pieces of practical or written work involving planning and research.

- Assignments – practical or written tasks to test your skills, knowledge and understanding.

- Case studies – these require you to produce a report, identifying problems, analysing issues, discussing and justifying solutions and presenting recommendations.

- Audio or video recordings – these can be used to support observation or discussions.

- Simulations and role plays – these are sets of tasks in a 'realistic working environment'.

You will discover that it is often the case that when you provide evidence for one part of a unit it can also be used as evidence or part-evidence for another unit. This is known as a holistic approach to assessment and your assessor will be able to guide you through this. It makes a great deal of sense to use this approach because it means you will not have to duplicate evidence. It also means that your evidence will come from a range of activities. It is a far more efficient way of collecting evidence.

■ Organising your evidence

Each unit you study will have an evidence record sheet which links the evidence to the assessment criteria. You will give each piece of evidence a reference or location and identify the assessment method used and the assessment criteria covered. The assessment record sheet needs to be signed by you and, after it has been checked, signed by the assessor. In due course it may also be counter-signed by the internal verifier, who monitors and samples the assessment decisions of the assessors.

This means that your portfolio of work can be a combination of written material, observation records, witness statements, or a mix of some or all of the different types of evidence that we have looked at. Wherever possible, real work evidence is best, even if this means evidence that comes from you working on a voluntary basis or during work experience. Simulations are acceptable and these can be carried out in a realistic working environment at your centre. They tend to be used only when you cannot complete the units because you do not have the opportunity to practise them in a real work environment.

■ Managing the evidence

This is a business and administration course and a basic piece of advice is to start as you mean to go on. This means from the very beginning organising your evidence. It needs to be kept safe, logged and given reference numbers and you need to be absolutely clear about its location if it is not in your portfolio of evidence.

By systematically completing the evidence record sheets and then the evidence summary sheets you will be able to identify each piece of evidence, and which units, learning outcomes and assessment criteria it relates to. This will make the job of assessment much easier. It also means that you can quickly identify gaps and particular assessment criteria that are proving to be a problem. Discuss these problem areas with your assessor and they will be able to suggest solutions.

Acknowledgments

The authors and publishers would like to thank the following for permission to reproduce material in this book:

Figure 301.4 pressmaster / Fotolia.com; Figure 303.1 deanm1974 / Fotoloia.com; Figure 303.2 Gina Sanders / Fotolia.com; Figure 303.4: Monkey Business / Fotolia.com; Figure 312.2 pressmaster /Fotolia.com; Figure 312.3 AVAVA / Fotolia.com; Figure 322.3 Yuri Arcurs / Fotolia.com; Figure 328.1 uwimages / Fotolia.com; Figure 329.1 vgstudio / Fotolia.com; Figure 318.2 alphaspirit / Fotolia.com; Figure 329.5 The Fairtrade Foundation

Every effort has been made to obtain the necessary permission with reference to copyright material. The publishers apologise if inadvertently any sources remain unacknowledged and will be glad to make the necessary arrangements at the earliest opportunity.

Manage Own Performance in a Business Environment

■ Purpose of the unit

This unit is about taking responsibility for managing, prioritising and being accountable for your own work in a business environment.

■ Assessment requirements

There are four parts to this unit. The first two parts look at planning and prioritising and behaving in a way that supports effective working. The second two parts focus on your own efforts and abilities in these areas. The four parts are:

1 Understand how to plan and prioritise work and be accountable to others – the purpose and benefits of planning work, negotiating realistic targets, prioritising targets and setting timescales, the purpose and benefits of keeping people informed about progress and of letting them know in good time if work plans need to be changed, recognising and learning from mistakes, the purpose of guidelines, procedures and codes of practice that are relevant to your own work. (K)

2 Understand how to behave in a way that supports effective working – the purpose and benefits of setting high standards, ways of setting high standards and dealing with pressure, accepting setbacks and dealing with them, being assertive and its meaning in work tasks, situations where it is necessary to be assertive, the purpose and benefits of taking on new challenges and adapting to change, treating others with honesty, respect and consideration, types of behaviour that show these characteristics and those that do not, the purpose and benefits of supporting others at work. (K)

3 Be able to plan, prioritise and be accountable for own work – negotiating and agreeing realistic targets and achievable timescales, prioritising targets, planning work tasks to make best use of time, effective working methods and resources, keeping others informed of progress, completing work to agreed deadlines or renegotiating timescales and plans, taking responsibility for your own work and accepting responsibility for mistakes, evaluating results of mistakes made and making changes to work and methods, following agreed work guidelines, procedures and codes of practice. (P)

4 Behave in a way that supports effective working – setting high standards for own work, demonstrating drive and commitment to achieve these standards, adapting work and work methods to deal with setbacks and difficulties, using own needs and rights to achieve tasks and priorities when

necessary, engaging with opportunities and taking on new challenges, looking for opportunities, changing ways of working to meet new requirements, treating others with honesty, respect and consideration, helping and supporting other people in work tasks. (P)

◾ 1. Understand how to plan and prioritise work and be accountable to others

1.1 Explain the purpose and benefits of planning work and being accountable to others for own work

The importance of planning

One of the most frustrating aspects of work, no matter what your role, is the feeling you are constantly working hard just to cope with the flow of work passing across your desk. Being effective in any role requires a degree of planning. You also need to prioritise the work which is presented to you.

There are many ways of achieving effective planning, but this is only part of being effective. You need to provide information and carry out work according to the timetable of others, as they may need what you are doing by a particular date, as well as being careful with the information which you receive, as it may be confidential.

Most senior members of staff who ask you to carry out work on their behalf will wish to be updated and kept informed of progress. There may be many different demands on your time, and in this part of the unit we examine methods of dealing with this.

Action planning is an important part of objective, target and goal setting, and problem solving. Action planning can assist a business to plan for the future, ensuring that as situations change they can be controlled. It converts the goals or objectives into a series of steps, in order to decide what has to be done, by whom and by when. It involves the following steps:

1 Decide a goal or objective.

2 Identify the actions required to achieve this objective or goal.

3 Amend the plan by identifying where it may go wrong.

4 Having identified what may go wrong, make another plan or decide on more actions to deal with these problems.

The action plan should describe in detail how the business gets from where it is to where it wishes to be, and how it proposes to do this.

Effective action planning requires all those involved to be aware of their role in the process and includes the following:

1 Development of the rough action plan – this will combine the work of all individuals involved. It will list their proposed activities to reach the goal. Once this has been completed, all of the activities are then discussed and the most appropriate ones are chosen. These then need to be arranged in the correct order to make sure the tasks are completed by the time they are needed.

2 Each step in the action plan needs to be detailed in terms of what, when and who.

3 Constant checks are necessary to make sure the skills, time, finance and materials involved will be available when required. Those involved also need to consider how problems may be dealt with if an unexpected problem arises.

The importance of planning cannot be stressed enough. Good planning skills mean you should be able to:

● waste less time

● make fewer mistakes

● stick to deadlines

● not have to start tasks again

● get more job satisfaction out of your work

● generally work better

● have the opportunity to take on more challenging work

● be valued by others for your abilities.

Each task or project is given to you or a team on the assumption that it will be completed. Making the best use of your time and resources in order to achieve a successful outcome, by the deadline, is important.

At the outset you should have a clear idea as to how, when and why you are undertaking particular work and precisely what the person who has allocated the work to you wants. Only by knowing what is required of you will you know what it is you have to produce or complete.

You need to know precisely what is wanted, who wants it, when they want it and, above all, how you are going to do it. You may wish to use a log sheet, or perhaps amend one so that it has sections covering the following:

● What is the required outcome.

● Tasks needed to achieve the required outcome (break down complex tasks or projects into manageable chunks which can be dealt with stage by stage).

- Appropriate methods to be used. (How are you going to go about doing the task? What will it involve you having to find out and where is that information? Do you have access to or knowledge of the methods which are the most appropriate?)

- Timescale. (The first real question is whether the timescale is reasonable. Is it possible for you to meet the deadline which has been set? If you have any doubts about meeting the deadline, you should say so as soon as possible.)

- Resources required. (Note down any people, equipment or materials which you will need in order to complete the task.)

Your priorities may not be shared by those who give you the tasks. Neither will your priorities necessarily be the same as those of the people with whom you may have to work to complete the tasks.

Prioritising is therefore a matter of personal judgement, but also negotiation with the task setter and other members of staff on whom you will need to rely to get the job done.

Organisational skills are important. In the business world, disorganisation can lead to time wastage and mistakes, some of which may potentially damage the business. Organisational skills include the following:

- Being neat and tidy.

- Keeping a diary of dates and times when meetings should be attended or a record of any expected visitors.

- Having an efficient way of storing and retrieving documents, whether this is paper-based or on a computer system.

Figure 301.1

- Having a follow-up procedure in place so that documents are always available at the correct date and time.

- Managing time efficiently. Time management does not apply just to those people who are in authority and have many responsibilities at work.

- Having a to-do list. This list can be weekly and/or daily and should detail the duties that have to be carried out.

Planning does not involve just daily or even weekly routines – sometimes you have to plan weeks or months in advance (for example, on a wall planner).

Increasingly, people use personal digital assistants (PDAs). These are mini-computers which have a function which allows you to enter information regarding deadlines and will alert you to the fact that deadlines are coming up. They can also alert you when you need to be in a particular place, at a particular time, so that you do not miss meetings or appointments.

Some organisations may use an electronic diary method of logging appointments and meetings. This information can be stored on the main computer system, or on a laptop or in a personal organiser. The electronic diary enables the user to scroll forwards or backwards by day, month or year. It can store around five years' worth of days and dates, for example provisional or confirmed appointments, mark out holiday periods and set reminders for particular days, weeks or months in the future. The electronic diary can also be used to detail appointments and cross-reference appointments or tasks.

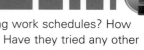

Gathering information

Does your organisation have a preferred way of planning work schedules? How do your colleagues keep track of what has to be done? Have they tried any other means of planning that have not worked for them? Which method of planning do you prefer to use?

Organised employees are self-disciplined and keep their work area neat and tidy, and have lists of things to be completed. They carry out tasks in a strict order, rather than concentrating on work which they enjoy doing. Without some organisation, work can become chaotic and put unnecessary pressure on you. It is therefore important to become organised at work in order to:

- be able to find what you need

- not keep everything in your head but on paper, where you can use it to remind you

- make the best use of your time

- finish jobs quicker

- be more confident

- be less stressed

- be more efficient.

A work area needs to be used to its best effect. Things which you use on a daily basis should be on your desk. Things you do not use very often should be put away in drawers. Stationery items and files and any other spare paperwork or equipment can also be placed in drawers. This means that what is on your desk should be what you are working on, together with any equipment you need to do that work. Many people use a series of trays on their desk – in-trays, pending trays and out-trays – so that paperwork can be categorised.

Being accountable to others

It is rare to be working in a situation where you have no dealings with others, or you do not rely on them or them on you to carry out work. In most work situations tasks carried out by individuals are part of a much larger series of activities. Each individual makes a contribution to an overall work goal or task. Others will rely on you to complete work and to manage that work. In a similar way you will rely on others to complete work to a suitable standard and in a timely manner.

These working relationships, commitments and mutual dependencies are based on professionalism and trust, and rely on each individual involved taking responsibility for their own work and recognising how important it is to others.

In some situations the allocation of work, the order in which it is carried out and to whom it needs to be passed will follow a strict set of guidelines. Your contribution to the overall task may be at a precise step or phase of the work. You may have to rely on others to have carried out certain tasks before that work passes to you to complete the next stage. Alternatively, it may be you who initiates the work and then passes it on to others for completion.

Gathering information

How do your work tasks fit into the work schedules of others? Are you reliant on others to complete work before you can start your tasks? Who do you have to pass completed, or partially completed, work on to? Ultimately, to whom are you accountable?

1.2 Explain the purpose and benefits of negotiating realistic targets for work and ways of doing so

You will often have routine jobs to complete as part of your workflow, as well as new or specific tasks assigned to you. Setting a realistic target is always a matter of judgement. You need to be sure that whatever target you agree takes into account the rest of your workflow. However, it may also be the case that you will need to give a particular task priority, which will have an impact on the rest of your work.

Setting a realistic target is best achieved by negotiation. Give a reasonably realistic estimate of how long a particular task may take, taking into consideration when the work is needed. The purpose of this is for both the task setter and the task completer to know what has been agreed and when the work can be expected. The benefits are to be able to plan for the task to be completed by a specific date, for the task setter to know when the work will be ready and for there to be agreement as to the priority of that task.

Some tasks and responsibilities may be obvious and do not require you to have to confirm your responsibilities with anyone. But many job roles within a team can become confused and will change over time. The term 'working arrangements' may mean a variety of things, including:

- start and finish times of the day
- days of the week to be worked
- times of breaks, including lunch
- who is in charge if the team leader or manager is not available
- when work and progress will be reviewed
- who has the right to instruct the team
- how the team goes about getting additional resources when they need them.

One of the tried and tested ways of target setting is to remember the word SMART. It stands for:

- Specific
- Measurable
- Achievable
- Realistic
- Timely or time bound.

This is a good way of approaching each target. Specific means that you know precisely what is involved in the task and what you are expected to do. Measurable means that you know the range of the task and when it has been completed. Achievable means having the skills and resources available to carry it out. Realistic means not only that the task should be possible given your skills, expertise and resources, but also that the task is not asking for something that is not possible given the circumstances. Timely, or time bound, is all about knowing when the task has to be completed and whether this is a reasonable amount of time to carry out that task.

As far as deadlines are concerned, it is useful to think about three different sets of timescales which could apply to a task or an objective:

● short term – this really means that the activity has to be done immediately or certainly over the next few days

● medium term – possibly a couple of weeks or perhaps months, but certainly not immediately or some vague time in the future

● long term – probably reserved for really major objectives, perhaps as long as a year, but certainly several months.

Working with resources and to a timescale involves a degree of planning and forward thinking. The more complicated an objective, the more resources may be needed and the longer the timescale may be. It is always valuable to think about complicated tasks or objectives as a series of mini-tasks or mini-objectives. This means that it is useful to break down the major job into manageable chunks. You need to know what has to be done first before you can get on with the next phase of the work.

In business, breaking down large tasks and objectives (sometimes referred to as projects) is known as setting up milestones. This means identifying key things which have to be done en route to completing the main objective. It also means identifying resources and how long each of the milestones is likely to take you as a team. Table 301.1 gives an example.

Table 301.1

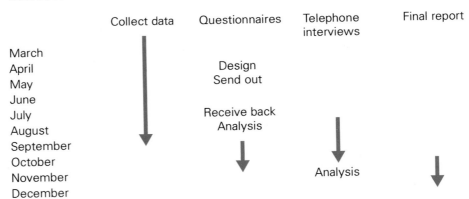

Using this kind of table, the team would be able to work out where they would need resources and when the most work would have to be done.

Give it a go

Look at the milestone diagram and answer the following questions:

1 When would the team need to have a stock of envelopes and stamps ready?

2 When would the team need to be using the telephones for the interviews?

3 What months could be used to analyse the information they have collected?

4 What is the overall length of the task?

5 When must the final report be ready?

1.3 Describe ways of prioritising targets and setting timescales for own work

Timescales refer to both the time that you have been given to complete a task and the deadline you have been given. This means that any task needs to be prioritised in terms of its importance. Broadly speaking, tasks can be divided into the following categories as far as priorities are concerned:

● urgent and important tasks

● urgent but not important tasks

● important but not urgent tasks

● not urgent or important tasks.

The natural thing is to concentrate on the first two priorities and to put the other two to the side. The problem is that they are often forgotten.

Give it a go

Using the four different sets of priorities in the above list, try to categorise your immediate workload at work. Where do most of the tasks or jobs you have to do fall? If there are many tasks in the higher priority categories, how do you prioritise them?

Timescales and priorities can often involve a mix of different routine, non-routine, urgent and non-urgent work. Typically, at any time you will have a variety of different tasks awaiting completion:

● First, you will have a series of fairly routine tasks to complete.

● Second, you will have large tasks to complete.

● Third, you may have sets of tasks which do not occur that often.

● Fourth, you will have small tasks which tend to crop up when you least expect them to.

Broadly speaking, all of these tasks can still be considered to be either:

- important or not important
- urgent or non-urgent.

You will ultimately decide whether a job is important and urgent enough to drop everything else and get on with it. The following have to be borne in mind when making that decision:

- What will happen if you don't manage to meet the deadlines you have been set?
- Who actually gave you the work? How senior are they in the organisation?
- How long will the job really take to do if you concentrate on it (assuming that you can)?
- Can the deadline be altered?

Give it a go

Have another look at the list of tasks which you prioritised in the last activity. Which of the tasks could be set aside for now? Which of the tasks could have their deadlines renegotiated? Have you prioritised your tasks because some of them have been demanded by senior or important people?

Gathering information

In your normal working week you may begin with a clear idea of your workload and when specific tasks have to be completed. Inevitably, as the week progresses, changes will have to be made to this as new work comes in and priorities may change. How do you keep track of the work that you know you need to complete by a specific day or time? How do you balance this against new work that arrives? How often is it the case that priorities suddenly change and urgent work becomes non-urgent, or new work becomes the priority?

1.4 Describe the types of problems that may occur during work, and ways of dealing with them

There is some additional information in 1.6, as encountering problems and solving them will often have an impact on others and they will need to be informed that work may be delayed.

All sorts of problems can arise during the course of the working day. Some problems will require assistance or guidance, but on many occasions it will be up to you to decide how to deal with the problem and whether to carry on. Each time you need to make a judgement once you have encountered a problem. By carefully looking at the situation you may find an answer to the problem without having to consult someone else. Showing your initiative becomes second nature as you become more experienced. You will be able to solve problems quicker and more easily.

Depending on your work role, you may encounter any number of problems during the course of a working day. Some examples of typical problems and possible solutions could include the following:

- Work colleague phones in sick – if possible, check with them to see whether they had any urgent or important work that needed to be completed. Find out how far they have got with this work and where all the information is being kept. Someone else may need this information to complete the task. If necessary, complete the task yourself, or find a member of the team who is not only competent but has sufficient time to finish the task.

- Computer network goes down – the first thing you will need to know is how long the network may be out of action. Once you know this you can then plan for the rest of the time. How much of the work can be carried out manually? Is there information on the network that is necessary to finish ongoing tasks? Has this been backed up anywhere else that does not require access to the network? If there is no immediate prospect of the network being fixed, or the ability to complete the tasks manually, then anyone who will be affected by the work schedule delay must be informed.

- Meeting room has been double-booked – is there an alternative venue for one of the meetings? Which is the smaller and/or less important of the two meetings? Could one of the meetings be rescheduled or relocated? If an alternative venue is available, have all the participants been notified of the change? Is it necessary to place notices in reception to direct the participants to the new venue?

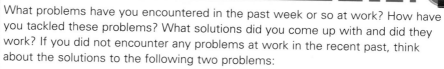

Gathering information

What problems have you encountered in the past week or so at work? How have you tackled these problems? What solutions did you come up with and did they work? If you did not encounter any problems at work in the recent past, think about the solutions to the following two problems:

1 A member of your team is not pulling their weight. This has been noticed in recent weeks. Before this they were hard working and a valued member of the team. Now everyone is complaining about them.

2 You were expecting information from another department to arrive at the beginning of the week. You and your team were relying on this information to carry out a series of tasks that needed to be ready by the end of the week. You have now been informed that the information will not be available until the middle of the week. You will not have enough time to finish it by Friday.

When you encounter a problem the first thing to do is to shape that problem and work out how it has occurred and what it is affecting. Once you know the scope of the problem you can look for solutions. Usually there is a way around the problem, but on some occasions solutions are more difficult to come by, so you may need to be creative. Some people solve problems simply by using trial and error, looking at different solutions until they come up with the right one.

Problem solving is all about decision making. Typical problems will have a series of options or solutions. This means that you can approach the problem in a standard way:

- What exactly is the problem? Define it.
- Gather any facts to help understand what the problem is and what it affects.
- Think about possible options and solutions.
- Consider and compare each of the options.
- Select the best option. Try not to compromise, but choose a way forward.
- If necessary, explain your solution to someone else, particularly if they are involved or affected.
- Follow through the solution and assess its effectiveness.

1.5 Explain the purpose and benefits of keeping other people informed about progress

By keeping others informed about progress you can warn them at the earliest possible date if you are experiencing problems in meeting their deadline. You can then ask for additional help, or time. It also means that the person waiting for the work can factor in these delays and change their plans accordingly.

Deadlines state the latest date by which a particular task must be achieved. Some people actually respond well to having a series of deadlines as they are challenged by the prospect of having to complete jobs by a particular date. At the earliest stage possible, it is important that you begin to take account of deadlines and work towards the completion of tasks by the time you are required to complete them. This becomes all the more difficult if you have to rely on others in the team to contribute towards the completion of work.

What happens when it becomes obvious that the deadline is not going to be met for whatever reason? It would be rare in working for a business to ever enjoy the opportunity to work on one task, finish it and then start on another. Work is never quite that simple. Therefore, as we have seen, prioritising jobs is the only real way forward.

Each deadline and task needs to be looked at on an individual basis. The best policy, however, is that as soon as it becomes obvious to you and the team that a deadline will not be met, you should inform your team leader or the individual who has set you the task. There may well be room for renegotiation of the deadline (pushing the deadline back) or for work that is not a priority to be put aside so that you can concentrate on the most important deadline.

Unexpected problems which could lead to a deadline becoming difficult or impossible to meet could include the following:

- staff shortages (either not enough staff or staff off sick or on holiday leave)
- other work piling up which has the same degree of priority
- difficulty in collecting information to do the task
- difficulty in contacting individuals you need to communicate with to complete the task.

In many cases, difficult deadlines and unexpected problems arise out of not having thought about the task and its implications in enough detail at the very beginning.

Progress reporting is particularly important if a certain task or complex series of jobs is scheduled to take place over an extended period of time. It is usual for there to be progress meetings, during which individuals involved in the overall task feed back to the rest of the group on the general progress that they have made, together with any problems they may be encountering. It is an opportunity to streamline information gathering and any procedures that may be holding up the task as a whole.

These meetings can help improve the efficiency of the overall project. They can deal with problems as they are arising. They can also assist in dealing with potential hold-ups before they become a major concern. By keeping everyone involved in the project informed about progress, bottlenecks or hold-ups in information exchange and work can be identified. Solutions can then be applied to them, perhaps by giving individuals access to information quicker or more easily. Additional resources can be allocated where necessary, as can additional assistance if required by particular individuals, and, perhaps, some work can be passed on to others.

On a daily basis, with smaller tasks that you need to complete in order for others to use your work for their own tasks, you should try to adopt a similar approach by:

- confirming with individuals that work will be completed by an agreed date
- informing them if there have been delays, the reason for those delays and anything you have done to deal with them
- telling them if you need more information or are awaiting more information and any impact that is likely to have.

Regular updates on work progress are always valuable to others, as they can amend their own schedules if you inform them in a timely manner that a delay is possible.

Gathering information

Do you have routine project progress meetings? How often do these take place? How effective are they in informing others and ensuring that the project remains on schedule?

1.6 Explain the purpose and benefits of letting other people know in good time if work plans need to be changed

One quality that many employers are looking for in employees is flexibility. This means not necessarily doing things which you are not trained to do but rather being prepared to help or adapt what you do to make sure that jobs are completed as soon as possible. The more multi-skilled you become through your experience of different types of work, the more valuable you will become to your employer.

Flexibility is important as you need to put aside any fears of not knowing precisely what to do in a new situation. You need to show that you have a desire to learn new things. Flexibility cuts across nearly all work and, as we will see, it is often impossible to set your mind to carry out a task in a particular way, on a particular day, without either being interrupted or having to change your plans.

Once you have planned a job and have a clear understanding as to what is required of you, you are in a position to actually begin work. Team leaders, supervisors and managers may want progress reports. So it is important that you know where you are, how much you have done and when you are likely to finish.

With other work and activities going on around you which may drag you away from the task at hand, it is vital that you remember where you are. When you return to the work you can then pick it up from where you left it. As your work on the task continues, you may foresee some difficulties – perhaps a vital piece of information is missing or you discover that there are insufficient envelopes or paper. Anything could happen. Rather than waiting until the problem stops you from working, you should try to make sure that whatever the difficulty is has been dealt with before you reach that point. If you realise that information is missing and that you will need it before the end of the week, take steps to acquire it immediately. In the case of the missing envelopes, a timely order to the stationery supplier would solve this potential difficulty.

It is rare to work in a business where things do not change. Workloads change, priorities change, the availability of staff changes with sickness and holiday leave. Sometimes the business is busier for no apparent reason and there may be pressures on you to carry out other duties which take you away from the tasks which you had expected to be doing. If you are aware of where you are with a task and you know where all the information is because it is filed away safely, you can return to it as soon as you have a chance.

If you are working with several other people, or carrying out work for various supervisors or managers, they will not necessarily know that you have had to abandon the work you were doing for them. Contingencies are situations which arise that could affect your ability to continue working on a particular task. What this means is that you will have to think about what is necessary in order to complete the task if you cannot spend the amount of time on it that you expected. If the task is not completed, who will be affected? What will happen if you cannot meet the deadlines? Providing the person who has set you the work knows what your alternative plans are, they may be happy for you to reschedule the work and delay its completion.

Some work cannot be rescheduled, however, because it is important and urgent. In order to think about how to handle this, you should set aside a short period of time and think through the implications of not finishing the work before you decide that you must put it aside. At all times you must contact the person who has set you the work, or the person who is relying on you to finish the work. They must be aware and then they can put their own contingency plans into action.

Gathering information

How do you handle situations when you have to tell others that work plans need to be changed? Do you do this formally or informally? In other words, is there a meeting where this kind of information can be exchanged? Do you inform them verbally or in writing? How do people react to such changes in work plans? Is there a set procedure within your organisation for this purpose?

1.7 Explain the purpose and benefits of recognising and learning from mistakes

It is always a good policy to admit that you have made a mistake and to then apologise. This avoids unnecessary workplace friction. In order to learn from that mistake you need to work out what went wrong. Once you have identified this you can then try to improve on that area of your work. You can learn from others in this way. They may be able to suggest solutions to common mistakes. If, for example, you are consistently missing deadlines, you may want to use either a to-do list with dates and prioritise the work you have, or to use Post-it note reminders of particular deadlines.

There will be occasions when there is no one to ask for assistance or guidance and it will be left to you to decide whether to carry on with a task or to wait. You will need to make a judgement as to whether you can proceed with the work or not. You must use your initiative (or judgement) in these situations. There may well be an answer to your questions without having to wait and ask someone.

It is also the case that you will be expected to show your initiative and not ask for assistance every time there is a problem which you cannot immediately solve yourself. Gradually, you will be able to make these judgements as to whether to continue or whether you really do need to wait for help.

It is inevitable that no matter what stage of your career, you will encounter situations where you made the wrong choice. This could be a question of doing something wrong or maybe failing to remember a task deadline. In recognising and then learning from such mistakes you can improve your overall administrative abilities. It also helps to prove the fact that planning is extremely important and that the value of very simple tools such as to-do lists is huge.

It is certainly the case that everyone will make mistakes. But you can turn mistakes into an advantage. The first thing to remember is that you will undoubtedly make mistakes and you should be prepared for them. You need to spot the warning signs. A prime example would be a situation where you have been given a task that you may not be able to complete. You may know from experience that this particular task will cause problems and you need to ask for additional resources and skills (assistance from others) in order to ensure the job is completed on time.

Another key is to not blame others for mistakes. If you are a team leader then you will have to take responsibility even if it was not your direct fault. Blaming others will only mean that some members of the team will become less loyal in the future. Share the blame as a group.

It is never a good idea to simply hope that a mistake will disappear. If there is a problem, come up with a solution – it will show that you have thought the problem through, dealt with the mistake and are capable of problem solving.

There are five golden rules in recognising and learning from mistakes:

1 Identify your position – how serious is it? How much of it are you responsible for?

2 Take a positive attitude – mistakes can be embarrassing and painful and can affect confidence, but do not let it affect your work abilities.

3 Work out how to resolve it – you need to come up with steps to solve the problem. You may need to apologise, but you need to come up with a way of dealing with the mistake.

4 Learn from it – remember how the mistake came about so that you can avoid being in the same position in the future.

5 Do not dwell on it – resolve to learn from the mistake and move on.

Gathering information

Some people believe that making mistakes is actually a good thing. No one is fault-proof. Have you made mistakes in the past? How have you dealt with them? What have you learned about yourself, your colleagues and the organisation you work for as a result? Has it made you more or less mistake proof?

1.8 Explain the purpose of guidelines, procedures and codes of practice that are relevant to own work

Codes of practice are principles, values and standards that aim to guide the decisions, procedures and systems of an organisation. The aim is to ensure that the organisation respects the rights of anyone affected by its operations and takes into account the welfare of its key stakeholders. In many organisations these are often referred to as professional codes of practice or ethics.

Guidelines are designed to give clear and concise advice and steps to take in relation to most normal working situations. They aim to ensure that the organisation is consistent and deals with the same issues, problems or procedures in the same way across the whole of the organisation.

Policies are broad guidelines that determine the way in which an organisation operates. Its procedures are the preferred ways in which it wants specific tasks or activities to be performed. The systems are the supporting mechanisms that allow the procedures to be followed. The values of an organisation are often part of its organisational culture and may include providing excellent customer service and feedback, value for money, open and honest dealing, and public accountability.

All organisations work in different ways and have different systems and procedures which they expect their staff to carry out in the course of their day-to-day duties.

The operation of administration procedures is important since the activities of the organisation must be coordinated and planned. If inadequate administration procedures are in operation, the organisation may suffer from a lack of efficiency and effectiveness since it does not have access to all relevant information. Administration procedures inevitably involve some form of filing, whether it be a paper-based filing system or one housed within a computer system.

Businesses and organisations will also have a series of other procedures. These will include the following:

- Health and safety – this will need to follow the requirements of health and safety legislation and will provide guidance to employees on ensuring that the workplace remains a healthy and risk-free environment.

- Security and confidentiality – these will include procedures to ensure that the building, the business or organisation's property, and confidential information remain safe.

- Grievance and disciplinary procedures – these will also follow legislation, but will state how an employee can bring a complaint to the notice of the employer and the procedures to be followed to investigate that grievance. The disciplinary procedure will state unacceptable behaviour and the sanctions that can be brought against the employee. It will also state the stages involved in the disciplinary procedure.

The systems which an organisation has in place should aim to establish a means by which the operations it carries out can be assessed. Most administrative systems are a series of sub-systems which can be split into additional sub-systems. It is, therefore, important that the organisation monitors all parts of the system. The systems should be designed in such a way that they can be changed to meet the requirements of the organisation.

Administrative procedures obviously play a vital role. They are the means by which the organisation is able to operate as a whole. Any organisation can have good ideas and well-motivated employees, but without procedures to ensure that functions are carried out, these may be unsuccessful. Information received into the organisation has to be processed in some way before it can either be stored (in which case it could later be retrieved) or disseminated (sent to different people) around the various departments. Alternatively, the information may need to be sent out from the organisation in a different format.

Table 301.1 shows us what information may come into a business, what the business may need to do to that information, and the type of information that may leave the business.

Table 301.2

Type of information that may enter a business	How information may be processed by the business	Type of information that may leave a business
Fax	Filed on a computer	A reply or response in writing
Telephone message	Sent around the different departments	A reply or response via the telephone
Email message	Filed in a filing cabinet	A bill to a customer
Business letter	Discussed at a meeting	A payment to a supplier
Money from a customer	Followed up by a member of staff	
Bill from a supplier	Analysed by managers	
	A report produced	

A business would not want procedures just for the sake of having them. They have to be an advantage to the business, particularly if setting up the procedures and then running those procedures costs the business money. Procedures, or guidelines and codes of practice, set out the way in which businesses prefer to carry out their activities and what is expected of individuals who work for the business.

Procedures allow a business to carry out all of its activities in an organised way. The decisions about the organisation's objectives will be made and then the procedures will help the business's managers and employees to achieve those objectives.

If a business's employees are organised in the way in which their activities or tasks are carried out, then the impression or image they give their customers and the general public is good. A good image is important for businesses. They will want their procedures to give this image and will try to make sure, for example:

- all paperwork that leaves the business gives a good impression because it is neat, accurate and well presented
- all information requested is sent out quickly to the right person, at the right time
- all messages received are dealt with promptly and efficiently
- all customers, or people likely to become customers, receive the same high level of service from employees
- employees are aware of the need to keep confidential or sensitive information safe
- the business's buildings and employees are kept healthy and safe
- they are following government laws in the way in which they carry out their activities.

Organised businesses will also have the following benefits:

- The business's customers are more likely to return and buy again (repeat business).
- The business's customers are more likely to recommend the business to others, which could bring new customers.

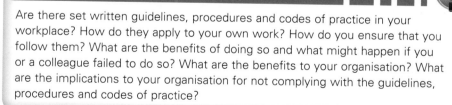

Gathering information

Are there set written guidelines, procedures and codes of practice in your workplace? How do they apply to your own work? How do you ensure that you follow them? What are the benefits of doing so and what might happen if you or a colleague failed to do so? What are the benefits to your organisation? What are the implications to your organisation for not complying with the guidelines, procedures and codes of practice?

■ 2. Understand how to behave in a way that supports effective working

2.1 Explain the purpose and benefits of setting high standards for own work and
2.2 Describe ways of setting high standards for own work

In a busy office there are literally dozens of things which could prevent you from concentrating on a job, or being able to do that job to the best of your ability. Offices are usually busy and noisy places, with frequent comings and goings, phones ringing, people talking across the office to one another and visitors appearing when you least need to see them.

The key benefits of setting high standards for your own work are that they establish you as a valued team member whose work is consistently good. This can lead to you being given more challenging tasks, as you will have proven your ability to cope and to produce consistently high levels of work. This in turn means that you will have a far more varied, interesting and rewarding job role.

Concentration is not always possible. There is often little opportunity to confirm what it is someone is asking you to do and, above all, the person you need to speak to is often either busy or unavailable. These factors and many more can impact upon both your ability to meet high standards and the efficiency of others in the office. There are a number of ways in which you can reduce the negative impact on meeting high standards, including the following:

- Listen carefully to instructions.

- Ask the appropriate questions to confirm what it is you need to do and if necessary write down the instructions.

- Make sure you follow the instructions given to you.

- Try to use your time as efficiently as possible by not getting sidetracked.

- Don't allow other people to distract you.

- If you need to concentrate and the office is particularly noisy or busy, if possible take yourself off to a quiet area to work. Make sure you tell someone where you have gone and why.

- Make the best use of any chance you have to communicate with others involved in the project or task. Effective communication means giving or receiving information in an easy-to-understand and clear way. It also means receiving information at the right time.

- Make sure you follow organisational procedures and that those working with you do the same.

Although standards need to be high, they should not be unrealistic. It is often said that if you set standards too high then everyone will fail because they are unable to reach these high expectations.

The standards need to be set by the organisation, reinforced by team leaders and supervisors and then taken on by all members of the team. This sets an acceptable level of performance. It also reminds team members what an acceptable level is. It could make things difficult in the short term but improve everything in the longer term.

By setting the bar too low in terms of standards, the work output will be poor. It is not usually helpful to compare the work of one team with that of another. The team needs to set its own standards for work, whether this is completing work ahead of schedule or being able to perform work tasks consistently and efficiently.

Setting high standards is only the first stage. You need to try to constantly meet them and exceed them. Exceeding your own high standards at work is a vital part of continuous improvement and career development. The business itself will play its own part in this – it may establish guidelines, procedures and codes of practice. These should be seen as the basic standards that are expected, but they should not be the level at which you are satisfied to work. You should seek to better them and continue to better them by constantly improving your standards and seeking the most effective way of carrying out your work.

A good way of setting your own standards and then exceeding them is to do what is known as the Plan – Do – Check – Act improvement cycle. This means:

- Plan – look at tasks and find out what goes wrong, such as slowing them down, and come up with a solution.

- Do – try out a selected solution and see whether it makes an improvement.

- Check – how effective was the solution? Has it made you more efficient? Is the work being completed at a higher standard?

- Act – if the solution has achieved this, then implement it from now on.

You should review the way you carry out work on a regular basis using this model and see where improvements can be made.

Gathering information

Does your organisation have set standards that you need to achieve during the course of completing your tasks? Are you always:

- told what the task means to the business?
- aware of where it fits into the broader picture?
- aware of how the work was done by others before you?

- aware of and conform to any procedures or policies that should be adopted?
- aware of a standardised way of performing the task?
- given feedback on your completion of the task?
- able to respond and change how you did the task as a result?
- able to set your own new standards for doing the tasks?

Do you have your own views about how the tasks could be improved regarding efficiency? Have you ever discussed your ideas with anyone else? If so, what was the outcome?

2.3 Describe ways of dealing with pressure arising from work tasks

According to the Health and Safety Executive (www.hse.gov.uk), one in six working people in Britain stated that their job was either very or extremely stressful. This often arises out of pressure to perform, or from having too great a workload. Work-related stress is probably the biggest cause of people taking sick leave. However, not everyone deals with workplace pressure and stress in the same way. What may be stressful for one person may not be stressful for another. It very much depends on an individual's personality and how they are able to deal with pressure.

Work-related pressure and stress can cause a number of physical and emotional health problems, such as:

- blurred vision
- backache or neck ache
- muscular tension
- raised heart rate
- headaches
- tiredness and sleep problems
- skin rashes.

Pressure can be recognised in a number of ways:

- You may have to be constantly on the move at work and are needed in too many places at the same time.
- You may have to work through your breaks.
- You may always leave work later than you expected.
- You may need to take work home with you.
- You may not have enough time to relax at home or spend time with your family.

There are ways in which you can try to ease pressure at work. The most effective ways include:

- managing your time more effectively

- prioritising tasks

- delegating work when you can

- ensuring that you do not take on more work than you can handle

- taking regular breaks at work

- trying to finish one task before starting another

- ensuring that your work environment is comfortable

- not working long hours – if you are tired then the quality of the work may suffer

- trying to improve relationships with colleagues in order to mutually support each other.

In organisations where there have been cuts in budgets and staff, fewer people will be doing more work and working longer hours. It is important to learn to say 'no', particularly to tasks that are not part of your main job role. By overloading yourself you will become vulnerable to ill-health, resulting in lower standards of work.

Delegating work to others is important in order to lighten a workload and relieve pressure. It also means that others will share the responsibilities and it will make them feel more trusted and secure.

Gathering information

Does your workplace take pressure and stress seriously? Do you know what is meant by occupational health? Is there an occupational health officer at your workplace? What parts of your job role do you find particularly stressful?

2.4 Explain the purpose and benefits of accepting setbacks and dealing with them

Overcoming setbacks at work is a way in which to continually develop. Setbacks can affect most people and they are often referred to as 'two steps forward and one step back'.

The first thing to do in attempting to overcome a setback is to try to identify what caused it. Why do you think you have had a setback? What did you expect to happen? This will help to identify what you expected the outcome to have been. Do not focus on reasons or excuses at this stage.

The next thing to do is to try to compare the difference between what you expected and what actually happened. This will help you to identify exactly how much of a setback you have actually encountered. It may just mean that you need to make a small adjustment. But if it is a serious setback, you may need to start all over again.

The final step is to identify what corrective steps you need to take in the future. What do you need to do to overcome the setback? This is the most critical stage. You should do the following:

- List the reasons why the setback occurred. What happened?
- Identify what you can do to deal with the setback.
- Is the setback within your control to fix?
- Do you need the help of others?

It is important to be patient as you work through a setback. You must not be tough on yourself. By carefully thinking about the setback, there will be a solution. It is often a case of adopting the right attitude and moving on. You should:

- give yourself time to deal with any disappointment
- focus on the positive: you will have learned from the setback – what has it taught you?
- consider the bigger picture – this is one event and you are now aware that this kind of thing can happen
- move forward – think about what you need to do now and give yourself time to deal with the setback and learn from the experience.

Gathering information

Have you suffered any setbacks in your working life? Was it career related? Did you expect a promotion or to be given more responsibility but this failed to happen? How did you deal with the situation? What did you learn from it? Have you been able to avoid getting into a similar situation since then?

2.5 Explain the purpose and benefits of being assertive and its meaning in work tasks and 2.6 Give examples of work situations where it is necessary to be assertive

Many people mistake assertiveness for aggressiveness and rudeness. You can be assertive in both a respectful and a professional way.

Assertiveness does not necessarily mean being pushy, confrontational or rude. Assertiveness is about being straightforward and strong. In other words, if you have an opinion, an idea, a solution or a problem, you can tell others without upsetting them or affecting relationships at work.

There are some key considerations to bear in mind about being assertive:

- Do not be demanding – make reasonable requests, be prepared to compromise and negotiate.

- Be direct – if you have a problem then confront the situation head on.

- Be confident – be self-assured, even if you are slightly in doubt. This also means learning how to say 'no' when it is appropriate.

- Control your emotions – do not get frustrated or angry. Some people will feel that if you are being over-emotional, you are being weak. You need to focus before being assertive.

- Remember that you are important – your contribution should be valued, so you should have an opinion or a point of view. If you are assertive in the correct way, it will improve your reputation.

The purpose of assertiveness is to allow yourself to communicate honestly. It also means influencing the behaviour and gaining the cooperation of others, but not at their expense. Assertiveness means being decisive and confident in dealing with people without being aggressive or appearing to be superior.

Figure 301.2

Assertiveness should be seen as a useful communication tool, but it is not always appropriate to be assertive in all situations. You should always have a healthy regard for the opinions of others, although you may actually discover that your viewpoint is wrong.

In any workplace you will encounter people with different styles of communication. You may think they are all being assertive in their own way, but in fact being assertive is about being direct, honest and responsible, accepting and often being spontaneous. Other types that are not assertive are:

- direct aggression – arrogant, bossy, intolerant, overbearing and opinionated people
- indirect aggression – manipulative, guilt-inducing and sarcastic people
- submissive – moaning, indecisive and apologetic people.

In order to be assertive you need to:

- maintain eye contact – it shows interest and sincerity, as well as a degree of determination and confidence
- be aware of your body posture – do not lean too far forward as this can be mistaken for aggression
- use gestures – highlight your points by using appropriate gestures to emphasise them
- moderate your voice – keep it level, otherwise it may be intimidating
- choose the right time – make your point at the right moment to maximise its impact
- be aware of the content – make sure that you focus on the points you want to get across and have answers to possible questions
- be prepared to use the word 'I' – this means that you are expressing your own needs and feelings.

Some good examples of when to be assertive at work include:

- when being poorly treated by a colleague
- when being taken for granted
- when having an unreasonable workload thrust upon you
- when unreasonable deadlines are being suggested
- when being asked to carry out a task that you know from experience should be carried out in a different way
- when being asked to work in an unsafe manner
- when being asked to work outside the conditions of service.

Gathering information

Are you assertive in your workplace? How do you think people view your level of assertiveness? Are others more or less assertive? What happens when two very assertive individuals clash? Have you ever received feedback from others about your own level of assertiveness?

2.7 Explain the purpose and benefits of being ready to take on new challenges and adapt to change

Being prepared to take on new challenges and changes highlights you as an individual who is adaptable, competent and reliable. This can mean that you will be given more challenging work and, ultimately, your work will be far more interesting and varied.

Many employees face changes in their working conditions as a result of their employer's drive to beat off the competition. For example:

- Retail employees now find themselves in a position where they have to work across the whole weekend.

- Some employees may find that their employer wishes to change their working hours.

- Manufacturers or factories wish to run their machinery for 24 hours a day, 365 days of the year. This means that a proportion of their employees will work regular hours during the day, while others will get into work very early and leave at lunchtime; others will start in the evening and finish in the early hours of the morning.

Sometimes these changes suit employees and there has been a trend for employers to bring in what is known as a compressed working week. If, for example, an employee had to work 42 hours per week, instead of spreading out those hours over 5 days they would work just 3½ days. Each of the days would consist of 12 hours and the half-day would consist of 6 hours. This would mean that the employee, although they were working for longer hours in a single day, would have 3½ days' leave per week.

There may also be changes in the way the employee carries out their work. Perhaps the introduction of new technology would change what may have been a paper-based job to an electronic-based series of duties. Jobs also change in manufacturing as new machinery and equipment are developed, making the jobs far more to do with checking and monitoring machinery than actual physical work.

When employers expect their employees to change the very nature of their jobs they usually provide re-training and assistance in order to help their employees make the transition.

Employers are increasingly looking for people with skills that they can transfer to any job. For example:

- a willingness to learn
- good verbal and written communication skills
- self-motivation
- team work
- commitment
- energy and enthusiasm
- reliability and honesty
- problem-solving and analytical ability
- organisational skills
- adaptability and flexibility
- ability to meet deadlines
- information technology skills.

Employers are looking for employees who can display the widest possible range of skills. Increasingly, because even low-level job roles are more demanding, employees need to have a wide range of skills and show the willingness to learn new skills. This multi-skilling provides employees with a range of skills that can be transferred from one job role to another, for example an individual who has used the Microsoft Office package for an administrative job and has sufficient typing skills to take on secretarial work.

If an employee is multi-skilled and has a wide range of transferable skills, their employment prospects are improved. Employers look for flexible, well-trained and highly skilled individuals who can adapt to various changes in their job roles as well as accept and welcome the need to continually update their bank of skills and knowledge.

Certain areas ideal for personal development will be highlighted in appraisals or annual reviews. The personal development plans that arise from such appraisals will outline the key areas that the employee, supported by their supervisor or manager and ultimately the human resources department, feels are relevant to their job role.

The human resources department will routinely inform employees of training opportunities and employees should also look in the local press and libraries for notices announcing training programmes in the area. Many of these external training programmes will either be paid for or subsidised by the employer. If this is not the case, many of the courses have sliding scales of payment to make them affordable to almost any employee.

Figure 301.3

2.8 Explain the purpose and benefits of treating others with honesty, respect and consideration, 2.9 Describe types of behaviour at work that show honesty, respect and consideration and those that do not and 2.10 Explain the purpose of helping and supporting others at work, and the purpose and benefits of doing so

Businesses attempt to strike a balance between ensuring all work is completed effectively and efficiently and trying to maintain good working relationships between different members of staff.

Despite some very bad examples of employers who bully and harass their staff, the majority of businesses prefer their employees to be happy. Happy and cooperative members of staff work together far more efficiently. They are not distracted by problems, so they can concentrate on producing good quality work.

You will have contact with a variety of people within the organisation, either on a routine and daily basis or just occasionally. Hopefully you will have established a productive working relationship with people. Productive working relationships can mean some or all of the following in Table 301.2

- that those involved are cooperative
- that others' feelings are considered
- that there is courtesy
- that people are respected and supported
- that people are loyal to each other
- that managers, team leaders and supervisors thank and praise people for doing a good job when appropriate
- that decisions are reasonable
- that the reasons behind decisions are explained to those involved
- that people should listen to one another and try to understand the views of others.

An unproductive working relationship atmosphere could include:

- the fact that people blame and distrust each other
- that a manager, supervisor or team leader is a bad leader and has favourites
- that some people will not listen to others
- that there is fighting between team members
- that some team members refuse to work as hard as others.

Table 301.3

Appropriate behaviour	Inappropriate behaviour
Listen to others when they are speaking	Interrupt others
Take the blame for your mistakes	Blame others
Give your best at all times	Work hard only when you feel like it
Avoid gossiping	Listen to gossip and pass it on
Support other team members at all times	Criticise team members publicly
Show respect for others, whatever their position within the business	Behave differently to those in senior positions and show little respect for those you do not like
Be prepared to carry out additional work to help others	Never do more than you need to do and leave work dead on the finishing time

Very few people will have all the necessary personal qualities to be an ideal team member, but many will hope to acquire some of these qualities over time. Typical personal qualities could include some of the following:

- having good judgement
- showing initiative
- showing integrity
- showing foresight
- having energy to show continued commitment to tasks
- having drive and enthusiasm
- being decisive
- being dependable
- being emotionally stable
- showing fairness and understanding to others
- being dedicated
- being cooperative.

Decisions will always have to be made and people will have different views about how to approach things. Most teams will try to make decisions together. In imposing decisions or ways of doing things on the team, there is no guarantee that the team will accept or understand the decision that has been made. The team will discuss decisions before they are made and try to reach an agreement on the way forward.

Negotiations and agreements may occur formally at a meeting, or may develop through a series of informal conversations as work is being done. The important aspect is that everyone feels that their view has been listened to, even if the rest of the team have not necessarily agreed with them. Decisions and agreements need to bring in the views of as many of the team as possible to make everyone feel that they have made a contribution. The way forward should be decided democratically, that is by majority decision.

Sometimes decisions have to be made quickly by the team leader, or by the team members who are directly involved in the work. The team may have no choice whatsoever as to the way in which a task must be approached as this decision has been determined by more senior management.

Teams rely on cooperation and to be cooperative means having a number of qualities:

- being loyal to the team and supportive to the others
- communicating easily and listening to what others say
- being happy to drop what you are doing and help another team member if they are in difficulties
- having a flexible approach to work
- being prepared to learn new skills
- keeping promises about work schedules
- not expecting other team members to always be cooperative, communicative or helpful
- being as happy with the team's successes as you are with your own.

Personality represents the way in which people think, feel, behave and relate to others. Some are extroverts and are lively and sociable people; others are introverts – they can be shy and find it difficult to communicate with others.

Different personalities have to be dealt with in different ways. Most extroverts are friendly and confident. They can be loud, lively and sociable, quite excitable and highly strung. Introverts, meanwhile, can also be highly strung but are usually confident, calm, shy and trusting.

> ### Gathering information
>
> How close are you to the other people in your team or the people you work with regularly? Do you trust and respect one another and are you supportive? Is it common for others to help if one of the team members is under pressure with work? Are there those in the team whom you can confide in and rely on for help and support? How does the way you treat one another help or hinder your work?

3. Be able to plan, prioritise and be accountable for own work

3.1 Negotiate and agree realistic targets and achievable timescales for own work

Refer to 1.2 and then consider the following.

> ### Gathering information
>
> In a busy office environment or an administrative post there will always be jobs that compete for time. Many of the tasks may be considered by others to be urgent and a priority. Setting yourself realistic targets and agreeing achievable timescales is important: it will reduce stress and avoid conflict with others.
>
> How do you negotiate and agree realistic targets and achievable timescales? In effect, how do you plan your time? How do you identify what needs to be given priority?

3.2 Prioritise targets for own work

Refer to 1.3 and then consider the following.

> ### Gathering information
>
> It can be difficult to judge how much time is needed for a particular task. It is difficult to predict when work will be received or completed. There will always be competing demands on time. You can identify some tasks as being urgent or non-urgent. Some of them will be important and others not so important. What may be urgent and important for someone else may have a lower priority as far as your workload is concerned.
>
> How do you distinguish the urgent from the non-urgent and the important from the not so important? Has this process caused problems?

3.3 Plan work tasks to make best use of own time, effective working methods and available resources

Refer to 1.1 and then consider the following.

Gathering information

When do you plan your working week? Are you able to do this on a weekly basis, or do the demands on you mean that this has to be carried out daily, or perhaps hourly? Is it possible for you to plan your work so that you can make the best use of your time, be effective in what you do and use the resources available? How does this work in practice?

3.4 Identify and deal with problems occurring in own work, using the support of other people if necessary

Refer to 1.4 and then consider the following.

Gathering information

Problems can arise during the day, but how do you deal with them? How supportive are others? Are you expected to show initiative to solve problems or do you have to refer them to someone else? At what point do you turn to others for help rather than sorting out the problem yourself?

3.5 Keep other people informed of progress

Refer to 1.5 and then consider the following.

Gathering information

Communication is a vital part of team work. If others know that you are experiencing problems they may be able to offer help.

How crucial are the tasks that you carry out to others? Do they rely on your completing a stage of the work? How do you feedback information and progress between one another? Is this formal or informal?

3.6 Complete work tasks to agreed deadlines or renegotiate timescales and plans in good time

Refer to 1.6 and then consider the following.

Gathering information

Part of being a member of a team means constantly updating others. You will have agreed certain deadlines for particular tasks. If there is a risk that the deadline will slip, it could have an effect. How successful are you at completing work tasks to agreed deadlines? How common is it to have to renegotiate timescales? At what point do you begin that negotiation?

3.7 Take responsibility for own work and accept responsibility for any mistakes made and 3.8 Evaluate results of mistakes made and make changes to work and methods, as required

Refer to 1.7 and then consider the following.

Gathering information

List some examples of mistakes that you may have made in the recent past. Did you take responsibility for them and what was the result of the mistakes? What were you able to learn from having made those mistakes and what were the consequences of the mistakes to others? Did the results of the mistake lead to you changing the way in which you work?

3.9 Follow agreed work guidelines, procedures and, where needed, codes of practice

Refer to 1.8 and then consider the following.

Gathering information

How clear are you about specific work guidelines, procedures and codes of practice? How were these explained to you? Were they part of specific training programmes or have you simply learned them on the job? Have these processes and expectations changed? How are you able to keep up with these changes? What is the purpose of following them? What are the consequences if you fail to do so?

■ 4. Behave in a way that supports effective working

4.1 Set high standards for own work and demonstrate drive and commitment in achieving these standards

Refer to 2.1 to 2.2 and then consider the following.

Gathering information

All employees are expected to operate to specific standards in terms of their work quality and output. Often an assessment of an individual's drive and commitment to achieve these standards is part of performance appraisal or work reviews. In between these appraisals and reviews there may be a formal or informal process that aims to support and monitor individuals.

What are your employer's expectations of you? How do you show your drive and commitment to achieving, maintaining and perhaps exceeding these standards? How formal is the process in your organisation? How does your organisation monitor this? Have you had feedback about your standard of work and how have you responded to it?

4.2 Adapt work and working methods to deal with setbacks and difficulties

Refer to 2.4 and then consider the following.

Gathering information

Setbacks and difficulties are inevitable. But they are a measure of your abilities to adapt to them and deal with them in an efficient manner.

What kind of setbacks have you encountered? What actually happened? How did you identify what needed to be done to deal with the setback? Did you require assistance? Were you able to deal with the setback alone? How did you deal with any disappointment as a result? How did you move forward from the setback? What steps did you take to try to ensure that this kind of setback or difficulty did not happen for a second time?

4.3 Use own needs and rights when necessary to achieve work tasks and priorities

Refer to 2.5 to 2.6 and then consider the following.

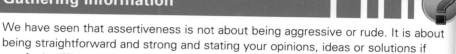

Gathering information

We have seen that assertiveness is not about being aggressive or rude. It is about being straightforward and strong and stating your opinions, ideas or solutions if you feel sufficiently confident about them.

Does your organisation support open communication, cooperation, collaboration and the sharing of ideas to solve problems? Are there those in your workplace who are overly assertive? How does this affect your dealings with them? Do you consider yourself to be an assertive individual? When did you last have occasion to be assertive in order to achieve your work tasks and priorities?

4.4 Look to engage with opportunities, and agree to take on new challenge(s) and
4.5 Look for opportunities, and change ways of working, to meet new requirements

Refer to 2.7 and then consider the following.

Gathering information

Looking for new opportunities and taking on new challenges are vital parts of career development. Also, looking for ways in which you can change the way you work to meet new challenges or requirements shows flexibility.

Does your organisation encourage you to take on new tasks and duties? Do you offer to do so? How do you identify these opportunities? What benefits are there to you of taking on new opportunities and challenges? Has this assisted you in meeting your career goals? Give some examples of opportunities and challenges that you have taken on. What has been the result of doing so?

4.6 Treat other people with honesty, respect and consideration

Refer to 2.8 to 2.9 and then consider the following.

Gathering information

The day-to-day interaction between individuals in the workplace can have a marked effect on the way in which the organisation runs. Honesty, respect and consideration for each other can have huge benefits.

What kind of relationship do you have with others in the workplace? Is it one of honesty, respect and consideration on both sides? Have you had feedback from others regarding this? Are there those who do not show these attributes? What is your view of them and how do they fit into the team or the organisation as a result?

4.7 Help and support other people in work tasks

Refer to 2.10 and then consider the following.

Gathering information

Collaborating, helping and supporting others to carry out tasks are at the heart of all team work.

How much of your job role relies on collaboration? Do you help and support? Do others help and support you? How often does this happen and are the help and support given freely, or do they have to be requested? How does your organisation benefit when employees show help and support to others? How important is this help and support in terms of getting work tasks completed? Could the work tasks be completed without this collaboration?

What is Evidence ?

A single piece of evidence can cover more than one learning outcome. Several assessment criteria can be dealt with by the one piece of evidence. You can also use the same evidence for other assessment criteria from other units. Your assessor will use a wide range of assessment methods for the learning outcomes in this unit, including:

- observing your performance in the work environment
- examining work products that you have created
- questioning you
- discussing work with you
- using witness testimony from work colleagues
- looking at your learner statements
- recognising your prior learning.

The range of evidence can include:

- annotated organisational policies and procedures
- work plans and revised work plans
- to-do lists
- emails or other communications seeking clarification or reporting problems
- appraisal or work review documents
- work requests and instructions
- minutes of team meetings
- feedback from others
- personal development plans.

Unit 302 Evaluate and Improve Own Performance in a Business Environment

■ Purpose of the unit

This unit is about looking at ways to evaluate and improve your own performance in the workplace.

■ Assessment requirements

There are three parts to this unit. The first part looks at understanding how to evaluate and improve your own performance. The remaining two parts focus on the way you can use feedback and how to agree, develop and use a learning plan. The three parts are:

1 Understand how to evaluate and improve own performance – the purpose and benefits of continuously improving own performance, the purpose and value of encouraging and accepting feedback, evaluating your own work, the purpose and benefit of trying out improvements to own work, evaluating learning and development in relation to improving own work, its benefits to the organisation and furthering of own career, comparing possible career progression routes and development opportunities and justifying the value of developing a learning plan. (K)

2 Be able to evaluate and improve own performance using feedback from others – encouraging and accepting feedback, evaluating own work using feedback to identify areas for improvement, identifying changes in working practices required, completing work using changed ways of working, evaluating work completed using changed ways of working. (P)

3 Be able to use evaluation of own performance to agree, develop and use a learning plan – evaluating own performance and identifying where further learning and development could improve own work, agreeing and developing a learning plan, following a learning plan, reviewing progress and updating a learning plan for improving own work and further learning. (P)

1. Understand how to evaluate and improve own performance

1.1 Explain the purpose and benefits of continuously improving own performance in a business environment

Employees and organisations should strive to improve their performance. It can help to improve the overall performance of the organisation and at an individual level help to improve the job satisfaction of the workforce.

Improvements in performance can be achieved by considering everything done to be a process of continuous development. Every time a new task is carried out, new skills are learned and work flexibility is enhanced. Skills and confidence will also be improved.

A good manager will set aside time to assess work and give advice as to the approach to that work. This may be formal or informal and may also take place as a scheduled event, or simply when the manager is checking progress.

Having an experienced member of staff review the work can be very useful as they will be able to identify mistakes and advise in terms of making your job easier and more efficient. These reviews can look at general work during an appraisal or ongoing work as and when the opportunity arises.

Self-assessment does not mean having to be critical of yourself. Neither does it mean that you should praise yourself over the efficiency or quality of your work. It means trying to step away and look at what is being or has been done. Have you met the targets which have been set? Are you able to stick to deadlines? Are you being cooperative, reliable, accurate and following procedures?

Even if you only take time at the end of the working week to reflect on how your week has gone, this is a step in the right direction to making a self-assessment of how you have worked.

More than 80 years ago a continuous development cycle, or the Deming Cycle, was developed. It remains a very useful tool. It is also a way to identify where work improvements can be made, how they can be improved and the progress that you have made towards that goal. There are only four steps in the cycle:

1 Plan – look at your current situation, gather information, identify problems and develop solutions.

2 Do – try out your solutions on a trial basis without disrupting your normal work patterns.

3 Study – did your solutions work and achieve the desired results? Modify your plans and solutions if necessary.

4 Act – now implement your modified solution to your work pattern.

Gathering information

Try to identify some areas of your work that you are unhappy with. Apply the four-stage process to it. Think about the benefits of improving your work performance. How will it impact on your working life? How will it improve your efficiency and that of your organisation?

1.2 Explain the purpose and value of encouraging and accepting feedback from others

Feedback is responses received from colleagues in reaction to your work or your performance. The feedback provides an opportunity to improve your overall performance in the workplace – you can be more efficient, a greater asset to the organisation and to your colleagues, and you can enjoy your job role by knowing that you are able to deal with the majority of different problems that you might face.

Much feedback is informal; however, both positive and negative feedback should be expected. Many businesses use formal feedback, usually in the form of an appraisal system, to review progress and assess abilities. Appraisals are opportunities to set targets and plans to improve performance. These appraisals will allow you to talk about your job, what you plan to do in the future and whether you would benefit from additional training. Appraisals are confidential and aim to be positive. They are a good opportunity to have uninterrupted conversations about work with immediate supervisors or team leaders. It is rare to receive totally positive feedback as most appraisals have some negative aspect.

Feedback sessions should be planned in advance. Action planning is useful as it helps you identify areas where you are working well, in addition to areas in which you are not performing as well. Action planning suggests ways of dealing with these situations.

Being defensive about criticism should be avoided unless it is unfair. When dealing with negative feedback it is sensible to ask what you should have done, or what you could do in order to improve.

Overall, any appraisal should provide you with the means in the future not to make the same mistakes as you may have made in the past.

Setting targets to improve your performance is very useful for the following reasons:

- They give you a clear idea of what you must do.
- They identify the key areas which you want to develop.
- They will give you satisfaction when you have achieved them.

- They will improve your confidence about your abilities.
- They will give you a vision of the future.

Figure 302.1

Targets must always be reasonable and realistic. In this respect, when setting targets you must:

- set specific targets about what you intend to achieve
- set realistic targets which are achievable
- not be too ambitious
- focus on the positive
- be as precise as possible by setting dates for reviews
- write down the targets so you can remember them
- not set too many targets, otherwise none may be achieved
- try to set targets which you can achieve yourself, rather than having to rely on others to help you achieve them
- make them your own targets and try not to have targets imposed upon you.

1.3 Describe ways of evaluating own work and 1.4 Explain the purpose and benefits of trying out possible improvements to own work

So far we have considered the value of feedback, as well as the purpose and the need to encourage and accept it from others. No one should rely just on other people's opinions in order to identify areas to improve their own work performance. By relying only on the feedback of others, an individual simply reacts to feedback and then adjusts their behaviour or performance as a result.

Evaluating your own work is a way to be proactive. It can allow you to identify areas that you are unhappy with and seek ways to improve them yourself. The most important aspect about evaluating your own work is to focus. This means looking at specific areas of your work performance systematically and then doing something about it if you have found that it is below your expectations. Here are some prime examples:

- Planning and organisation – can you think ahead? Can you arrange work logically? Can you re-evaluate your priorities? Can you cope with several projects at the same time? This all requires the ability to think ahead and to see future needs clearly and distinctly. Being able to handle several projects at the same time means having the ability to instantly refocus as you switch from one task to the next.

- Use of time – can you meet deadlines? Can you spend a reasonable amount of time on each project by wasting the least amount of time and remaining 'on task'? By focusing on how you are using your time you should be able to meet these objectives.

- Thoroughness – can you identify problems that are developing at the earliest possible stage? Are you aware of what could go wrong? Have you paid attention to detail? You may need a few minutes to focus once you have finished a task, simply to double-check it to make sure that all the necessary areas of the task have been covered.

Table 302.1 Professional

Skill	Current assessment	Improvement target
Personal appearance		
Level of confidence		
Enthusiasm and positivity		
Level of professionalism		
Level of respect		
Speed of learning		
Knowledge of work role		
Knowledge of work duties		
Ability to adapt to change		
Ability to communicate		
Ability to remain up to date		

Table 302.2 Information handling

Skill	Current assessment	Improvement target
Written and verbal communication skills		
Problem-solving skills		
Research skills		
Ability to accept diversity		
Ability to reason		
Ability to prioritise		
Ability to meet deadlines		
Level of flexibility		
Level of accuracy		
Ability to plan effectively		
Ability to make conclusions and recommendations		

Table 302.3 Interpersonal

Skill	Current assessment	Improvement target
Verbal communication		
Ability to summarise		
Ability to present information to a variety of audiences		
Accuracy of information		
Ability to use questioning techniques		
Ability to listen		
Ability to identify relevant information		
Ability to interact with others and move a discussion forward		
Ability to cascade information		
Level of respect from others		

Table 302.4 Self-application

Skill	Current assessment	Improvement target
Problem solving		
Level of work initiative		
Decision making		
Enthusiasm		
Work ethic		
Monitoring skills		
Adaptation skills		
Ability to work under pressure		
Numeric skills		
Ability to work to tight deadlines		

Give it a go

Complete the four tables yourself and then ask a colleague to complete them as their view of your performance and skills. How does your own review compare to that of your colleague's impressions? Has your colleague identified something that you had not noticed? What action could you take to bridge any gaps in skills that have been identified?

Career development helps you recognise and seize opportunities that could increase your employability, general level of education, experience and skills. Opportunities arise at different times and such opportunities will provide you with a chance to gain training, experience or qualifications.

Typical types of career development include the following:

- Induction – this is a primary training programme that takes place in the first few days or weeks of a new member of staff starting work with the organisation. Induction covers all the basics, including policies, procedures, guidelines and the general work approach of the organisation.

- Training needs analysis – for new employees and on a yearly basis with existing employees. The business will use the job specification, person specification and the employee's current abilities to identify gaps. The process should reveal any training that may be required.

- Development plans – to identify longer-term career plans and to match any training or qualifications needed. These are normally carried out on an annual basis and have agreed targets.

- Performance targets – these are minimum levels of work or output that you will be required to complete by the employer. Performance targets are difficult to set for some individual workers, so a departmental or section target may be set. These will require work to be completed by specified deadlines and very much depend on the type of work involved.

- Certificated training – this is training for recognised qualifications, such as an NVQ, and is useful for personal development as it allows you to demonstrate your ability to work at a particular level.

- Uncertificated training – in-house training programmes, designed specifically for the business, perhaps to update on policies and procedures.

- Personal development – training needs analysis, various types of training and development plans.

- Flexible working – willingness to work in different areas of the business, leading to multi-skilling.

- Progression opportunities – promotion opportunities, higher pay or a more valued post. As skills and experience improve, progression opportunities will present themselves. With each step you will gain access to higher-level work and begin the process once again of improvement and the chance to seize the next opportunity for progression.

Gathering information

To what extent have you considered your future career? At what stage of your career would you say you are now? Do your career progression routes suggest that you will be able to achieve them in your current workplace? Are there sufficient career progression opportunities? Does your current workplace encourage development opportunities?

1.8 Justify the value of developing a learning plan

Personal learning plans are very effective learning and career development tools. They benefit the individual and the workplace. They should be seen as positive tools and need to be updated periodically so that they remain relevant to the current circumstances.

As far as the individual and the workplace are concerned, Table 302.5 outlines the key benefits of a learning plan.

Table 302.5

Individual benefits	Workplace benefits
Increases motivation and responsibility for learning	Provides an opportunity for the organisation to talk about career goals and how they fit in with the needs of the organisation
Make the individual personally accountable for their own development	Improves relationships with management
Increase belief in own abilities	Encourages managers to talk about career development in a structured way
Develops self-awareness of strengths and weaknesses (based on own evaluation and feedback)	Provides a formal way of talking about performance at work
Provides a structure behind career plans	Allows the organisation to tailor-make training to match its own needs and that of individuals
Sets measurable goals	Helps prioritise training goals and objectives, by coordinating the training and reducing costs
Underpins career development and learning	Useful in identifying the skills of the employees and those who could be leaders in the future
Encourages flexibility and allows the individual to tailor-make their learning to suit them	If training and opportunities are offered by the organisation, it could mean that valuable employees do not look elsewhere
Encourages coaching and mentoring sessions in the workplace	May help identify the need to recruit new employees with different sets of skills and abilities

Gathering information

Are you encouraged by your workplace to develop a learning plan? If so, is this seen as part of a formal or informal process? Do aspects of a learning plan appear as part of performance appraisal or work reviews? How does the organisation prioritise development opportunities? Does your organisation encourage internal promotions or recruitment? How often would you need to update a learning plan? Who in your organisation would have sight of your learning plan?

■ 2. Be able to evaluate and improve own performance using feedback from others

2.1 Encourage and accept feedback from other people

Refer to 1.2 and then consider the following.

Gathering information

Perhaps the best way of not only encouraging and accepting feedback from others but also acting upon it is to document it. Each job role will be different. You will have interaction with different colleagues, supervisors and managers in the workplace. Some of them may be more or less able to pass comment and provide feedback on your performance.

Create a basic feedback form that you could use for a variety of individuals. You may need to create slightly different versions to suit different circumstances and individuals. Consider the following as you create your form:

● What do others routinely see you performing in terms of work?

● What areas of work do you feel uncomfortable with at present?

● Which individuals could offer you valuable feedback?

● How can you use this feedback to help improve performance and confidence?

Bear in mind that different people seeing you perform different tasks will have differing opinions about your performance.

2.2 Evaluate own work and use feedback from others to identify areas for improvement

Refer to 1.2 and 1.3 and then consider the following.

Gathering information

Hopefully you will have received feedback from a variety of individuals. You should also have begun to evaluate your own work. Now you should:

- compare the feedback from others to your own evaluation of your work
- comment on the feedback that you have received
- identify your strong areas
- identify areas of weakness and suggest how they could be addressed.

2.3 Identify changes in ways of working needed to improve work performance

Refer to 1.3 and then consider the following.

Gathering information

The process so far should have identified areas where you may need to change the way you work to improve performance. What advice have you been given in the feedback that may mean a change in the way you work? Are you comfortable and confident about these potential changes? How do you think they will impact on your overall work performance?

2.4 Complete work tasks using changed ways of working

Refer to 1.4 and then consider the following.

Gathering information

Having identified changes in the way you work, you should now try out some tasks using these changes. Ask the individuals who provided you with feedback that led to the changes to witness you carrying out the work in the new way. Try to document their comments. A work diary may be useful, as it can identify when you will be carrying out the task and when they can observe you doing this.

2.5 Evaluate work completed and changed ways of working for improvements and effectiveness

Refer to 1.4 and then consider the following.

Gathering information

Changing the way that you carry out work is all part of the learning and development process, aimed at improving your work performance and effectiveness. Comment on the impact that these changed ways of working has had. Have they made you more efficient, faster, reliable or confident in what you are doing?

3. Be able to use evaluation of own performance to agree, develop and use a learning plan

3.1 Evaluate own performance and identify where further learning and development will improve own work

Refer to 1.5 and then consider the following.

Gathering information

Your evaluation of your own performance may have highlighted areas that you still feel uncomfortable with. You may have identified areas where further learning and development would be beneficial. This is the first stage in developing a learning plan. It identifies areas where further learning and development are necessary. Ideally, this should be a collaborative process. You will need the support of your organisation and, specifically, your manager or team leader to help you. There need to be realistic opportunities for this learning and development. Exactly how this is delivered will differ from organisation to organisation. It can include:

- specific training
- mentoring or coaching
- shadowing a more experienced individual
- access to manuals outlining policies, procedures and processes.

3.2 Agree and develop a learning plan to improve own work performance, that meets own needs

Refer to 1.5 and then consider the following.

Gathering information

Learning plans need to be personal. Although there are many learning plan templates, they may not necessarily suit your own purposes. Ideally, they need to incorporate the following:

- A set of learning goals that you hope to achieve within a specified period of time.
- Each large goal needs to be broken down into sub-goals that can be achieved as a series of steps.
- Each goal or sub-goal should have actions that you need to take in order to achieve them.
- Your actions should be actual behaviour, such as practising, reading up on a particular topic, attending a training course, etc.
- Each action should be associated with resources that you might need.
- You should also note what evidence you will collect to prove that you have achieved the goal.

It is very important to make the learning plan as interactive as possible, as it will need to be evolved. You will attain goals and collect evidence. The goals that you have achieved will become your learning records. The learning plan itself needs to look forward. The learning record documents what you have accomplished.

3.3 Follow a learning plan for improvement to own work and
3.4 Review progress against learning plan and make updates for improving own work and further learning

Refer to 1.8 and then consider the following.

Gathering information

You should set yourself milestones for your learning plan by breaking down major goals into sub-goals. You should then be able to achieve the sub-goals stage by stage and show progress. You may be able to arrange to have an informal session at work to review your progress against your learning plan, perhaps on a monthly or quarterly basis. At this point you can remove but retain documentation of the goals that you have already achieved. This can then be replaced with the next stage in your learning plan. By reviewing and updating your learning plan you will continue to improve your work and identify learning goals. Support from your organisation may be essential in this. A learning plan should be seen as an ongoing process of improvement.

What is Evidence ?

A single piece of evidence can cover more than one learning outcome. Several assessment criteria can be dealt with by the one piece of evidence. You can also use the same evidence for other assessment criteria from other units. Your assessor will use a wide range of assessment methods for the learning outcomes in this unit, including:

- observing your performance in the work environment
- examining work products that you have created
- questioning you
- discussing work with you
- using witness testimony from work colleagues
- looking at your learner statements
- recognising your prior learning.

The range of evidence can include:

- appraisal or work reviews and subsequent reviews
- feedback received from colleagues
- learning or development plans
- self-assessment or reviews
- minutes of meetings
- internal communications related to methods of working.

Work in a Business Environment

■ Purpose of the unit

This unit is about being able to behave and make positive contributions to work tasks and procedures. It means behaving in a way that supports diversity and the reduction of waste, improves efficiency, shows respect for property and security, and minimises risk.

■ Assessment requirements

There are 12 parts to this unit. The first six introduce working relationships, dealing with security and confidentiality, risk, waste reduction, hazardous materials and sustainability. The remaining six parts of the unit provide you with the opportunity to show your ability to perform these duties in the workplace. The 12 parts are:

1 Understand the purpose and benefits of respecting and supporting other people at work – purpose of supporting others, what is meant by diversity, benefits of diversity, treating others in a sensitive way, respecting others and learning from others at work. (K)

2 Understand how to maintain security and confidentiality at work and deal with concerns – purpose and benefits of maintaining security and confidentiality, organisational requirements for security and confidentiality, legal requirements, procedures for dealing with concerns about security and confidentiality. (K)

3 Understand how to assess, manage and monitor risk in the workplace – sources of risk, assessing and monitoring risks and minimising risks. (K)

4 Understand the purpose of keeping waste to a minimum in a business environment and the procedures to follow – purpose and benefits of waste reduction, causes of waste, ways to minimise waste, purpose and benefits of recycling, organisational procedures for recycling, minimising waste through regular maintenance of equipment. (K)

5 Understand procedures for disposal of hazardous materials – purpose and procedures for the recycling and disposal of hazardous materials, describing the organisational procedures for recycling and the disposal of hazardous materials. (K)

6 Understand ways of supporting sustainability in an organisation – benefits of improving efficiency and minimising waste, ways to continually improve working methods and use of technology to achieve maximum efficiency

and minimum waste, outlining ways of selecting sources of materials and equipment that give best value for money. (K)

7   Be able to respect and support other people at work in an organisation – completing work tasks with others in a way that shows respect for their background, ability, values, customs and beliefs, being sensitive to others' needs, using feedback and guidance to improve own way of working and following organisational procedures and legal requirements in relation to discrimination legislation. (P)

8   Be able to maintain security and confidentiality – keeping property secure and following organisational procedures and legal requirements, keeping information secure and confidential, following procedures to report concerns about security or confidentiality. (P)

9   Be able to assess, manage and monitor risk – identify and agree possible sources of risk in own work, identify and agree new risks, assess and confirm the level of risk, identify and agree ways of minimising risk, monitoring risk in own work, use outcomes of assessing and dealing with risk to make recommendations. (P)

10 Be able to support the minimisation of waste in an organisation – complete work tasks keeping waste to a minimum and use technology in ways that minimise waste. (P)

11 Be able to follow procedures for the disposal of hazardous waste in an organisation – follow procedures for recycling and disposal of hazardous materials in work tasks. (P)

12 Be able to support sustainability in an organisation – follow procedures for the maintenance of equipment, review own ways of working and make suggestions for improving efficiency, select and use equipment and materials that give best value for money, support others in ways that maximise their effectiveness and efficiency. (P)

■ 1. Understand the purpose and benefits of respecting and supporting other people at work

1.1 Explain the purpose of supporting other people at work and
1.2 Explain the purpose of helping other people to work effectively and efficiently (a) for individuals, (b) for organisations

Creating effective working relationships is an important part of being satisfied at work. Being able to work together enables team work. Many organisations are team orientated, where individuals contribute to the success of the team. Even though individuals may have specific job roles, they join together as a team to accomplish larger objectives.

Team work can operate only when each participant makes a positive contribution and this means supporting other individuals' efforts, pulling together and being self-directed. Not only will supporting others in the workplace make the team and organisation more efficient, it is also beneficial to the individuals involved.

Individuals need to understand why they are participating in the team:

- It can help solve problems (individuals may not be able to come up with a solution themselves).

- It can identify improvements (individuals may not be able to bring about these improvements alone).

- It can encourage creativity and the exchange of ideas (sharing ideas and pooling ideas is more effective).

- It can break down tasks (smaller, simpler individual tasks contribute to the whole).

Every person who works for an organisation is slightly different. They have different skills, abilities and experiences. Some may have energy; others may have ideas or enthusiasm. Taken together, all of these different skills and abilities can be moulded to make an effective team. Each individual can contribute and the others can support that individual.

For an organisation, this means far more efficient working practices. Most people enjoy working as a member of a team. Businesses recognise this and employees who enjoy their work have greater job satisfaction and are generally more productive.

Collectively, the team is able to do almost anything: mixing and matching the skills and abilities while supporting each other to ensure that tasks are carried out in an effective and efficient way.

Gathering information

Do you work as a member of a team? How supportive are others towards you? How supportive are you towards others? Do you think that the team works more effectively when they pull together? What benefits are there to the individual members of the team? How do you think the organisation benefits?

1.3 Explain what is meant by diversity and why it should be valued and
1.4 Outline the benefits of diversity to an organisation

Not only do businesses need a broad range of skills and talents, they also benefit from having a diverse workforce. Regardless of the background, values, customs and beliefs of individuals, all employees have similarities and this is the starting point for understanding them and appreciating diversity in the workplace.

Everyone has needs, interests and outlooks. Learning about these can contribute to a good working relationship. They will also have different interests outside of work. Whatever their background, at work the employees are there to accomplish mutual goals and to work effectively as a team. It is possible to pool common interests.

Diversity arises out of different backgrounds, different sets of values, customs that may be related to family history or different religious beliefs. Factors such as race, disability, age, gender and working patterns all make the workplace a diverse environment.

Some businesses and organisations have schemes to ensure that everyone is treated equally and that their differences are valued, as they make a major contribution to the workings of the organisation. They allow the organisation to look at things from different perspectives.

Figure 303.1

Businesses try to promote equality of opportunity, to support unlawful discrimination and harassment and, on a daily basis, promote good relations between employees, regardless of their differences.

Gathering information

Diversity is not just about different ethnic backgrounds or religions – it is far broader and includes age, experience, values and customs. How diverse is your workplace? Is it representative of the population in your area? What can be learned from the broad range of very different individuals in your workplace? How does their outlook on life differ?

1.5 Explain how to treat other people in a way that is sensitive to their needs and
1.6 Explain how to treat other people in a way that respects their abilities, background, values, customs and beliefs

Colleagues and supervisors will have different priorities, workloads and commitments. Much work relies upon negotiating suitable times and cooperating to fit around one another's busy schedules. However, more senior members of staff may decide the priorities; they may also decide how workloads will be organised.

In order to ensure that you treat others with the respect they deserve, you should always:

● be courteous, polite and kind

● encourage others to express their opinions or ideas

● listen to what others are saying and do not interrupt them

● be prepared to use the ideas of others even if it means changing your own work and credit them for coming up with the idea if it is a successful one

● avoid insulting people

● avoid unnecessary criticism

● treat people the same, regardless of their age, race, religion, gender or origin

● include everyone in conversations, discussions and meetings and allow them to participate.

There are laws and regulations related to discrimination in the workplace and their key purposes are shown below. It is unlawful to discriminate against a person at work on the grounds of:

● sex

● race

- disability

- colour

- nationality

- ethnic or national origin

- religion or belief

- sexual orientation

- age.

Discrimination can be classed as either direct or indirect. Direct discrimination is when a person is treated less favourably at work because of their sex, race, religion, age, sexual orientation or disability – for example, a man is not selected for promotion because he is male.

Indirect discrimination happens when a particular employee cannot meet a requirement that is not supportable in terms of the work and they are disadvantaged as a result. For example, if an employer gives training only before 08.00, this would discriminate against people with young children.

Harassment is another form of discrimination. Harassment can include:

- verbal abuse

- suggestive remarks

- unwanted physical contact.

An employee can also be discriminated against if they are victimised after trying to take action about discrimination.

It is unlawful for an employer to discriminate against an employee on the grounds of their sexual orientation. They cannot be discriminated against or harassed in the workplace because they are gay, lesbian, bisexual or heterosexual. All employees are protected, whatever their sexual orientation.

It is unlawful for an employer to discriminate against employees on the grounds of their religion or belief. Religion generally means any religion, religious belief or similar philosophical belief. It does not include political beliefs. Employees are protected from discrimination whatever their employer's religion or belief, and whether they are already working for them or are applying for a job. If an employee has been discriminated against because of their religion or belief, they should seek help from an experienced adviser as there is a strict three-month time limit for taking legal action on these grounds.

Unlawful discrimination takes place when an employee is paid less than an employee of the opposite sex for doing the same or similar work.

The Sex Discrimination Act (SDA) 1975 makes it unlawful for an employer to discriminate because of a person's sex or marital status when appointing someone to a post:

Watching someone carry out a series of tasks, observing work in progress, listening to people's descriptions of their normal working day and any opportunity to see other parts of a business or organisation at work can all be valuable, as is linking up with a senior or long-serving member of staff. Drawing on their experience is a valuable form of individual training and learning. The experienced employee has a thorough practical working knowledge and is able to highlight potential difficulties, together with tips on how to deal with problems.

Most businesses create procedures by talking to those who carry out the duties which the procedures will cover. These individuals are aware of the difficulties and steps which need to be taken in relation to particular types of tasks. By asking the experts how they would ideally do a particular job, the business can begin to create a handbook outlining the procedures. Such manuals become reference books for individuals carrying out these tasks in the future. The manuals can be updated as procedures change or are amended for various reasons.

Businesses do not usually circulate copies of a manual and expect people to read it from cover to cover and understand what is now required. New procedures are often supported by training events, or individuals who were involved in the writing of the manual provide support for others who were not more directly involved. The mentor or expert in these procedures can assist others through what may be a difficult process of understanding the new way of working.

A business may create a series of documents or forms to track the procedures. These documents would be used to confirm that particular steps outlined in the procedures have been followed. This tracking can also serve as a useful way of highlighting difficulties with the new procedures.

In larger organisations it may be impossible to contact those who have designed the procedures. Larger organisations instead provide support by having named people responsible for dealing with the difficulties.

Gathering information

Some organisations make a point of putting together an experienced employee and a new employee, particularly at the beginning of the new worker's career with the organisation. This is known as mentoring or coaching. It has long been recognised that experienced members of staff can pass on valuable information. Is this common practice in your organisation? What have you learned from existing employees that has helped you with your work? Is there an experienced employee you turn to as a source of information and assistance?

■ 2. Understand how to maintain security and confidentiality at work and deal with concerns

2.1 Outline the purpose and benefits of maintaining security and confidentiality at work,
2.2 Outline requirements for security and confidentiality in an organisation,
2.3 Outline legal requirements for security and confidentiality, as required and
2.4 Describe procedures for dealing with concerns about security and confidentiality in an organisation

The key purpose of security is to protect the buildings, employees, equipment and information. Part of this is obviously to prevent theft or deliberate damage to the business or organisation's property.

Information dealt with as part of a task may involve the need to respect confidentiality. Information may not only be confidential, it may also be sensitive and therefore security needs to be paramount. Confidential or secure information should not be left lying around on your desk. Neither may it be appropriate for you to ask others their opinion of it, or what to do with it. Here are some examples of confidential information:

- personal details about other employees

- appraisal information or confidential notes, letters or memos about employees

- payroll details

- business information (for example, product details, suppliers, costs and prices)

- business plans

- customer lists.

Confidential or sensitive information is not always labelled as such and an informed judgement may need to be made before letting anyone else see it. The following list suggests some basic steps to take:

- Be vigilant when photocopying confidential information.

- Lock confidential information away.

- Seal envelopes containing confidential information.

- Shred unwanted copies of confidential documents.

- Switch off the screen or close the document before leaving the computer if you are working on confidential information.

- Never write down computer or network passwords.

- Never disclose confidential information over the telephone.

A business's or organisation's knowledge, inventions, ideas and written material that have been created by the business or organisation are known as intellectual property. Certain inventions and ideas can be protected by a patent. Confidential information or copyright material, which has been created by the business or organisation, has a commercial value. A good example would be a list of customers, which, if it were to be passed on to a competitor, might cause the business or organisation to lose sales. Work and material created during work hours is normally owned by the employer and the employer takes steps to protect that information.

Most businesses and organisations will have procedures related to security and confidentiality. If an employee feels there is a problem, they should report the situation to their immediate team leader, supervisor or manager. Some larger organisations have security personnel whose sole responsibility it is to deal with these matters.

The following information should never be disclosed:

- personal information about other employees

- information about other customers

- information about the business's plans

- information about the business's financial situation.

Sometimes departments or sections within a business are very competitive. A manager's plans may be considered confidential as they may not wish any other manager to know what they are aiming to do in the future.

Access to confidential information will depend upon which part of the business you work in. Human resources, for example, will have access to confidential information about other employees; sales will know where the business orders its supplies and how much it pays for them. Some information must not be divulged to people outside the organisation. There may be clear organisational policies and procedures which determine this aspect of confidentiality.

Equally, some information must not be passed on to those outside the department, for example:

- salary scales

- plans for the department

- new project planning

- promotion prospects.

The Data Protection Act requires businesses to handle personal information held on individuals within certain principles. There are eight principles that must be applied by any business that processes personal information, as follows:

1 It must be fairly and lawfully processed.

2 It must be processed for limited purposes.

3 The information held must be adequate, relevant and not excessive.

4 It should be accurate and up to date.

5 It should not be kept for longer than is necessary.

6 It should be processed in line with individuals' rights.

7 It should be secure.

8 It should not be transferred to other countries without adequate protection.

These eight principles apply to both computer-based and paper records.

The Data Protection Act was brought into force as computers were becoming more powerful and easier to use. Much more information was being stored about individuals. It is relatively easy to set up a database on a computer and it takes far less space than paper records. Businesses found that data stored in this way could be used far more easily and it was flexible as different types of searches could be made. However, over time people became concerned that the information held on individuals could be misused or passed on to unscrupulous individuals. Just over 20 years ago the first Data Protection Act came into force. It covers all information or data related to living people that might be stored on a computer or in a paper filing system. The act sets up the rules that businesses have to follow and the Information Commissioner enforces these rules. The key phrases to remember regarding data are:

● Information Commissioner – the individual who enforces the act

● data controller – a named individual in a business who collects and keeps data about individuals

● data subject – a living person who has data stored about them which is not under their control.

Any organisation that wishes to store personal data has to register with the Information Commissioner. It has to state what type of data will be stored and how it will use it. The actual register entry will contain the following information:

● data controller's name and address

● description of the information that will be stored

● what the information is going to be used for

● whether the data controller will pass on the information to other individuals or businesses

- whether any of the data will be passed on to countries outside the UK

- how the data controller intends to keep the data safe and secure.

Copyright and patents are examples of what is known as intellectual property. Patents protect the features and processes that make things work. This lets inventors profit from their inventions. Copyright is automatic once text has been written – it can include manuals and some forms of databases. Written work, as long as it is original and not copied from another source (the original copyright holder), is protected by law. Patents aim to protect the features and processes that make things work. This allows the creator of the invention to profit from their work.

Clearly, if a patent falls into the wrong hands then another individual or organisation could simply copy the invention and profit from the work of the inventor. If an organisation does not patent its inventions, then anyone can use them, make them or sell them without its permission, and it can be a long and expensive business trying to protect an invention that does not have a patent. However, if a patent does exist then the inventor can prove that they created the invention and that someone copying it has no right to do so.

Gathering information

Do you work in part of an organisation that deals with sensitive or confidential information? Are there policies and procedures in place to protect that information? Are you aware of the legal requirements? What procedures exist in your organisation to deal with any security or confidentiality concerns?

■ 3. Understand how to assess, manage and monitor risk in the workplace

3.1 Describe sources of risk in an organisation, including health and safety

An office-based environment may appear to have few risks. Certainly there are fewer than in a factory or warehouse. Simply walking around the office environment will identify a number of potential problems and hazards:

- Fire risks – this can be an ever-present danger. Any electrical item is a potential fire risk and employees need to know what to do if a fire breaks out.

- Slips, trips and falls – even without steps and trailing cables, items placed on the floor can create hazards and these types of risk are significant in any workplace. This is particularly true if new equipment or desks are added to the office environment in an unplanned way, as they will create new hazards.

- Hazardous substances – printers and copier toner cartridges have poisonous substances. Employees should not be exposed to these and they should always follow manufacturers' instructions.

● Catering – simple items such as kettles can cause serious injury. Shared resources such as fridges can harbour germs.

Many of these considerations fall under the general title of health and safety. Health and safety should incorporate any major risks or hazards that employees could face in the office environment. Health and safety also involves looking at the best ways of reducing the probability of incidents occurring.

It is important that all employees share the responsibility for ensuring health and safety in their working environment. Protecting employees or visitors is a legal responsibility under the Health and Safety at Work Act. Complying with health and safety rules is extremely important and many organisations will have their own health and safety policy. In fact, it needs to be in writing if the employer has five or more employees. Health and safety rules also involve:

● carrying out a risk assessment

● ensuring that the workplace meets minimum standards in terms of comfort and cleanliness

● recording serious injuries or accidents in an accident book (in some cases reporting them to a relevant authority)

● reducing the amount of harm that the business does to the environment.

Gathering information

Look around your working environment and try to identify any potential sources of risk. Have there been any instances of accidents in the workplace? What caused the incident? Has the cause of the incident now been removed?

3.2 Explain how to assess and monitor risks in an organisation

To comply with health and safety legislation employers need to risk assess the working environment. It is not the case that all risks can be eliminated, but the rule is to try to protect people as far as is reasonably practicable.

A risk assessment will identify areas that require improvement. Out of this an action plan should aim to deal with the most important first. In order to evaluate potential hazards, they are identified as being high, medium or low in terms of the harm that they could cause.

In a typical working environment workplace hazards can easily be spotted. This means dealing with the following:

● loose or trailing cables

- wet, slippery, badly surfaced or unclean floors
- poorly lit areas
- poorly ventilated areas
- poor storage of cleaning substances and chemicals
- faulty or inappropriate electrical equipment
- poor drainage
- poorly maintained tools, equipment and machinery
- poorly designed work stations
- areas that are exposed to prolonged, sudden or loud noises
- insufficient rest breaks
- insufficient training
- excessive work pressure
- providing protective devices, such as wrist supports or anti-glare screens.

It is important to make sure that each risk is carefully considered:

- Can equipment be used to control the hazard?
- Can the hazard be isolated?
- Can better working practices and systems be brought in?

It is equally important that all risk assessments are written down. Under the Health and Safety at Work Act, whoever is carrying out the risk assessment needs to be able to show that:

- they made a proper check
- they asked who might be affected
- they dealt with obvious hazards
- they took reasonable precautions and any remaining risks are low
- others were involved in the process.

A plan of action is drawn up that can include a number of approaches:

- a temporary solution until a longer-term solution has been put in place
- a long-term solution that will effectively eliminate the risk
- additional training for employees to help avoid the risk
- regular checks to ensure that control measures stay in place
- clear responsibilities as to who will undertake the work and monitor the risk.

Gathering information

Who is responsible in your workplace for carrying out risk assessments? How are these risks monitored? What kind of control measures are put in place? Risk assessments are effective only if people act on them. How is this ensured in your organisation? The Health and Safety Executive has an online office risk assessment tool, which may be of use to you if you are not involved on a regular basis (www.hse.gov.uk/risk/office.htm).

3.3 Describe ways of minimising risk in an organisation

Very few workplace environments remain the same. From time to time new equipment and procedures are brought in that could lead to a range of new risks and hazards. This means that there has to be an ongoing review. The review will also help ensure that the organisation is still improving and not ignoring identified risks.

In order to ensure that risks are continually assessed, the following questions need to be asked:

● Have there been any major changes?

● Are there still improvements that are necessary?

● Has a problem been identified?

● Have there been any accidents or near misses?

Having carried out a risk assessment it is easy to ignore the situation until something actually goes wrong. It is therefore advisable to have a review date for the risk assessment.

If there is a significant change in the working environment, a risk assessment should be carried out immediately. Typically, new risk assessments should be carried out when:

● new equipment or machinery is brought into the working environment

● new processes or working practices are adopted

● new substances are used (such as a change of photocopier or its toner)

● new employees join the organisation

● the working environment is significantly altered

● a department moves premises

● the business expands

● there has been an accident or a near miss.

Gathering information

Have there been any significant changes in your working environment? Was a new risk assessment carried out? Who would you consult to see whether basic health and safety procedures comply with regulations? Is there a process in place that allows individuals to report potential risks? How are these reports dealt with?

4. Understand the purpose of keeping waste to a minimum in a business environment, and the procedures to follow

4.1 Describe the purpose and benefits of keeping workplace waste to a minimum, 4.2 Describe the main causes of waste that may occur in a business environment and 4.3 Describe ways of minimising waste, including using technology and other procedures

Producing any kind of waste is inefficient and costs the business or organisation money on materials and disposal costs. Businesses try to get the most value they can out of their resources by using renewable resources and minimising waste at the same time. Businesses benefit from waste reduction by saving time and money.

Approximately 5 per cent of what an average business makes as profit each year is lost due to wastage. Reviewing all activities and processes can help. Simple changes, such as printing or photocopying on both sides of the paper, can be effective. It may not always be necessary to have a printout of a document. An email attachment is a good alternative that can be circulated to all those who need to see the document. However, many people still prefer to work from a hard copy and to read paper documents rather than electronic ones.

Businesses and organisations have high energy and waste disposal costs, as well as legal obligations to deal with the waste. In an office, the bulk of the waste is paper. Ways to reduce the amount of paper wastage include:

- reusing paper
- changing printer settings to print double-sided or in draft mode
- cancelling junk mail and other unwanted communications

- using email instead of printed documents
- reusing scrap paper for message pads
- reusing envelopes for internal mail.

According to the government group Envirowise (http://envirowise.wrap.org.uk), office waste costs British organisations and business £5 billion each year. The average worker in an office prints off more than 1,500 sheets of paper each month. This is despite the fact that approximately 70 per cent of all office waste is recyclable.

Gathering information

Do you know the level of waste your team or office generates in a month? Is the waste generated by your office or team, or is it generated elsewhere and you have no need for it once it has been processed or used? What alternatives are there for sharing information? Do you have a high failure rate in printing and photocopying and what is done with scrap paper?

4.4 Explain the purpose and benefits of recycling,
4.5 Describe organisational procedures for recycling materials, and their purpose and
4.6 Describe ways in which waste may be minimised by regularly maintaining equipment

Recycling involves reprocessing used materials that would otherwise be discarded and put into landfill as waste. Recycling involves reusing or remaking the materials into new products. Paper can be recycled, as can printer or toner cartridges, which can be cleaned and refilled. The main benefit of recycling is in reducing the need to produce wholly new materials.

Britain has one of the lowest recycling rates in Europe. Although 70 per cent of all office waste is recyclable, less than 8 per cent is in fact recycled. By recycling 1 ton of paper, 7,000 gallons of water are saved, as are 17 trees, landfill space, an enormous amount of energy and oil. It has been estimated that the average office worker wastes 50 pages every day.

There are some key tips to ensure that recycling works in the office environment, including:

- set the default on printers to print on both sides of the paper or in draft mode
- don't print out emails unnecessarily
- don't print off too many copies of documents

- place recycling bins in every office

- don't use vending machines that use paper or plastic cups

- avoid buying catering products that use milk pots, sugar sachets or paper plates.

Businesses need to be more environmentally aware and stress the importance of cutting waste. Transparent bin bags for recycling waste allow everyone to see what is being recycled. This has proved to be more effective than hiding it away and can be a valuable part of showing how recycling schemes actually operate.

Regular maintenance of printing equipment is important in keeping waste to a minimum because machines will encounter fewer paper jams. Using the recommended paper weight is also beneficial, as thinner, cheaper paper, while more economical, can cause jams and problems with the majority of faxes, copiers and printers.

Good practice also involves using email attachments to pass on work rather than printing hard copies of documents.

Gathering information

Is there a recycling policy at your workplace? Are you aware of the waste disposal costs and the impact that your activities have on the environment? Offices are often seen as having little impact on the environment, but they use significant quantities of resources, including paper, energy and water. How often is equipment maintained or serviced in your workplace? Are engineers called in only when there is a problem? Who has the responsibility for this?

5. Understand procedures for disposal of hazardous materials

5.1 Explain the purpose of procedures for the recycling and disposal of hazardous materials and
5.2 Describe procedures for the recycling and disposal of hazardous materials for an organisation

All employees must be aware of their responsibilities regarding the recycling and disposal of hazardous materials. Employers will put procedures in place to prevent employees from damaging themselves and other employees, or contaminating the working environment. Businesses and organisations have to ensure that chemicals or dangerous substances are stored and handled in a way that minimises any risks. The Control of Substances Hazardous to Health

(COSHH) Regulations 2002 require organisations to assess storage risks and handling and take into account any environmental damage.

While most substances that could be considered dangerous or hazardous may be found in manufacturing, there are some used in the office environment, such as printer ink and toner. Printer cartridges were classified as hazardous waste in 2005 and precautions have to be taken to control risks, including:

- following manufacturers' instructions for safe storage
- having only the minimum quantity of hazardous substances on site
- storing substances that could react with one another separately
- making sure there are no leakages
- training staff to deal with spills and having a spill kit prepared
- cleaning up spills or leaks
- using protective clothing and having adequate ventilation when handling the substances
- making sure that anyone who has to handle the substances has been trained
- ensuring the containers are properly labelled
- ensuring the containers are intact.

Businesses should have a series of best practice measures and procedures, which could include:

- ensuring liquids are stored above ground
- ensuring they are not placed near major employee traffic areas
- ensuring all deliveries are supervised
- preventing overfilling of containers
- putting in drip trays in case of leakage.

Hazardous substances can include those that:

- are flammable
- are toxic
- are corrosive
- give off fumes.

Some can cause headaches, skin rashes or sickness and can be dangerous for asthmatics. Even common substances used in the workplace, such as glue, can be hazardous. Some prime examples of hazardous substances that can be found in an office environment include:

- photocopier toner

- glue

- paint

- bleach

- furniture polish

- pest control substances.

If hazardous substances are present a COSHH risk assessment has to be carried out. The Health and Safety Executive (HSE) suggests using a risk assessment form, such as the one shown in Figure 303.3, which is included on its website (www.hse.gov.uk).

Company name: Architect's office	Date assessment made					
Department	Date discussed with employees					
Dept 1 Substance	**Step 2**	**Step 3**		**Step 4** Action		
What's the hazard?	What harm, and who?	What are you doing already?	What improvements do you need?	Who	When	Check
Breathing in solvent vapours Wide format inkjet printer	Irritation					
	Everyone in the office	Leave prints in well-ventilated room to dry	Move printer to ventilated room			
Skin contact with ink	Anyone filling printer cartridges	Skin cleanser provided	Get sealed cartridges			
Skin contact with solvent	Anyone cleaning a print head - skin damage	Use nitrile gloves and lidded bin for waste	Begin skin checks			
Indoor air quality	Everyone from time to time - irritation					
	Sore eyes/throat, stuffy nose		Better fresh air provision, provide plans to increase humidity. Use questionnaire			
Photocopier – breathing in emissions	Toner dust (not harmful), odour (not ozone)					
	Anyone nearby	Change filter and corona wires	Vacuum up dust. Get a new copier			
Also:		Action taken	Action needed			
Thorough examination & test – COSHH						
Supervision						
Instruction and training						
Emergency plans			Spill of print head cleaner			
Health surveillance		None	Some checks			
Monitoring						
Step 5 Review date:		1 Review your assessment - make sure you are not sliding back 2 Any significant change in the work? Check the assessment and change if necessary				
Other hazards needing attention: slips and trips, lifting, electrical appliances						

Figure 303.3

Computer monitors are also hazardous waste as they require recycling. Rather than disposing of old computers and monitors, businesses will take them to be refurbished and used by voluntary organisations or shipped out to developing countries. Legislation encourages the reuse of computers, printers and monitors.

The Waste Electrical and Electronic Equipment Regulations (2006) recommend what is known as Best Available Treatment Recovery and Recycling Techniques. This means that the business has to find the most appropriate way in which to protect the environment when it disposes of equipment. Some examples of best practice include:

- removing whole toner cartridges intact so that the toner does not enter the water system

- careful handling of computer monitors so the glass or screen is not broken – a professional organisation would have to remove any pollutants, such as lead

- not burning electrical cables but shredding or reusing them

- recycling the printed circuit boards in mobile phones.

Gathering information

What kind of recycling and environmental schemes are run at your workplace? Are you encouraged to think about minimising waste and recycling? If so, how is this done at your organisation? Who has responsibility for ensuring it is being done?

6. Understand ways of supporting sustainability in an organisation

6.1 Explain the benefits to an organisation of improving efficiency and minimising waste over time and
6.2 Describe ways of continuously improving own working methods and use of technology to achieve maximum efficiency and minimum waste

The key benefits to an organisation of improving efficiency and minimising waste over time are:

- greater productivity

- reduced costs

- increased profit

- reduction in impact on the environment

- the creation of a sustainable operation

- fewer complaints

- an ability to identify new efficiency areas and new ways to further minimise waste

- a culture that encourages employees to maintain sustainability

- improved working conditions for employees.

The whole concept of sustainability infers environmental friendliness across all processes, products or manufacturing. It is also broader than this, as sustainability tries to balance the needs and impacts on people (employees and others) with the impact on the globe (in terms of environmental impacts) while still trying to be profitable. This is often referred to as the three Ps (people, planet, profit).

Sustainable development of a business means meeting customer needs while treating the environment in a considered way and being able to be profitable at the same time. From an employee's point of view, working conditions and the technology used, as well as the surroundings or the number of people with whom an employee works, can differ from business to business. Qualifications and skills differ, as do the ways in which these are used in a specific job.

Government legislation can also impact on working conditions as these are governed by health and safety rules. Employees work much better if the employer ensures the following:

Figure 303.4

- the workplace is well lit

- the workplace is kept at a constant temperature, regardless of the weather

- the workplace is well decorated

- efforts are made to encourage health and fitness and to reduce sickness

- the hours worked can be flexible to take account of employees' personal commitments

- employees receive regular training and the opportunity to gain qualifications

- employees' skills are rewarded and this is reflected by salary or promotion

- experienced employees are encouraged to stay with the business

- pay and conditions are attractive and compete with those of local competitors.

Environmental conditions, such as heating and ventilation, lighting, noise and the availability of working space, can impact on efficiency. Businesses organise work areas to try to make the best use of the space they have available. Some businesses have tried different office layouts and design and have decided to make the best use of the space they have available and reduce the number of individual offices. Other businesses have kept the more traditional approach of individual offices. Many businesses and employees consider an individual office to be prestigious and indicative of importance.

As the nature of the work being carried out by employees differs, there will always be a need to allow others to access information and equipment which is used daily. A poor environment can affect the way in which employees are able to perform their duties. Considerations include:

- heating and ventilation – in a cellular office the employee can control the temperature; in an open-plan office this has to be agreed by all

- lighting –a designer or an architect may need brighter lighting than someone who works on a computer

- décor – open-plan offices restrict wall space and the space required by other people

- noise – open-plan offices are often noisy, but cellular offices can have the door closed

- working space – there are restrictions on the amount of working space each employee is allowed. Cellular offices can be used differently and the door can be locked overnight.

There are a number of ways that small changes in working practices and the use of technology can improve efficiency and reduce waste. Reusing paper and setting the printer to produce draft copies are good practice, but other simple measures include:

- using paperclips instead of staples – 72 tons of metal would be saved every year

- replacing disposable pens with refillable ones

- reusing padded bags and polystyrene beads

- reusing cardboard boxes

- repairing equipment rather than replacing it

- ensuring all mailing lists are up to date

- encouraging employees to cycle or walk to work, or use public transport or car sharing.

Gathering information

Does your workplace consider itself to be a sustainable organisation? What steps has it taken to improve efficiency and minimise waste? What could you personally do, as far as your own working methods and use of technology are concerned, to be more efficient and to minimise waste?

6.3 Outline ways of selecting sources of materials and equipment that give best value for money

Whenever the term 'value for money' is used, the natural inclination is to believe that it is purely price that drives the selection of sources of materials and equipment. However, value for money is far broader than this and includes the following:

- Fitness for purpose – do the materials and equipment actually perform sufficiently well for their intended use?

- Technical performance – do they have a technical advantage over similar products? Other factors could include the reliability or even the economic life, which is particularly relevant for equipment. It is important to think about whether the item is too expensive to maintain or whether it will quickly become replaced with new technology.

- Capability of the supplier – can they continue to supply materials or equipment of the same quality at the required time?

When considering value for money, the real cost of materials and equipment is in fact their whole-of-life cost. This includes:

- acquisition costs – how much to buy

- operating costs – particularly for equipment, including its energy use and safety costs

- maintenance costs – costs of consumables, spare parts and repairs

- upgrade costs – costs of spares and modifications and training

- support costs – costs to insure the item
- disposal costs – how much the item may be worth at the end of its useful life or how much it will cost to dispose of it in an environmentally friendly way.

Many businesses will have approved or existing suppliers of materials and equipment. They will have already negotiated deals with them. However, many other businesses have specific purchasing departments. They respond to requests to source materials and equipment from other parts of the organisation. The purchasing team's responsibility is to find materials and equipment that match the specifications or needs and to negotiate the best possible price from the most reliable supplier.

Some organisations will have more complex systems, such as tendering. A good example would be the supply of photocopy paper for the whole year. A number of potential suppliers would be contacted. The quantity and quality of the paper would be specified, the frequency of delivery would be included. Each potential supplier would then give the organisation a written quote based on this information. The supplier that offers the best value for money and most acceptable terms would get the order.

Gathering information
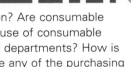

How are purchasing decisions made in your organisation? Are consumable materials purchased centrally? Who keeps track of the use of consumable materials? Is their cost allocated to different teams and departments? How is equipment purchased? How are suppliers selected? Are any of the purchasing decisions made with sustainability in mind? Who has to authorise major purchases?

7. Be able to respect and support other people at work in an organisation

7.1 Complete work tasks with other people in a way that shows respect for (a) backgrounds, (b) abilities, (c) values, customs and beliefs

Refer to 1.2 and 1.6 then consider the following.

Gathering information

Ideal situations will include team-work tasks. Your workplace will have a wide variety of people. Each individual will have something to offer and it is your ability to recognise this that is important. You could obtain witness testimony or your assessor will be able to observe and comment.

7.2 Complete work tasks with other people in a way that is sensitive to their needs

Refer to 1.5 then consider the following.

Gathering information

It is always important to be attentive to what others are saying. You would want others to be sensitive about issues that you feel strongly about. Again, this can be best tackled through observation or witness testimony. You need to show that you value the opinion of others. Always be aware, however, that other people's priorities may be different to your own, so you also need to be sensitive to their needs.

7.3 Use feedback and guidance from other people to improve own way of working

Refer to 1.7 then consider the following.

Gathering information

You should try to use feedback and guidance from others. You could do this in a slightly more formal way, in order to ensure that you have collected sufficient evidence. You could create a simple form that could cover your timekeeping, your availability, your organisational skills, your approachability, your communication skills and your contribution to the team. You could ask individuals to grade you, with 1 being excellent and 6 needing improvement. Leave a space for general comments on the form. You can use this form as the basis to help you improve your own way of working.

7.4 Follow organisational procedures and legal requirements in relation to discrimination legislation in own work

Refer to 1.6 then consider the following.

Gathering information

The equal opportunities policy of your workplace is a good place to start. Most organisations will have a policy and a series of procedures that will be in line with legal requirements. Try to obtain a copy of this and indicate which parts of the policy could apply to you.

■ 8. Be able to maintain security and confidentiality

8.1 Keep property secure, following organisational procedures and legal requirements, as required and
8.2 Keep information secure and confidential, following organisational procedures and legal requirements

Refer to 2.1 to 2.3 then consider the following.

Gathering information

Many businesses will have specific procedures to fall in line with legal requirements regarding the security of property (the business's own property and that of the employees) and information. The policies will identify security management, the sharing of information, restrictions on communications, responsibilities of employees, potential risks, equipment security, access to data and steps to be taken in the case of an incident. Organisations will often:

● provide a lockable space for employees' personal property

● have a security tag and/or alarm equipment

● have clear instructions regarding the access to data, whether it is printed or on a network.

These will fall in line with legal requirements. It is important to remember that most data will be considered to be confidential and sensitive.

You will need to demonstrate that you follow any existing organisational procedures and legal requirements.

8.3 Follow organisational procedures to report concerns about security/confidentiality to an appropriate person or agency, as required

Refer to 2.4 then consider the following.

Gathering information

Procedures for reporting concerns about security and confidentiality will differ across organisations. The procedures will be entirely different in a small to medium-sized business compared with a larger organisation. Larger organisations will tend to benefit from having more elaborate security measures. Even smaller businesses will have areas that are not accessible to visitors or members of the general public. However, most businesses will have systems put in place to protect data, particularly if it is kept on a network. You will need to identify how you would go about reporting any security or confidentiality concerns. In some cases the reporting will be to another employee. In other cases it may be to an external agency, such as a subcontracted security company.

9. Be able to assess, manage and monitor risk

9.1 Identify and agree possible sources of risk in own work,
9.2 Identify and agree new risks in own work, as required and
9.3 Assess and confirm the level of risk

Refer to 3.1 to 3.2 then consider the following.

Gathering information

If you have not been involved in carrying out a risk assessment of your own then you will need to carry one out. You will have to identify possible sources of risk. If you have already done this you should reassess your working environment, focusing primarily on any new potential risks. You can use downloadable templates from the Health and Safety Executive website (www.hse.gov.uk). You will need to assess the level of risk – high, medium or low – and confirm that your assessment of the risk conforms to generally accepted assessments.

9.4 Identify and agree ways of minimising risk in own work

Refer to 3.3 then consider the following.

Gathering information

Focusing on your working environment, incorporating the equipment and materials that you routinely use, suggest how you could minimise any potential risks that you have identified.

9.5 Monitor risk in own work

Refer to 3.2 then consider the following.

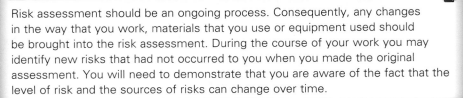

Gathering information

Risk assessment should be an ongoing process. Consequently, any changes in the way that you work, materials that you use or equipment used should be brought into the risk assessment. During the course of your work you may identify new risks that had not occurred to you when you made the original assessment. You will need to demonstrate that you are aware of the fact that the level of risk and the sources of risks can change over time.

9.6 Use outcomes of assessing and dealing with risk to make recommendations, as required

Refer to 3.1 to 3.3 then consider the following.

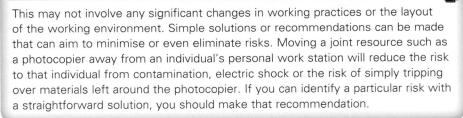

Gathering information

This may not involve any significant changes in working practices or the layout of the working environment. Simple solutions or recommendations can be made that can aim to minimise or even eliminate risks. Moving a joint resource such as a photocopier away from an individual's personal work station will reduce the risk to that individual from contamination, electric shock or the risk of simply tripping over materials left around the photocopier. If you can identify a particular risk with a straightforward solution, you should make that recommendation.

10. Be able to support the minimisation of waste in an organisation

10.1 Complete work tasks keeping waste to a minimum and
10.2 Use technology in own work tasks in ways that minimise waste

Refer to 4.1 to 4.6 then consider the following.

Gathering information

There are simple ways of providing evidence to show that you make an effort to minimise waste and to use technology in the correct way. A straightforward example would be checking a document thoroughly on-screen before printing it out, reading it and then discovering that there are errors. In many cases you can use technology to minimise waste by printing documents on both sides of the paper. The majority of office printers and photocopiers are capable of achieving this simple waste reduction method. But in many cases these are rarely used.

11. Be able to follow procedures for the disposal of hazardous waste in an organisation

11.1 Follow procedures for recycling and disposal of hazardous materials in own work tasks, as required

Refer to 5.1 to 5.2 then consider the following.

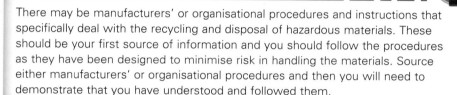

Gathering information

There may be manufacturers' or organisational procedures and instructions that specifically deal with the recycling and disposal of hazardous materials. These should be your first source of information and you should follow the procedures as they have been designed to minimise risk in handling the materials. Source either manufacturers' or organisational procedures and then you will need to demonstrate that you have understood and followed them.

12. Be able to support sustainability in an organisation

12.1 Follow procedures for the maintenance of equipment in own work,
12.2 Review own ways of working, including use of technology, and make suggestions for improving efficiency,
12.3 Select and use equipment and materials in own work in ways that give best value for money and
12.4 Support other people in ways that maximise their effectiveness and efficiency

Refer to 6.1 to 6.3 then consider the following.

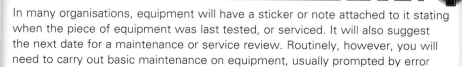

Gathering information

In many organisations, equipment will have a sticker or note attached to it stating when the piece of equipment was last tested, or serviced. It will also suggest the next date for a maintenance or service review. Routinely, however, you will need to carry out basic maintenance on equipment, usually prompted by error messages. A printer, for example, may require head cleaning or a photocopier may require function keys to be pressed so that it can carry out a self-maintenance and cleaning program. The instructions or procedures for such work will normally be found in the manufacturer's instructions or in specific instructions put together by the organisation. These should be in manuals or documents close to the equipment.

As part of your contribution to sustainability you should also look at the way in which you work. Are there simple steps that you could take, such as reducing the number of documents that you print, or the turning off of equipment that is not being used? Other straightforward efficiency improvements could include moving frequently used documents or resources closer to your own work station.

It is not always an individual's responsibility to select and use equipment and materials, but you need to show that you are aware of the fact that certain equipment and materials offer better value for money, both in the short and the long term. A prime example is paper. Many businesses buy standard paper in bulk and use it for most things. Yet cheaper, unbleached paper could be used for draft internal documents. Printers and photocopiers could be set to provide draft quality only rather than high-quality copies that should be reserved for documents that will be seen by customers, for example.

You should encourage your work colleagues to look at these areas and see what aspects of their working practices could contribute towards sustainability in the organisation. For the purposes of evidence you may wish to circulate an email or form to your work colleagues, with your suggestions and a request that they make their own suggestions based on their working practices.

What is Evidence ?

A single piece of evidence can cover more than one learning outcome. Several assessment criteria can be dealt with by the one piece of evidence. You can also use the same evidence for other assessment criteria from other units. Your assessor will use a wide range of assessment methods for the learning outcomes in this unit, including:

● observing your performance

● examining work that you have produced

● questioning and discussing issues with you

● using witness testimony from work colleagues

● looking at your learner statements

● recognising your prior learning.

The range of evidence can include:

● annotated organisational policies and procedures

● appraisals or job reviews and subsequent reviews

● self-evaluation

● work plans and amended work plans

● learning or development plans

● feedback from colleagues

● minutes of meetings

● review of work methods

● communication relating to security issues

● risk assessment of work area or task

● documentation monitoring ongoing risk

● communication regarding recommendations as a result of monitoring risk.

Work with Other People in a Business Environment

■ Purpose of the unit

This unit is about working in a team. It highlights the importance of sharing responsibility with others to ensure that the team achieves agreed goals and objectives for the organisation and the team.

■ Assessment requirements

There are nine parts to this unit. The first six parts look at teams and team working. The remaining three parts focus on your performance as a member of a team and the dynamics within that team. The nine parts are:

1 Understand how to support an organisation's overall mission and purpose – how the organisation works, its mission and purpose, how it compares to other organisations, your main responsibilities and how these fit into the organisation's structure and contribute to achieving the organisation's mission, organisational policies, procedures, systems and values relevant to your role and where to seek appropriate guidance on these. (K)

2 Understand how to work as a team to achieve goals and objectives – the purpose and benefits of working with other people, how team work can bring about positive results, sharing work goals and plans, supporting other team members and the purpose and benefits of agreeing quality measures. (K)

3 Understand how to communicate as a team – communicating with others within the team, different methods of communication and when to use them and the benefits of effective communication within a team. (K)

4 Understand the contribution of individuals within a team – the purpose and benefits of acknowledging the strengths of others and respecting individuals working within a team. (K)

5 Understand how to deal with problems and disagreements – types of problems and disagreements in a team and ways of resolving those problems and disagreements. (K)

6 Understand the purpose of feedback when working as a team – the purpose and benefits of giving and receiving constructive feedback and the ways of using feedback to improve your own work, the work of others and that of a team. (K)

7 Be able to work in a team to achieve goals and objectives – working to support the organisation's overall mission, following policies, systems and

procedures relevant to your job role, and seeking guidance when necessary, contributing to improving objectives, policies, procedures and values, putting the organisation's values into practice, communicating effectively with other team members, sharing work goals, priorities and responsibilities, agreeing objectives and quality measures, making best use of all abilities in a team, supporting other members of a team, showing respect for team members and ensuring that the team produces quality work on time. (P)

8 Be able to deal with problems in a team – identifying and resolving problems and disagreements in a team. (P)

9 Be able to share feedback on objectives in a team – sharing constructive feedback, receiving constructive feedback, sharing feedback to identify improvements in own work and that of a team. (P)

■ 1. Understand how to support an organisation's overall mission and purpose

1.1 Explain how the organisation works

The easiest way to visualise an organisation's structure is to think about a pyramid. At the top of the pyramid there are a few people making the most important and the biggest decisions about the business. As you go down the pyramid there are various layers of managers. After the managers are team leaders or supervisors. At the broadest part of the pyramid, the base, are the rest of the employees.

A functionally based organisational structure is usually designed around the different parts of the organisation that produce, market and sell the product or service. In other words, the different departments or functions will all be controlled by a board of directors, who elect or appoint a managing director. The managing director is supported by a range of senior managers, each of whom has the responsibility for one particular function of the organisation.

The functional areas of an organisation, often otherwise known as the departments, all have their own specific jobs to do. Examples are outlined in Table 305.1.

Table 305.1

Functional area	Purpose and responsibilities
Finance and accounts	The finance or accounts department of an organisation supervises all matters involving money.
Human resources	The main function of the human resources department is to recruit the most suitable employees and organise them so that they provide the right type of work which the organisation needs in order to meet its objectives.
Production	The production department is involved in all functions which revolve around actually producing the products or services for the customer. This department will monitor levels of wastage to ensure the most efficient use of resources. It will also check the cost of raw materials and parts purchased to make sure that profit margins are maintained.
Research and development	Working closely with the marketing department (which is keeping a close eye on competitors' products and services), the research and development department will attempt to come up with new products for the business.
Purchasing	The purchasing department is responsible for assisting the other departments of the business in ordering and buying the goods and services required.
Sales	The sales department's main responsibility is to create orders for the business's products or services. Many organisations employ a large sales force, which may be based either on a local level, in the case of retail outlets (shops), or in the case of organisations which supply other organisations, on a regional basis.
Marketing	The main function of the marketing department is to try to meet customers' needs and to predict what they may need in the future. Working closely with the sales department, the marketing department carries out a great deal of research to try to discover what customers want, where they want to be able to buy what they want and how much they are prepared to pay for it.
Distribution	The effective and efficient distribution of the business's products is the responsibility of the distribution department.
Administration	Some organisations have what is known as a central administration department. The main function of this department is to control the paperwork and to support all the other departments by providing them with secretarial or administrative work.
Customer services	Without customers a business is unable to survive. However large or small a business may be, it will always want to make sure that its customers are happy. Because the customers' needs, wants and requirements change all the time, the business will have to think ahead of its customers to make sure it always gives them exactly what they require to make them satisfied.
IT services	The information technology (IT) or computer services department will have the responsibility for the hardware and software that a business uses. It will also be responsible for maintaining the business's databases, telecommunication systems and other office technology. As most organisations now incorporate computers into many of their routine activities, this department will need to be up to date on any developments in the technologies used and know how to use new software.

Even the smallest organisation is a complex network of different factors. All organisations input resources in order to create products or provide services, which are then used (but not always sold) to supply customers or clients. In a business organisation the difference between the costs of the resources and the revenue it receives from sales is the business's profit or loss.

However, not all organisations are primarily interested in profit. They may have a budget, which is the set amount of funds or resources, to provide a range of services to a specific client group. A prime example would be a local council. It receives money from the community charge, from business rates and other sources. These are the inputs or resources. The local authority is then required to provide a range of services for the local population. This can range from refuse collection and street sweeping to the provision of parks, housing and swimming pools.

The exact nature of each organisation, regardless of its size, will differ. What does not change, however, is the use of inputs or costs to the organisation and the money that it receives in exchange for providing products or services.

Some organisations will be people and service based, such as banks. Banks do not have products as such; they provide a range of services. A small business such as a TV aerial company will provide a range of products and services to customers, including aerials, satellite dishes and cable installation. In order to provide these services and products and to pay for their employees, they charge customers for the products and services. Charging more for these products and services than it has cost them to buy (plus the cost of their employees, premises, etc.) represents the profit that the business has made.

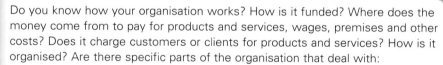

Gathering information

Do you know how your organisation works? How is it funded? Where does the money come from to pay for products and services, wages, premises and other costs? Does it charge customers or clients for products and services? How is it organised? Are there specific parts of the organisation that deal with:

- income
- expenditure
- buying
- selling
- decision making
- advertising?

1.2 Explain the organisation's mission and purpose

All business organisations, whether they are small, medium or large, will have a purpose – a set of aims or objectives which they wish to achieve. The purpose of most is to be successful and they will aim to achieve this objective in all of their day-to-day activities. However, there are some things that can affect whether or not a business is able to meet its objectives, which may be out of the control of the organisation itself, including the following:

- changes in legislation
- financial difficulties
- business ownership or legal structure changes.

Businesses will compile a list of their aims, purposes and objectives in their business plan. This requires flexibility, as the environment in which the business is operating could be changing constantly and its objectives may have to change along with it.

Examples of objectives included in a business plan are different for each organisation, but could include:

- to be successful
- to make a profit
- to break even
- to sell products
- to sell services
- to survive.

Business objectives can also differ from time to time. Objectives are the medium-to long-term targets which help the business to achieve its 'mission statement'.

Organisations have to ensure that their employees know about the business's objectives. Employees must have a true picture of what the organisation needs. Organisations will use some of the following to make sure they keep their employees up to date with changing objectives:

- staff meetings
- newsletters
- company newspapers
- bulletin boards
- notice boards
- email messages
- press statements or press releases

- organisational videos

- documents sent directly to all employees.

Mission statements

Mission statements contain an organisation's corporate objectives. An organisation's mission statement is different from its business plan because it describes what the organisation as a whole stands for. It is an agreement between the managers and the employees of the organisation regarding a number of goals. Everyone involved in the business will have an opinion about the way goals should be achieved, or at least share some ideas about how they will be achieved.

- A business's fundamental policy will be contained within a mission statement and this will describe the organisation's business vision, including its values and purpose. Mission statements are a statement of where a business wishes to be rather than a description of where it is at the present time. A business may choose to include within its mission statement a vision of how it wishes its employees to respond, react and fulfil the needs of its customers.

- Businesses will want whatever is contained within their mission statement ultimately to be achieved. Employee development programmes and training programmes help them meet the objectives stated in the mission statement.

Gathering information

Does your organisation have a mission statement? Is it clear what is meant by the mission statement? Does it clearly spell out the organisation's purpose? Is the statement updated from time to time or is it a general statement that does not require updating? What does the statement tell someone who is unaware of the organisation about the business's mission and purpose?

1.3 Compare how the organisation works with other different types of organisations

There are many different ways in which you can compare organisations, including:

- legal structure – is it a partnership, a limited company, a charity, a government organisation?

- size – is it based on a single site or are there multiple sites?

- purpose – what does the organisation produce or provide? Who are its clients or customers? What is its mission statement?

- employees – how many employees are directly or indirectly employed by the organisation?

- teams, departments and organisation – how is the organisation broken down? Are there specific teams for specific functions? Are there different divisions or groups?

● types of customer – what are the common customer types? Are they individuals, businesses or organisations?

● sector – is the organisation privately owned or publicly owned? Is it involved in raw materials (primary sector), manufacturing (secondary sector) or services (tertiary sector)?

Another way of making a comparison between organisations is to look at the mission or purpose. It is sometimes difficult to compare organisations with one another because they are so very different. Some organisations have grown and changed over a long period of time; others are new and have been created specifically to carry out a range of tasks.

An organisation in the private sector may be more interested in its share of the market, profit and its customers. A public-sector organisation needs to perform well and show that it provides value for money. An organisation in the voluntary sector is concerned with raising money and providing high-quality services to its clients.

When comparing how organisations work, all of these factors need to be taken into account. You would not expect a school working from a budget to provide high-quality education to pupils to operate in exactly the same way as a retail outlet that sells mobile phones. Added to this, all of the admin-istration and support would be entirely different – it would be focused on radically different areas. In the case of the school there would be a great deal of paperwork to complete, such as reports, attendance records and fulfilling legal obligations. For a retail outlet the administrative focus might be on purchasing, sales, marketing and stock control.

Gathering information

One of the best ways of approaching this is to look at organisations that you are familiar with. Knowing someone who works in a different type of organisation can also be valuable. Think about some of the factors listed, such as legal structure, size and purpose. Creating a table that highlights the key differences could be a valuable way forward. Sometimes you may not find it easy to categorise certain aspects of how organisations work, as they will be radically different.

1.4 Explain your main responsibilities, how these fit into the organisation's structure, and how these contribute to achieving your organisation's mission

An employee's job role should be explained at interview and then will be contained in the contract of employment, as well as the job description. This will outline the employee's role in the organisation, either as a team member or as an individual working to support others in the organisation.

All employees, however, have to be flexible and adaptable, as they are often required to carry out duties which are not necessarily part of the job description. The term 'clarity of roles' means knowing exactly what is expected of an employee in a variety of circumstances. The employee should be aware of how their job role and ultimate work relates to the larger activity of the business or organisation as a whole.

Organisational procedures can help an employee understand the processes involved in getting particular tasks completed and often will suggest the ideal ways in which the business wants particular things completed. These will be a series of steps, supported by checks, to make sure that everything has been covered and completed to the business's, and probably the customers', satisfaction. The organisational procedures will set out the requirements of a particular task, possibly as a series of instructions to alert or remind the employee that particular documents have to be referred to, other documents and forms completed and other individuals involved. Organisational procedures therefore help an employee to ensure everything has been done. They will also assure the business that all the necessary steps have been taken in line with its policies and procedures.

A job description explains what the job involves and would include:

- the job details
- the employee's position within the organisational structure
- the tasks and activities required
- the roles and responsibilities.

The amount of detail included on a job description will depend on the type of job involved – there will probably be more details given for a job with management responsibility than a job for a junior person with fewer responsibilities.

A business may also compile a person specification. This is a description of the kind of qualities the person should have to satisfactorily carry out the job. A person specification is the business's checklist of the ideal person for the job and will include a description of:

- experience required
- skills required
- physical characteristics, i.e. minimum height restrictions
- qualifications required
- personality and temperament – particularly important for team leaders or dealings with customers
- motivational qualities – can they work unsupervised?

An organisation's structure could look like a pyramid. At the top of the pyramid there are a few people making the most important and the biggest decisions about the business. As you go down the pyramid there are various layers of managers. After the managers are team leaders or supervisors. At the broadest part of the pyramid, the base, are the rest of the employees.

Instructions or orders are passed down the various layers of the organisation until they reach the employees. Information is provided by employees to their team leaders or supervisors, who check that information and pass it on to the various layers of management. The management in turn passes this information on to the owners of the organisation. Armed with this information the business's owners can make their decisions and create the orders and instructions. Figure 305.1 illustrates these issues.

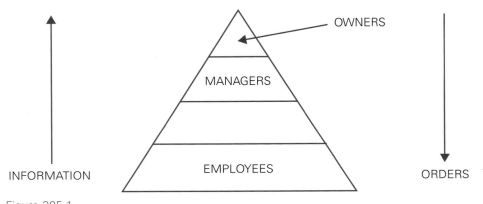

Figure 305.1

The way an organisation chooses its structure will depend on a number of issues, including:

- the size and nature of the market in which it operates
- the type of business in which it is involved
- the need for good communication throughout the organisation
- the size of the organisation
- the number of different branches or sites
- the type and number of customers
- how much the organisation is affected by legislation
- how much the organisation is affected by new technologies
- the organisation's responsibilities and obligations
- the organisation's previous structure
- the organisation's present structure

- the organisation's future plans

- the complexity of the organisation's activities.

A functionally based organisational structure is designed around the different parts of the organisation that produce, market and sell the product or service. The different functions will all be controlled by a board of directors, which elects or appoints a managing director. The managing director is supported by a range of senior managers, each of whom has the responsibility for one particular function of the organisation. Figure 305.2 explains a functional structure.

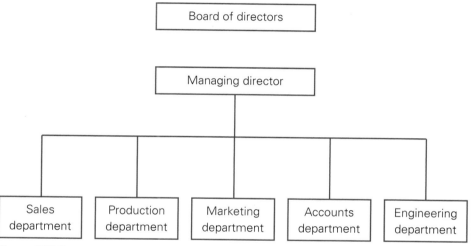

Figure 305.2

This structure is particularly relevant for larger organisations, where each function or area is a separate department. Each organisation that is structured in this way creates a number of departments to best suit its objectives. It also helps define what individuals do and the responsibility of each department. Effectively this is a way of grouping different employees, usually by their function or what they do for the organisation. In other cases it might be by location, so the organisation may be structured so that it has several different regional offices. Other businesses organise themselves by types of customer.

Each individual within the department will have their own specific job role.

Gathering information

Does your organisation have an organisation chart that shows the structure? Do you have a job description and can you see how your main responsibilities fit into the overall work of the organisation? What parts of your job role help achieve an aspect of your organisation's mission?

1.5 Define policies, procedures, systems and values of your organisation relevant to your role and
1.6 Describe when it is appropriate to seek guidance from others when unsure about objectives, policies, systems and procedures and values

Policies are the broad guidelines that determine the way in which an organisation operates. Procedures are the preferred ways the organisation wants specific tasks or activities to be performed. The systems are the supporting mechanisms that allow the procedures to be followed. The values of an organisation are often part of its organisational culture and may include providing excellent customer service and feedback, value for money, open and honest dealing and public accountability.

Administration procedures are important since the activities of the organisation must be coordinated and planned. If inadequate administration procedures are in operation, the organisation may suffer lack of efficiency and effectiveness due to lack of relevant information.

Businesses and organisations will also have a series of other procedures, including the following:

- Health and safety – following health and safety legislation and providing guidance to employees.

- Security and confidentiality – procedures to ensure that the building, property and confidential information remain safe.

- Grievance procedures – will also follow legislation and will state how an employee can bring a complaint to the notice of the employer and the procedures to be followed to investigate that grievance.

- Disciplinary procedures – will state unacceptable behaviour and the sanctions that can be brought against the employee, as well as the stages involved in the disciplinary procedure.

Most administrative systems are a series of sub-systems which can be split into additional sub-systems. The organisation will monitor all parts of the system, which should be designed so that they can be changed to meet the evolving requirements of the organisation.

Administrative procedures are the means by which the organisation is able to operate as a whole. Without procedures to ensure that functions are carried out, these may be unsuccessful. Information received has to be processed before it can either be stored or disseminated around the various departments or sent out of the organisation in a different format.

Depending on the type of business and the type of information there are generally accepted descriptions of administration procedures:

- rules and regulations laid down by senior management

- activities carried out by managers to meet the objectives of the organisation

- activities carried out to ensure the control of the day-to-day running of the business.

An organised approach is required for efficiency and effectiveness. In a larger organisation, administration will be carried out by the administration department, but in smaller businesses the administration may be carried out by a single individual who will be responsible for all forms of administration. The basic purpose for these procedures is the same, however:

- to provide support systems for all resources used by the organisation

- to keep a record of the organisation's activities

- to monitor the performance of the business's activities.

The organisation will need to ensure that:

- information is stored in the right place

- information can be found easily

- information can be copied or printed and distributed

- information can be sent and received easily by the business

- the physical resources are available to the business's employees.

Activities of an organisation may be classified as routine or non-routine. Routine activities are carried out on a regular basis and include opening the mail and filing. Others will be non-routine activities or those that cannot be predicted. Routine functions can be easily arranged throughout the organisation if the correct procedures are in place to handle them. An office organised in this way will base its procedures on experience and will know with considerable accuracy the demands that will be placed upon it. When non-routine tasks are involved the employees must be able to rely upon a separate series of procedures to support them. It may be the case that a support system has to be created for that specific purpose if the non-routine task needs to be carried out so frequently that it becomes routine.

Procedures need to be in place to track the activities of the business. All organisations will have their own procedures, but generally they will all have a way of keeping track of some of the following aspects of their activities:

- the cost of purchases

- the names of suppliers

- sales levels

- the customers

- enquiries made by customers

- payments made by customers

- payments outstanding from customers

- payments made to suppliers

- payments outstanding to suppliers

- information about employees

- details of training undertaken or required by employees

- information about the levels of stock

- records of meetings.

Larger organisations tend to have more procedures than smaller ones. Some procedures are very formal because they are dictated by law, such as health and safety procedures, but others are dictated by the business's objectives, or what they have discovered to be the best way to do things. Some procedures are required to ensure the business's confidential information is not leaked or because there is a need for security of information or the business's buildings. The following could be examples:

- All visitors to the business have to check into reception.

- Employees wishing to do photocopying or obtain a file have to complete a form.

- All mail being delivered or sent out of the organisation has to be dealt with by a mail room and distributed to each department.

Procedures have to be advantageous to the business, particularly if they are expensive to set up and run. A business could benefit from having procedures in place if they allow an organised approach to activities. Decisions about the organisation's objectives will be made and the procedures will help the business's managers and employees to achieve those objectives.

Effective procedures help provide a good impression or image to customers and the general public. A good image is important and the business would want:

- all paperwork to convey a good impression

- all information requested to be sent out quickly, accurately and efficiently

- all customers to receive a high level of service

- confidential or sensitive information to be kept safe

- buildings and employees to be kept healthy and safe

- government legislation to be adhered to.

This will bring the following benefits:

- Customers are more likely to return and buy again.
- Customers are more likely to recommend the business to others.

Gathering information

Are there clear policies, procedures, systems and values in your organisation? Are these specifically written down in a manual (printed or on the intranet)? Alternatively, have you learned these or had them passed on to you by other employees? Where do you go for guidance if you are unsure? How do you make the judgement as to whether or not you need guidance or you could reasonably work out what is necessary from your experience?

2. Understand how to work as a team to achieve goals and objectives

2.1 Explain the purpose and benefits of working with other people to achieve agreed goals and objectives

Teams are created for a variety of reasons, but most have the following objectives:

- To solve problems.
- To make improvements.
- To assist members to learn and develop.
- To create a team spirit.
- To encourage creativity.
- To exchange ideas.
- To work constructively.
- To develop the team's overall skill levels.
- To develop the abilities of team members.
- To break down complex tasks into a series of simpler tasks.

Teams can be set up to carry out a variety of work. They can be set up for a specific task or for a long-term task, such as developing better customer service.

Individual goals and talents often have to be forfeited for the team to meet its goals. Team work requires patience and understanding, but can be enjoyable, with strong friendships being developed.

Businesses create teams because they know that teams can produce better results and work more effectively than individuals working alone. Businesses will try to get teams working as well as possible, as quickly as possible and will give team leaders a major role in ensuring this happens.

Team-working situations are important because a manager, supervisor or team leader can create and control the way the team operates to provide particular answers to questions. The business will want the team to be capable of carrying out specific tasks and to fulfil a particular role in the business. The primary reasoning is that the team has to be effective and efficient at what it does.

Gathering information

How do you feel about working as a member of a team? Do the members of the team share the same view of work? How do members of the team communicate with one another and how often? Do you feel that working as a member of a team is more effective than working independently?

2.2 Describe situations in which working with others can achieve positive results

Teams can be capable of a variety of tasks, their purpose being to make sure that the tasks are carried out efficiently. Many employees find that working in a team promotes close social relationships at work.

According to the European Foundation for the Improvement of Living and Working Conditions, businesses are keen to develop team working because:

- productivity can be increased by up to 80 per cent
- quality of work increases in approximately 70 per cent of cases
- 50 per cent of teams reduce the amount of waste (in time and materials)
- 65 per cent of team members say that team work increases job satisfaction
- 60 per cent of teams managed to improve customer satisfaction.

Many businesses reorganise their structure to accommodate more team working, as shown in Figure 305.3.

Team functions can be broken down into three main areas:

- Tasks – the time and effort put into achieving the team's objectives or goals.
- Interaction – the contact between the members of the team. This changes over time. At the outset the interaction will be about deciding how things are to be done and sorting out conflict. Once the team is established, inter-action between team members will revolve around asking for support and help when needed.

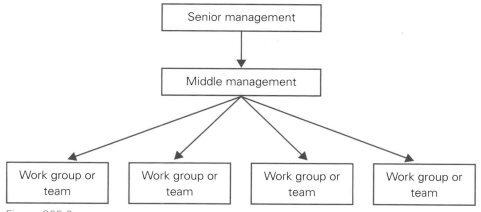

Figure 305.3

● Self – the time and effort involved in ensuring that individuals within the team are doing what is needed to support the team. It is also about being noticed and satisfying your own needs.

Individual roles within the group are important and there needs to be a good mix of different types of people, with skills and abilities to support one another.

Gathering information

Do you feel you are a member of an ideal team? Do individuals in the team have different roles? If so, what are they? How much more effective are you as a team than as a group of individuals?

2.3 Explain the purpose and benefits of sharing work goals and plans when working with others

The purpose of agreeing work goals and plans when working as a team is to ensure each individual knows their role and what is expected of them. The benefit of doing this is ensuring that the tasks and activities are carried out with maximum efficiency. Sometimes negotiation and splitting the work is required to make maximum use of each team member's strengths.

The classic way to approach target setting is to consider the acronym SMART. SMART stands for:

● Specific

● Measurable

● Achievable

● Realistic

● Timely.

All of the team's goals and targets should be broken down into manageable pieces so that short-term goals are achieved en route to achieving major goals. These steps must be prioritised and written down so that there is no doubt about what the goals or targets are. As the goals are achieved they can be ticked off and the next one concentrated on.

Planning is a crucial element of team work. A good plan needs to be 'alive'; it needs to be flexible and remove pressure from the team and its leader. It provides the team with a 'map' for achieving objectives and targets. Planning can involve:

● deciding on the team's objectives overall

● highlighting the main objectives

● deciding the order in which the objectives must be met

● deciding on the strategies needed to achieve the objectives

● deciding the roles of team members to achieve the objectives.

Team planning usually takes place at meetings where the following would be addressed:

● progress checks

● upcoming deadlines

● prioritising tasks to meet deadlines

● allowing individual input

● allocation of tasks

● allocation of resources.

Gathering information

What are your team targets over the next month? What are the most important priorities? Why is it important for the team to share goals and plans and agree on these?

2.4 Describe situations in which team members might need support and
2.5 Explain different ways of providing support to teams

The exchange, or swapping, of information between team members is absolutely vital in order to make sure that any tasks, series of tasks or major objectives are achieved. Continual communication between the team members means that everyone is kept up to date with the progress of the project and that any problems which occur can be dealt with by the team as a whole. It also means that information collected by one of the team is available to all of the others, as they may need these facts and figures to carry out their part of the task.

Exchanging information as a regular process is vital. The team must devise a foolproof way of collecting and disseminating collected information so nothing is missed or overlooked and not exchanged with the others. If this happens, then the whole idea of working as a team begins to break down.

The process of exchanging information can either be formal or informal, as we can see in Table 305.2.

Table 305.2

Formal	Informal
Meetings	Conversations
Reports	Email messages
Memoranda	Business notes
Circulated documents (with sign-off sheets to show they have been seen)	
Presentations	
Updates or newsletters to all team members	

Team work relies on cooperation. Cooperation means being helpful, available and open to suggestions. Cooperation between team members involves:

- putting the needs of the team first
- a friendly and sociable atmosphere
- avoiding conflict
- no competition between team members
- support and cooperation
- trust
- an acceptance of the rules
- adherence to legislation
- respect among members
- fulfilment of expectations.

Team members must learn that they need each other because they have mutual goals. They will all be striving to achieve the same thing, which can be achieved only if they all work together. In addition to this, the team has to share resources and fulfil any role which has been given to them.

Team members can assist and support by:

- helping
- sharing
- encouraging
- explaining
- discussing
- teaching.

Gathering information

How do you handle different situations when team members need support? How do you reallocate work if a team member is unavailable? What do team members do if they have finished their part of a task but others have not yet completed their tasks? How do you bring in new members of the team and help them adapt to team work?

2.6 Explain the purpose and benefits of agreeing quality measures within a team

The purpose of agreeing quality measures is to ensure that standards are kept high. It gives each team member the ability to strive to work to the same standard and produce quality work. It allows each team member to know what is happening and what is expected. It also ensures that resources and time are not wasted.

Standards of work reflect directly on the business or the department in which the team is working. The key to it is communication, so that everyone knows exactly what is happening and why actions or tasks have to be undertaken.

Businesses recognise that employees are the most important resource that they have. Teams are given clear guidelines as to what is expected of them, but it is the responsibility of the team to organise themselves and use the resources they have for the best possible outcome.

Gathering information

Quality can be affected by a number of different situations. How do you think the quality of your work can be affected by not having clear instructions, lacking a deadline, team members not being available due to other work commitments, or lack of resources? How would you tackle each of these problems?

■ 3. Understand how to communicate as a team

3.1 Explain when it is essential to communicate with the people working within a team and 3.2 Compare and contrast different methods of communication and when to use them

Effective communication in business is essential, as is communication between team members when carrying out the normal activities of a team. Even organisations which are not concerned with profit making must be able to respond effectively to pressures. Employees have to work fast, accurately and try to make the right decisions. At the heart of this is effective communication.

Day after day information will flow in and out of the business. This needs to be checked, read, understood and those in need of the information have to receive it. Communication can take various forms and be used in a variety of circumstances.

In order for the business to make the right decisions or take the right course of action, the information needs to be communicated as quickly as possible and accurately. This requirement extends to every role within the organisation.

Communicating effectively means:

● providing accurate detail

● providing comprehensible communication

● presenting information comprehensibly

● choosing the correct method of communication

● providing timely information to the correct person.

Face-to-face communication is one of the most important ways teams communicate. Face-to-face communications include:

● informal conversations

● informal meetings

● formal meetings

● providing advice, guidance or information on an ad hoc basis.

Important face-to-face communication considerations are:

● the clarity of information provided

● the pitch and tone of voice

● listening and paying attention

- not interrupting
- asking appropriate questions at the right time
- being aware of body language.

Face-to-face communication involves a mixture of both verbal and non-verbal communication. There are two considerations:

- having the ability to read other people's body language
- being aware that others can read your body language.

Since the main purpose of working as a member of a team is to share ideas and be more efficient, poor communication can undermine the whole effort. It is often a good idea to establish ground rules that will ensure that everyone is updated, communication is encouraged and any project or task is completed. An ideal way to start is to:

- create an outline of the project steps
- identify who is responsible for each step
- establish an email group, so that messages can be sent or answered along with updates and changes. Setting up the email group will mean that all team members will receive the emails and will be aware of the project guidelines.

Teams should meet in person and discuss deadlines and progress. Face-to-face meetings are ideal to solve problems and to assess each team member's progress. This can also be an opportunity to reassign duties if someone requires assistance or a team member has become available to take on additional work.

Ideal communication between teams is, therefore, a mix of face-to-face communication in formal and informal situations, backed up by written communication, usually in the form of emails or minutes of meetings.

Choosing the right time to use a particular form of communication can be difficult; Table 305.3 is designed to help make those choices.

Table 305.3

Circumstances when you should use written communications	Circumstances when you should use verbal communications
When you are passing on facts	When you are passing on emotions and feelings
When the message needs to be permanent and filed	When the message does not have to be permanent
When urgency is not a major issue	When there is some urgency in getting the message across
When you do not need feedback straight away	When the need for feedback is immediate
When the ideas or details are complicated	When the ideas or details are quite straightforward and easy to understand

Gathering information

When you are involved in team work, are guidelines set to ensure that the team communicates? What mix of different communication methods do you use? Which do you personally find more effective? Do you have the opportunity to pass on your thoughts and ideas?

3.3 Explain the benefits of effective communication within a team

The benefits of effective communication within a team are very broad and most are based on establishing a basic professional relationship:

- By encouraging communication, all team members feel involved.

- They will understand the requirements of the project and its targets.

- They will have the opportunity to ask questions or have discussions to clarify issues.

- Team members can offer solutions.

- Team members are informed about project updates and issues.

- There is less chance of confusion or team members carrying out unnecessary work.

- Each team member has an opportunity to contribute, either in conversations or in writing.

- It gives each team member a chance to listen and acknowledge other people's points of view.

- Feedback and suggestions can be gathered.

Making appropriate use of emails, telephone, voice messages and other communication methods is important. Communication provides the opportunity to avoid misunderstanding and to ensure that the team remains on track to complete projects.

Gathering information

When you have worked as a member of a team, what have you found to be the most effective way of communicating with other team members? Do you prefer face-to-face or written communication? How available are other team members to discuss team work informally? Are there set procedures that try to ensure that all team members remain updated? How effective are they? What are the benefits to your organisation and the efficiency of the team?

■ 4. Understand the contribution of individuals within a team

4.1 Explain the purpose and benefits of acknowledging the strengths of others and 4.2 Explain the purpose and benefits of respecting individuals working within a team

Passing judgement on the performance of others, particularly if you are not in a position of authority, is not recommended. The view of others on a team's performance may differ from your own. An objective view is required and can be achieved by an observer watching the interactions of team members. The observer will be able to judge how each team member contributes and is involved in the team work.

Self-assessment is a good starting point. Look at your own performance, contribution and relationship with other team members, then apply the same approach to recognising the strengths and weaknesses of other team members.

Strengths and weaknesses can be looked at individually or for the team as a whole. Some may be good at doing certain things; maybe they are more communicative than others. Some are extrovert and others are introverts. The mix of people in a team makes the team as a whole effective or ineffective. Consider the overall strengths and weaknesses of the team. Are they all too alike? Did one person take the lead and the others follow? Did the team fail to agree on anything? Was the task actually completed? Was there any conflict while the task was being completed? Judging the strengths and weaknesses of a team can be done when considering the success or otherwise of a particular task. But this does not identify how well the team members cooperated during the task.

Teams should attempt to use the best qualities of each individual and assign them to appropriate tasks that suit their abilities. Each team is made up of a number of individuals. These individuals may be from different age groups, backgrounds, religions, beliefs and experiences. This enriches the team and allows them to draw on the different approaches of each of the individuals. Diversity is important in a team, as it allows the team to look at things from different perspectives and to draw on individual strengths.

Deadlines for completion of tasks are a key issue regarding successful team work. Tight deadlines will add pressure. Team work is about pulling together and ensuring each member is supported.

External factors, such as a lack of resources, can add pressure. This is an important part of planning. Resources should be identified in the planning stage.

Respect is also a key issue, regardless of the circumstances. Team members should try to ensure that they do not:

- argue

- get angry

- shout

- blame others for errors

- make excuses for errors

- interrupt each other.

Teams work well if the members all respect each other. They should feel able to apologise if necessary, ask for help if needed and strive together to see a task through to completion.

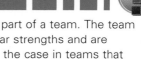

Gathering information

Individuals adopt specific roles over time when they are part of a team. The team members recognise that certain individuals have particular strengths and are best suited to specific roles in tasks and projects. Is this the case in teams that you work in? What are the key strengths of members? How are these strengths acknowledged? Do team members show mutual respect? How does this manifest itself? Why is this important?

5. Understand how to deal with problems and disagreements

5.1 Explain the types of problems and disagreements that may occur when working with others and
5.2 Evaluate ways of resolving problems and disagreements when working with others

Working as a member of a team inevitably means there will be conflict at some stage. The conflict may be as a result of disagreement about a task. These are the easier types of conflict to resolve because people naturally tend to have different ways of doing something.

Important issues can be more difficult to resolve and there may be major problems if someone is doing something differently to the rest of the team. Members may become angry and not be prepared to compromise. Conflicts such as these should be dealt with calmly and logically; any argument should be about the facts and not about personalities.

A frequent cause of conflict is when team members simply do not cooperate or communicate. Cooperation and communication within a team are vital, not only to avoid conflict but also to ensure the team is efficient and effective.

Alternative sources of conflict are personality clashes or team members bringing their problems with them to work. Some of the most frequent sources of conflict include:

- criticising a team member in front of an outsider
- leaving a team member out of the decision making
- allowing one team member to develop a strong dislike for another
- saying hurtful or tactless things to one another
- being intentionally awkward or unpleasant.

Team disagreements can become emotional. Team members tend to take sides. Issues are viewed as win or lose and team progress is halted.

Many team conflicts relate to one or more of the following, which collectively are known as PRIDE:

- Process – conflict based on how the team operates on a daily basis.
- Roles – who actually does what in the team.
- Interpersonal issues – team members not getting along.
- Direction – the way in which the team is progressing and trying to achieve its goals.
- External pressures – such as lack of time, tight deadlines or inadequate resources.

There are three ways in which conflict can be approached:

- Anticipate and prevent problems in the first place.
- Do not focus on one person causing the problem – it is a group problem.
- Do not over-react or under-react.

Typically, though, team leaders deal with conflict in very different ways:

- They do nothing, hoping it will go away.
- They may speak to individuals on a one-to-one basis.
- They may talk to the team but not be specific.
- They may confront individuals on a one-to-one basis.
- They may confront the whole team in a formal situation.
- They may expel a problematic individual from the team.

The most important consideration in dealing with conflict is to resolve it. This means:

- clarifying what the problem is by listening and asking questions
- figuring out where the team agrees and where the team disagrees

- treating the conflict as an opportunity to sort out problems and become more efficient

- asking for contributions and being creative in trying to solve the problem.

Many problems in a team arise from a lack of ground rules. The following is a list of basic ground rules that should apply to teams:

- Attendance – unless there is a legitimate reason, everyone should always attend.

- Promptness – meetings should start and end on time.

- Participation – contributions from every team member should be considered valuable.

- Interruptions – should be avoided, including phone calls, conversations with non-team members or non-task conversations.

- Courtesy – always listen and be respectful to others, do not interrupt and have only one conversation at a time.

- Work responsibilities – a lot of team work is done between meetings. It is important that each team member completes their tasks on time.

- Breaks – allow short breaks in the meeting so it is not so intense.

- Rotate roles – give people an opportunity to do something different and not always perform the same kind of tasks.

- Responsibility – ensure all team members are clear as to their role.

Evaluating ways of resolving conflict means having a precise way of dealing with the situation and weighing up the alternatives:

- Identify the problem and have a discussion with both sides.

- Define the areas of agreement and disagreement.

- Come up with several possible solutions to the problem. Aim to create several alternatives.

- Evaluate the alternative solutions by considering the pros and cons of each.

- Narrow down the possible solutions to workable ones that will suit each side of the disagreement.

- Decide on the best solution, preferably the mutually acceptable one, even if it is not perfect for both sides. It needs to be fair.

- Implement the solution.

- Continue to evaluate the solution and ask each side from time to time whether the solution has worked.

- Consider your solution to be open to revision if necessary.

6. Understand the purpose of feedback when working as a team

6.1 Explain the purpose and benefits of giving and receiving constructive feedback and
6.2 Explain ways of using feedback to improve individual work, the work of others and a team as a whole

One of the best ways of improving longer-term efficiency and effectiveness in relation to team activities is to evaluate previous tasks. Divide your experiences and ideas into good or bad and what went well or badly. Keep to the point and be honest.

Reviewing your own performance involves objective thinking about what you did and how you coped. Be honest about achievements and contribution. Key things to consider are:

- How was the task approached?

- How could the task have been more successful?

- Was there thorough planning, with consultation?

- How was the workload allocated?

- Was the outcome successful?

- How could performance have been improved?

Feedback is a very valuable tool. Feedback consists of comments and suggestions received from others in a constructive manner. It can help improve performance; it is not meant to be critical but to support individuals. Feedback gives an insight into team-work contributions. Simple, positive feedback can include:

- thanking

- praising

- celebrating successes and combined effort.

Good feedback assesses where help might be needed and finding solutions.

Feedback from others should be encouraged; even negative feedback can be of real value. Ask questions to clarify what went wrong and consider how the feedback could be used to show improvement. Good feedback can help improve working relationships, as it encourages openness and the sharing of ideas.

Feedback can come during team meetings or when a particular project is over. Of course, feedback can be positive or negative. However, it should always be constructive. Facts should be stated without exaggeration. Feedback will play a role within team meetings right from the beginning.

When giving feedback it is important to:

- be conscious of the words being used
- keep your temper
- listen patiently to others' responses
- concentrate only on the issue being discussed
- analyse what you are about to say before giving the feedback to other members of the team.

When receiving feedback it is important to:

- be open to what you hear
- let the person finish
- paraphrase what is being told to you so that you are clear that you have it right
- ask clarifying questions
- if the person giving feedback is not being specific, ask them to be so
- ask the person giving feedback how they feel you should have performed
- take time after the feedback to evaluate and come up with specific actions for improvement
- realise that there will be situations where you need to change the way you do things
- use the feedback to clarify your goals, track your progress and improve your effectiveness.

Above all, when receiving feedback you should not:

- take it personally
- become defensive or try to explain
- interrupt
- demand that the person defend their opinion
- make excuses.

Gathering information

How is feedback handled in your organisation, particularly when you are a member of a team? Is feedback only ever provided by the team leader? Are there opportunities for you to formally or informally give feedback? How does this work? How do you feel about receiving feedback in a group situation?

7. Be able to work in a team to achieve goals and objectives

7.1 Work in a way that supports your organisation's overall mission

Refer to 1.2 and then consider the following.

Gathering information

You need to be aware of your organisation's overall mission. A good place to start would be to look at your job description, a person specification and to outline the key duties that you perform as part of your normal working day. What aspects of your work tie in with the organisation's overall mission?

7.2 Follow policies, systems and procedures relevant to your job,
7.3 Contribute to improving objectives, policies, systems, procedures and values in a way that is consistent with your role,
7.4 Put your organisation's values into practice in all aspects of your work and
7.5 Seek guidance from others when not sure about objectives, policies, systems, procedures and values

Refer to 1.4 to 1.5 and then consider the following.

Gathering information

Annotated organisational policies and procedures are a good place to start. You should try to:

- identify those policies, systems and procedures that are relevant to your own work
- suggest ways in which they could be improved in relation to your work
- consider how your work reflects your organisation's values
- note potential sources of guidance from others if you are unsure about any aspects of your organisation's objectives, policies, systems, procedures and values.

7.6 Communicate effectively with other people in a team

Refer to 3.1 to 3.3 and then consider the following.

Gathering information

It will be evident that you are able to engage in effective communication with other team members in both formal and informal situations, using a variety of communication methods.

7.7 Share work goals, priorities and responsibilities within a team,
7.8 Agree work objectives and quality measures with a team, to achieve a positive outcome,
7.9 Make sure work goals and objectives are achieved in a way that makes best use of all abilities in a team and
7.10 Provide support to members of a team, as required

Refer to 2.1 to 2.6 and then consider the following.

Gathering information

This group of assessment criteria is team-work focused. You will need to demonstrate your contribution and integration into a team. You will also need to demonstrate how work objectives and quality measures are agreed and then ensure that the best use is made of the team's abilities to achieve them. You must also demonstrate that you are willing and able to provide support to other team members when necessary.

7.11 Show respect for individuals in a team

Refer to 4.1 to 4.2 and then consider the following.

Gathering information

Having identified the fact that different team members have different and complementary strengths, and that it is important to value and respect every team member, this again can be best achieved through observation and witness statements. You need to clearly demonstrate the purpose and benefits of respecting others in a team.

7.12 Make sure the team produces quality work on time

Refer to 2.6 and then consider the following.

Gathering information

Producing quality work on time should be a key priority for any team. You need to demonstrate how you agree quality measures within a team. This can be achieved by observation or witness testimony. It can focus on the agreement process and any monitoring and reviewing that takes place over the course of a task or project.

■ 8. Be able to deal with problems in a team

8.1 Identify problem(s) or disagreement(s) in a team and
8.2 Resolve problem(s) or disagreement(s), referring if required

Refer to 5.1 to 5.2 and then consider the following.

Gathering information

This can be evidenced by either a written statement or witness testimony. It is unlikely that it can be achieved through observation unless specific problems and disagreements have arisen at the right time. You will need to demonstrate how problems and disagreements were identified and the processes involved in resolving them.

■ 9. Be able to share feedback on objectives in a team

9.1 Share constructive feedback on achievement of objectives with a team,
9.2 Receive constructive feedback on own work and
9.3 Share feedback on achievement of objectives to identify improvements in own work, and that of the team

Refer to 6.1 to 6.2 and then consider the following.

Gathering information

The feedback should focus on the achievement of objectives of the team, constructive feedback from others on your contribution and your ability to identify improvements that may be necessary in your own work and that of the team as a result of the feedback.

What is Evidence ?

A single piece of evidence can cover more than one learning outcome. Several assessment criteria can be dealt with by the one piece of evidence. You can also use the same evidence for other assessment criteria from other units. Your assessor will use a wide range of assessment methods for the learning outcomes in this unit, including:

- observing your performance
- examining work that you have produced
- questioning and discussing issues with you
- using witness testimony from work colleagues
- looking at your learner statements
- recognising your prior learning.

The range of evidence can include:

- annotated organisational policies and procedures
- work plans involving others
- suggestions for improvements to objectives, policies, systems, procedures or values
- work requests and instructions
- internal communication with others
- appraisal or work reviews
- minutes of meetings
- report on how problems were solved
- documents relating to identified problems and how the problem was solved
- records of feedback given and received
- suggested improvements based on constructive feedback received.

Unit 309 Communicate in a Business Environment

■ Purpose of unit

This unit is about being able to select and use information and different styles of communication. The purpose is to be able to communicate in a clear, accurate and effective way using written or verbal communications in a business environment.

■ Assessment requirements

There are eight parts to this unit. The first four parts focus on your understanding of various aspects of communication. The remaining four parts ask you to demonstrate your own communication abilities. The eight parts are:

1 Understand the purpose of planning communication – the benefits of knowing the purpose of communication, knowing the audience, knowing the intended outcomes and the different methods of communication and when to use them. (K)

2 Understand how to communicate in writing – relevant sources of information for written communication, communication principles for using electronic forms of written communication, different styles and tones of language and the reasons for selecting them, organising, structuring and presenting written information for different audiences, checking written information, accurate use of grammar, punctuation and spelling, plain English, the purpose of proofreading and checking work, recognising important and urgent work and organisational procedures for saving and filing written communications. (K)

3 Understand how to communicate verbally – presenting verbal information and ideas clearly, making contributions to discussions, adapting contributions to suit different audiences, purposes and situations, using and interpreting body language, using and interpreting tone of voice, methods and benefits of active listening and the purpose of summarising verbal communication. (K)

4 Understand the purpose and value of feedback in developing communication skills – ways of getting feedback and the purpose and benefits of using feedback to develop communication skills. (K)

5 Be able to plan communication – identifying the purpose of communication and the audience, selecting and confirming the methods of communication to be used. (P)

6 Be able to communicate in writing – find and select information that supports

the purpose of written communication, presenting information suited to the purpose, using language and structure so it is clear, accurate and meets the needs of different audiences, using accurate grammar, spelling, punctuation and plain English, proofreading and checking, confirming important and urgent work, producing written communication to agreed deadlines and keeping file copies. (P)

7 Be able to communicate verbally – presenting information and ideas verbally, making verbal contributions to discussions, using appropriate body language and tone, actively listening, asking relevant questions and summarising communications to ensure correct meaning has been understood. (P)

8 Be able to identify and agree ways of further developing communication skills – getting feedback to confirm whether communication has achieved its purpose and using it to develop own communication skills. (P)

■ 1. Understand the purpose of planning communication

1.1 Explain the benefits of knowing the purpose of communication

Each communication, whether it is written, verbal or a diagram, is a message and has a purpose. The purpose may be to instruct, provide information or request information. The communication may have to be presented in a particular way and it could be formal or informal. Effective communication is essential. It is important whether the communication is internal or external.

Managers, teams and employees work under pressure and have to work accurately if the right decisions are to be made. Every day information flows in and out and around an organisation. This all has to be checked, read, understood and communicated to other employees, departments or to other organisations. Some types of communication suit the situation better than others.

In smaller businesses much communication is straightforward, by discussions, conversations and meetings. In larger businesses this can become more complicated as different departments may be in different parts of a building, or in different parts of the country or the world.

Some of the organisation's customers may be non-English speaking, or English may be their second language. Customers from different cultures may expect communications to be in ways familiar to them and others may have specific needs; they may have a hearing impairment, or they may be young children.

Above all, the purpose of planning communication is to be:

● clear about why the message needs to be sent

● clear about what you are trying to get across in the message

- clear about what you hope the message will achieve
- able to identify whether it needs to be a formal or informal communication
- clear about the language needed
- clear about the audience involved.

The main benefits of knowing the purpose of any communication are to enable that communication to be as effective as possible. The purpose of the communication needs to be established, as it will ultimately determine the method of communication used and the content.

Communication, for example, can be used in order to:

- persuade
- inform
- request
- direct.

A persuasive communication needs to put arguments to try to convince someone. An informative communication simply needs to pass on facts. A request can also be persuasive, but it is asking for someone to do something. A communication with directions will be a series of informative statements, which aims to explain how something should be done.

Each of these different purposes will require a different approach. Therefore the benefits of knowing the purpose can help frame the way in which the communication is constructed and how it can best be presented for the intended audience.

Gathering information

What is the purpose of the majority of communications that you make with others? How does this affect the way that you put that communication together and the method that you use? Do you have to plan your communications? What benefit does this planning bring to you and to your organisation?

1.2 Explain the reasons for knowing the audience to whom communications are presented and
1.3 Explain the purpose of knowing the intended outcomes of communications

Knowing the audience helps eliminate communication methods that are not appropriate and to focus on communications that are ideal for a particular job.

There are several golden rules about learning to identify the audience to whom you are communicating:

- What is the size of the audience? – are you directing the communication towards one individual, several or hundreds? This will determine the communication method used.

- What are the attitudes and biases of the audience? – you need to take this into account and show your awareness and sensitivity to their views.

- What motivates your audience? – do they have strongly held views or expectations?

- How much does your audience already know? – you need to say enough that they understand, tell them what they need to know and how to respond.

- Are they interested? – try to focus on their interests and not your own. They may have common interests or conflicts.

- What will they get out of the communication? – this is often referred to as 'what's in it for me?' or 'why should I listen?' You need to tell the audience what they will get out of your communication.

Communication aims to inform, persuade, change or establish goodwill. The target audience can be:

- an initial audience that will pass on your communication to others

- a primary audience that you hope will act on your communication

- decision makers who will ultimately decide whether or not to act on your communication.

Once you have identified the audience you can then decide whether a formal or informal channel of communication is appropriate. You can also decide whether the communication needs to be written or spoken. You will also have to decide how quickly you require a response, or whether you need the audience to participate and contribute in some way.

The key benefits of knowing about your audience is to allow you to correctly frame your communication in the most effective manner, ensuring that you get all of the key points across and that they are left in no doubt as to how they should respond to your communication.

Each communication will have a specific outcome. Part of the communication is to make this as clear as possible. The typical outcomes are:

- a decision

- a discussion

- information

- planning

- generating ideas

- getting feedback

- finding solutions

- agreeing targets or aims

- policy statement

- team building or motivation.

In combining the knowledge you have of the audience with a clear under-standing of what you hope to achieve from the communication you should then be able to create the communication using the most effective channel. For the most part intended outcomes are responses, feedback or some kind of action. In the majority of cases an effective communication will clearly state what is expected of the audience in terms of an outcome. It will also set a deadline and a method to respond or contribute.

Gathering information

What is the most common audience for your communications? How well do you know this audience? Do you create communications that have specific outcomes intended? How do you signpost those intended outcomes in your communications?

1.4 Describe different methods of communication and when to use them

Different communication options are available, dependent upon whether the communication is for internal or external purposes. Internally, the key options are as follows:

- Emails – ideal for short communications that may pass on information or request information. They need to have clear headings.

- Internal telephone systems – ideal as the communication is instant and can offer a more private way of discussing things in a direct way.

- Discussions in meetings – these can be effective if you can openly discuss problems, make suggestions and encourage others to become involved.

- Informal face-to-face conversations – which may be appropriate if you know the individual and are able to meet with them.

- Written and printed – these are considered more formal communications and include memos, newsletters, reports and other longer documents. These need to be distributed and read but sometimes they are the only way to get complex information to others.

External communication offers a broader range of possible communication methods:

- Letters – these need to be properly set out, look professional and provide information.

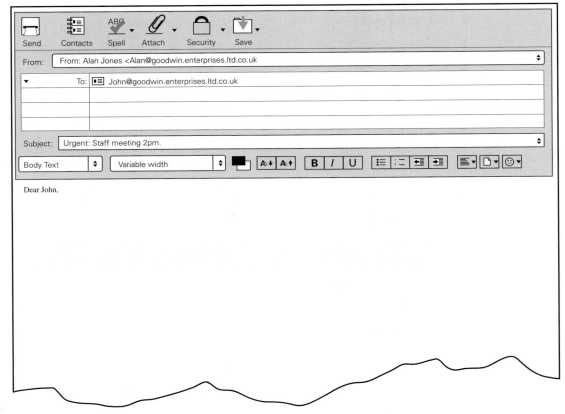

Figure 309.1

- Emails – these can be ideal for confirmations and exchanging ideas.

- Telephone – unless recorded there is no record of the communication, but otherwise it is an ideal communication tool.

- Fax – there are still occasions when hard copies of original documents are needed. Most printers are multifunctional and have a fax facility.

- Websites – if they are clear they are a good way of passing on information and providing a means to contact the organisation for more information.

- Posters, flyers and leaflets – effective ways of communicating and individuals do look at them if they are sent to the right place or distributed to the right audience.

- Advertisements – these are useful to pass on information and to be persuasive, but they must be in the right medium for the right audience.

The different methods of communication fall into two main categories: verbal and written. Communication in business is constant and varied and enables information and ideas to be passed from one person to another. A business will use a wide variety of methods of communication. Tables 309.1 and 309.2 identify the basic differences between written and verbal communication.

Figure 309.2

Table 309.1 Verbal communication

Advantages	Disadvantages
Communication is quick	Listener may not be able to hear clearly
Communication is cheap	The speaker has to be clear about what they are saying
The voice can be used to highlight important points	The messages cannot be too long or too complicated
Immediate feedback can be given by the listener	It is easy for the listener to be distracted if they are working in a noisy environment
Confirmation from the listener that they have understood	If the speaker and listener disagree there could be an argument or disagreement
Body language and facial expressions help make explanations easier	There is no record that the conversation took place

Table 309.2 Written communication

Advantages	Disadvantages
They are ideal for formal communication	Preparing the communication can be time consuming
A record is created	It must have no errors and be accurate
The record allows others to read the communication and refer to it	Poor layout and design looks messy
Copies can be made for others to read	Spelling mistakes give a bad impression
Long and complicated messages can be fully explained	Ideally it should not be handwritten, as it needs to be easy to read
Diagrams and instructions can help understanding	The communication may take longer to arrive than would be ideal

Gathering information

How many different types of communication do you use? How do you decide which is the most appropriate? Have you found certain methods of communication to be more effective than others? Why do you think this is the case?

■ 2. Understand how to communicate in writing

2.1 Identify relevant sources of information that may be used when preparing written communication

There is a wide variety of sources of information, although this will depend on the type of work involved and the nature of the organisation. Typically, sources of information include:

- documents – letters, reports, memos, company information, product details, financial reports

- directories – from telephone directories to specific industry directories, listing businesses and organisations involved in particular sectors

- telephone lists – customer or supplier contacts or telephone details of employees

- company catalogues – for the business or organisation itself or from customers or suppliers

- price lists – usually accompanying company catalogues

- the internet – researching information.

Someone within the organisation will have the responsibility of analysing the data and the figures to identify what may be relevant and what is not relevant. This is because many facts and figures are presented in ways which are not immediately useful to the business or to particular departments. The data will be analysed, finding what is relevant, and then it will be presented in its most useful format. The more relevant the information, and the shorter the summary of that information, the more likelihood there is of the reader being able to understand its relevance. It would be impossible and very time consuming for people attending a meeting to read through long and complicated documents beforehand. Equally, the meeting would be slowed down by those individuals having to refer to that document several times. The summaries present the information in a different, shorter way. More than one document or source can be used to extract information and compile it into a new format.

Gathering information

Having the relevant sources of information to hand is extremely important. When you need to prepare a written communication based on various sources of information do you know how to locate that information? How do you decide which information is relevant? How do you ensure that the information is complete?

2.2 Explain the communication principles for using electronic forms of written communication in a business environment

Emails enable text, pictures and files to be sent using email software, such as Outlook Express. You are able to write, send, receive, store and manage emails. Both the sender and the receiver have to have email addresses.

Emails can also be sent to several different people at the same time. It is a convenient way of sending messages to individuals, as they can be sent and received almost straightaway. It also allows contact with people without having to use the telephone, or write, print and post formal documents. Emails are ideal for sending simple messages, but they can also be useful in sending complex ones with other documents as attachments. The receiver can print or store emails and attachments if they wish.

Emails have many advantages, including the following:

- They can be sent instantly.

- They save on costs, such as postage and printing.

- They can be sent and received anywhere there is an internet connection.

- They can be stored for later reference.

- Email addresses can be stored.

- Hard copies can be printed out if necessary.

- Time differences around the world are not a problem.

However, there are also some disadvantages:

- It is not always clear whether the receiver has received the email, or whether it has been opened.

- Internet access and an email account are necessary for both sender and receiver.

- Computer failures could lead to the loss of all email records.

- Care has to be exercised in opening attachments on emails, or clicking links in emails. Attachments must be virus scanned and unless you trust the link being given in the email it should not be clicked on.

Gathering information

Do you routinely use email as a form of written communication? How do you ensure that you have worked through the emails received and have responded to them? What steps do you take to ensure a response from emails that you have sent? Are emails only used primarily for internal communications? Or are you encouraged to also use them for external communications?

2.3 Explain different styles and tones of language and situations when they may be used for written communications and
2.4 Explain the reasons for selecting and using language that suits the purpose of written communication

Vocabulary is the use and choice of words, which regularly has to change in different circumstances. Jargon terms or complicated words that the audience is not familiar with should be avoided. Use of vocabulary is not about intelligence, showing off by using complicated words, or even trying to impress others. It is about ensuring understanding. Talking and writing is about two-way communication; both sides need to understand.

Complicated information can be 'translated' into different formats to suit particular readers. Style is often a personal way of passing on that information to others. Sometimes an organisation will have preferred ways of doing this. Style can actually mean several different things:

- The business has a preferred way of formatting documents.

- The business has preferred spellings, such as using 'z' instead of 's' in words such as organisation (organization).

- Style can also be set out in the use of particular forms, which the business expects everyone to use (house style).

- Style may be conversational, technical (which assumes understanding of technical jargon) or formal (requiring tact, politeness and discretion).

Style, in most cases, means knowing how to speak or write in particular circumstances. The business may have codes or rules that have to be followed in all communications. Normally, the style of written communication differs:

- when dealing with colleagues on the same level as yourself

- when dealing with someone who is senior

- when dealing with customers or suppliers

- when different types of document are being produced

- when preparing a document which will be read by strangers.

Tone means putting a communication across in a way that receives the right kind of reaction from the recipient. Tone can depend on the type of individual being addressed and can be different in the circumstances identified in Table 309.3.

Table 309.3

Type of person	Tone to be used
Colleague on the same level	Friendly, familiar tone, not too formal, can use jargon if you both understand it
Senior colleague	Friendly, but not too familiar. You may need to be formal, you can use jargon
Customer	Friendly, polite and respectful but clear, forceful, and not rude
Supplier	Friendly, polite, quite formal and definitely clear

Gathering information

Is there a written communication style guide used by your organisation? Are there preferred ways in which certain types of written documents are put together in terms of language, style and tone? If not, how did you learn to adapt the style you use for different audiences?

2.5 Describe ways of organising, structuring and presenting written information so it meets the needs of different audiences

Adapted information may not always be required in its original format. Facts and figures, for example, may be hidden in paragraphs of text and may need to be converted into tables, charts or diagrams. Equally, charts and diagrams may have to be converted into text, with explanations as to what the figures mean.

When analysing, extracting and adapting information, it is important that the ultimate presentation meets the needs of the audience. Adapted information needs to be in a format which is easy to understand and can be used for quick reference.

Sometimes it will be obvious which type of document or format to choose, but at other times it may be useful to break down the document with headings, so that individual sections are smaller. Each paragraph may need its own heading, or numbered paragraphs may be required. When making a series of points rather than presenting information as a single paragraph it may be valuable to break them up by using either bulleted points or numbered points to automatically highlight their particular importance within the document. Graphics including pictures, tables and charts can often help to make information easier to understand.

The way in which written information is organised, structured and presented should reflect:

● order

● clarity

● accessibility.

It is undoubtedly the case that any audience reading written information may have a short attention span. This means that the information has to be broken up into manageable chunks. Organising, structuring and presenting can help break the document down into distinct sections, which can be read separately. Larger sections can be broken down into subsections or small units of information; perhaps only a paragraph or a diagram with a small caption.

When writing a document you should justify everything that you put in it. It should either serve a purpose or be removed. A paragraph, for example, should put across a single idea. Wherever possible, diagrams can be used to convey information more effectively. It is easier for someone to understand a pie chart rather than a list of numbers. Labels and titles should always be included.

All written documents should be drafted, revised and edited. This is part of the process of making them clearer and more effective. By spending time doing this the reader will waste less time struggling with the document.

Gathering information

Does your organisation use standard document templates? Have you created a series of templates or standard documents that you can use and amend for a variety of different purposes? How do you ensure that the way you have organised, structured and presented information is appropriate to the recipient or audience?

2.6 Describe ways of checking written information for accuracy of content

Business information must be accurate. Incorrect figures, dates or facts can cause enormous problems for the organisation's decision makers. The address on an envelope could cause an unnecessary delay, or a mistyped email address could result in a vital message not being received. Even jotting down telephone numbers needs accuracy – double-check at the end of the call, as sometimes it is too late to confirm the number once the call has ended.

It is sometimes impossible to see mistakes in your own work, so get someone else to check it. Some basic accuracy tips include:

- reading back information, facts and figures to a caller to ensure that you have written down the correct information

- getting someone to check documents before you despatch them

- proofreading everything thoroughly

- not relying only on the spell-check facility on the computer, as many such facilities are unable to recognise names of towns, people or the use of certain words, like 'whether' and 'weather'.

Accuracy is based on three key areas:

- Document accuracy – does the document cover what was needed? Is its focus covered in sufficient detail?

- Style accuracy – have paragraphs and sentences been used correctly? Is the word choice effective? Has the document been drafted, revised, edited and proofread?

- Technical accuracy – are the facts and figures correct? Are you stating what actually is the case rather than what you perceive to be the case? Have you used the most up-to-date facts and figures?

Gathering information

What is your procedure for checking the accuracy of written information that you have generated? Do you check it yourself? In fact, do you have the time to do so? Is there someone else that can check the documents for you? Is this actually part of the normal process?

2.7 Explain the purpose of accurate use of grammar, punctuation and spelling in written communication,
2.8 Explain what is meant by plain English, and why it is used and
2.9 Explain the purpose of proofreading and checking work

Poor or inaccurate spelling in a business document would be the last thing a business would want. It will give a very poor impression of the organisation and could upset its customers or suppliers. Nevertheless, these errors do occur and attention must be paid to:

- non-reliance on the spell-check facility

- using a dictionary – having a dictionary on the desk and double-checking for spelling will eventually improve general spelling

- double-checking the spelling with a colleague.

Some people have problems with plurals. A plural is usually formed simply by adding an 's,' but some words can be both singular (one) and plural, such as sheep.

Other words need more than an s to transform them into a plural. Words ending in 'y', such as library or facility, require the 'y' to be removed and '-ies' added to the end – 'libraries' and 'facilities'. Words ending in 'ss', for example 'mass', usually require an '-es' to be added to give the plural, i.e. 'masses'.

Some nouns ending in 'f' or 'fe' need to drop the 'f' to make a plural and replace it with a 'ves', for example 'calf' and 'calves', and 'knife' and 'knives'.

'Their', 'there' and 'they're' sound the same but have different meanings and many confuse them:

- 'Their' – means 'belonging to them' and could be used to describe 'their' work, or 'their' children, or 'their' home. 'Their' is the plural of words like 'his', 'her' or 'its'.

- 'They're' – means 'they are' and is like 'I'm' or 'We're' in that a letter is missed out.

- 'There' – this relates to a place or indicates something, for example 'There is' or 'Go over there' or 'I'll meet you there'.

Some golden rules regarding punctuation include:

- A full stop should be used at the end of a sentence.

- A capital letter should be used at the beginning of a sentence and when using the names of people and places (proper nouns).

- A question mark is used to replace a full stop at the end of a sentence when a question has been asked in the sentence.

- A comma is a way of identifying a pause in the middle of a sentence and can sometimes be replaced with a dash (–).

- A semi-colon is used almost as a replacement for a full stop, but it breaks up one complete sentence which needs a break in it, but which has to remain as one sentence rather than two short ones.

- Colons are used when a list is included in a sentence.

The apostrophe is commonly used. There are two different uses for the apostrophe:

- It shows that a letter or letters have been missed out of a word, e.g. 'I'm' for 'I am' or 'won't' for 'will not'.

- It shows that something belongs to someone or something, e.g. the manager's car or the dog's tail. This is known as the possessive apostrophe.

There is only one exception to the use of the possessive apostrophe and that is the word 'it', when the possessive apostrophe is never used.

The use of plain English is important as it tries to eliminate jargon or confusing information. Plain English aims to make sure that everything is clear and concise. In Britain, businesses and organisations can apply for a Crystal Mark. This is a system that was set up by the Plain English Campaign. It is a seal of approval for the clarity of a document and is now internationally recognised. The Plain English Campaign produces a number of free guides that explain how to write in plain English and a list of alternative and clearer words that can be used instead of jargon. Plain English aims to ensure that anyone reading a document can understand it without being bombarded with jargon, odd terms or phrases and unnecessary complexity.

The impression given in a business document will be greatly enhanced if the writer's use of the English language is good.

It is very important that all documents are proofread to make sure there are no errors. A word processor cannot be relied upon to identify words that are spelt correctly, but where the wrong word has been used.

All documents, from memos and business letters to reports, articles and job descriptions, need careful checking. Mistakes can creep in, particularly in the use of punctuation, grammar, spelling and the general English. Such errors can make a sentence or paragraph confusing and hard to understand.

Proofreading written work can be done on two levels:

- Micro level – this involves looking for errors in spelling, punctuation, use of capital letters, word usage, and all other aspects of English usage that the spell checking facility may have missed.

- Macro level – ensuring the document is clear and concise and that your thoughts flow logically and smoothly. Read the document word for word and not sentence by sentence. This will help you to spot and correct errors that may have slipped through initially.

The purpose of thorough proofreading is to:

- allow you to read the document as if you were the intended audience
- make sure the message is clear and to the point
- highlight any errors before a colleague, supervisor, senior member of staff or customer sees them
- provide you with an opportunity to clarify sentences if necessary
- maintain the image of the organisation.

A poorly written and badly presented document does not successfully allow the recipient to understand and appreciate the message.

Gathering information

What steps do you take in order to check your grammar, punctuation, spelling and use of English? Do you always proofread and check your work? Are there organisational procedures in place for this? Also think about the communications that you receive. What kind of effort has been put into addressing these areas? What impression did you get of that business or individual?

2.10 Explain the purpose of recognising work that is 'important' and work that is 'urgent'

Tasks and communications will have different priorities. These priorities can be broken down into four different groups:

- Urgent and important – this needs to be done immediately and needs maximum priority.
- Urgent but not important – this is not as vital as urgent and important, but still needs immediate attention.
- Important but not urgent – this is vital information that must not be forgotten, but does not need immediate attention.
- Neither urgent nor important – this does not need immediate attention and is usually routine work, but it still needs to be done.

Communications will not always be marked as important or urgent. In fact some work, which is both urgent and important, can be complicated and may take time to complete.

Work is likely to be required from a variety of different places and forms:

- Correspondence or documents
- emails or voicemail messages
- as a result of meetings or discussions
- from decision makers.

Balancing all of these competing tasks is difficult at times and requires organisation. The ability to identify priorities is a key way of managing our own personal effectiveness. Not identifying priorities can lead to stress, frustration, panic and chaos for oneself and others.

Some organisations use a priority grid in which tasks can be listed according to their level of priority, as shown in Figure 309.3.

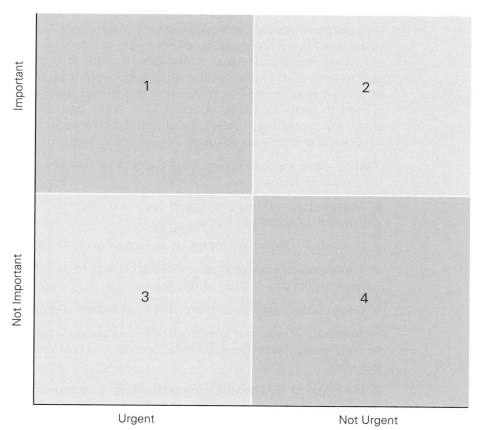

Figure 309.3
Source: www.wrightcoachanddevelopment.co.uk

Tasks are written into the relevant section of the grid, together with deadlines where appropriate.

2.11 Describe organisational procedures for saving and filing written communications

This assessment criterion requires you to identify the procedures in place in your organisation for saving and filing written communications. The procedures in place may include computerised files and paper documents.

Businesses and organisations need information. It is vital that their records are carefully organised and systematically maintained. This means the organisation will have worked out an efficient way in which to store information so that when a search for that information is made it is straightforward to be able to retrieve it. Businesses and organisations still keep an enormous amount of paper-based records, however, and this means that principles have to be applied to daily filing tasks. Efficient filing is the basis of record-keeping and entails the processing, arranging and storing of the documents so that they can be found when they are required.

When paper documents are filed, it could be that this is done using any of the following systems:

- Alphabetical – the document is filed according to the first letter of the surname or the organisation.

- Numerical – linking by means of an index card to the alphabetical method.

- Chronological – documents are filed according to date, with the most recent being at the top or front of the file.

- Geographical – documents are filed in alphabetical order by location.

Information security and confidentiality is extremely important and it applies to both manual and computer data. Security or confidentiality incidents often include:

- disclosure of confidential information to an unauthorised person

- putting the integrity of the system or the data at risk

- the availability of the system or the information being put at risk.

As far as computer files are concerned, data can be put at risk if any of the following take place:

- password sharing

- not logging off

- unauthorised access by hackers or accidental downloading of viruses

- not complying with the organisation's internet or email policies

- deliberate damage of information by an employee

- downloading unauthorised software

- siting computers in the wrong place, which could allow unauthorised people to view what is on the screen.

Gathering information

Does your organisation have procedures in place for saving and filing written documents? Are there procedures in place for ensuring security of computer files? Is your computer networked or stand-alone? Do you have to use a password to log onto your machine? Can you access other machines? What proportion of documents needs to be stored as paper copies in your organisation? Is there a procedure that determines how long these copies are stored? Are electronic copies sufficient? Is there a standard procedure for saving and filing both paper and digital copies of written communications?

■ 3. Understand how to communicate verbally

Any form of verbal communication involves exchanging information between a sender and a receiver. The sender will have a particular reason for sending the message and will expect a certain response from the receiver. The receiver has to understand what is being said, otherwise there will be misunderstanding and confusion.

Verbal communication can have one or more of the following purposes:

- to inform

- to confirm

- to promote

- to make a request

- to instruct.

It is important to establish in advance:

- the purpose of the verbal communication

- the best way to get the message across in the clearest manner

- the most appropriate timing

- whether a record of the verbal communication is required
- feedback needed from the recipient.

Verbal communication options are:

- face to face – either in a one-to-one formal or informal situation or in a meeting
- remote verbal – using the telephone, teleconferencing or videoconferencing
- voice messages.

In a business environment verbal communication can include:

- informal conversations and brief chats
- informal meetings
- formal meetings
- oral presentations
- instructions from or to another employee
- talking to customers, either in person or on the telephone.

There are many points that need to be considered when carrying out any form of verbal communication. These include:

- whether or not the message is being made clear
- the pitch and tone of the voice being used
- whether the recipient is listening or paying attention to what is being said
- whether the recipient feels free to ask questions
- when not to speak or interrupt
- the body language used.

Body language can take several different forms and includes the following:

- facial expressions
- gestures
- posture
- eye contact.

We look at how to use and interpret body language later in this unit.

Gathering information

How many different methods of verbal presentation do you routinely use? Do you know which are more appropriate in different situations? How much preparation do you give yourself before verbal presentation? How effective are you in getting your ideas across? Have you received feedback from others about your verbal communication skills?

3.1 Explain ways of making contributions to discussions that help to achieve objectives and 3.2 Describe ways of adapting verbal contributions to suit different audiences, purposes and situations

Preparation is often the key to being able to make a valuable contribution to discussions. Preparation involves reading through agendas and being aware of the purpose of team meetings and discussions. Going into a meeting or discussion without knowing the purpose or subject of the meeting will inhibit your ability to make valuable contributions.

Good team meetings encourage those attending to make a contribution, as good teams recognise that individuals have their own perspective on situations and tried and tested ways of dealing with them.

Every team has its own mix of individuals. Some quietly work in the background and are happy for others to make the important decisions. Some teams are a combination of difficult characters, often competing with one another to make decisions and to appear to be in charge. A team needs to be a good mix of individual members, each with their own set of skills, abilities and experience. They are there to support one another.

3.3 Describe ways of verbally presenting information and ideas clearly

The most famous attempt to explain the roles of individuals in teams was suggested by Dr R. Meredith Belbin in the 1980s. The Belbin types, or roles, outlined in Table 309.4, remain one of the best ways of describing the various roles of individuals within a team.

Table 309.4

Overall	Belbin type	Description
Doing/ Acting	Implementer	Well organised and predictable. Takes basic ideas and makes them work in practice. Can be slow.
	Shaper	Lots of energy and action. Challenges others to move forwards. Can be insensitive.
	Completer/ Finisher	Reliably sees things through to the end, ironing out wrinkles and ensuring everything works well. Can worry too much and not trust others.
Thinking/ Problem solving	Plant	Solves difficult problems with original and creative ideas. Can be a poor communicator and may ignore the details.
	Monitor/ Evaluator	Sees the big picture. Thinks carefully and accurately about things. May lack energy or the ability to inspire others.
	Specialist	Has expert knowledge and skills in key areas and will solve many problems. Can be disinterested in all other areas.
People/ Feelings	Coordinator	Respected leader who helps everyone focus on their task. Can be seen as too controlling.
	Team worker	Cares for individuals and the team. Good listener and works to resolve social problems. Can have problems making difficult decisions.
	Resource/ Investigator	Explores new ideas and possibilities with energy and with others. Good networker. Can be too optimistic and lose energy after the first flush of it.

Another way of dividing them is shown in Table 309.5.

Table 309.5

Overall	Belbin type
Leading	Coordinator
	Shaper
Doing	Implementer
	Completer/Finisher
Thinking	Monitor/Evaluator
	Plant
	Specialist
Socialising	Resource/Investigator
	Team worker

Teams work best when there is a balance of primary types and when team members know their roles, work to their strengths and actively manage weaknesses. To achieve the best balance there should be:

- one *coordinator* or *shaper* (not both) as the leader of the team
- a *plant* to stimulate ideas
- a *monitor/evaluator* to maintain honesty and clarity
- one or more *implementers, team workers, resource investigators* or *completer/ finishers* to make things happen.

In team meetings it is important to consider the information available, tasks and objectives to be met and any factors that may affect the team's methods of operating. Team meetings or discussions may involve:

- considering the current situation
- considering deadlines and their possible achievement
- prioritising deadlines and goals
- asking for opinions
- reaching agreement
- allocating tasks
- identifying and requesting resources.

Some discussions flow naturally, but others have to be prodded along. There may be a limited amount of time and a large agenda or several decisions to be made. The conversation needs to be driven along so that the team can agree a particular way forward.

It is very difficult to make a valuable contribution to a discussion if you have not prepared in advance. Having done this it should be easy to contribute to the discussion. You may worry that you have misunderstood something in your preparatory work and that everyone else understands the issue more than you do. In order to overcome any anxieties that you might have, contribute in a simple way and bear in mind the following points:

- You do not have to make a major contribution – say something simple or straightforward as this is still a contribution to the discussion.

- Share some of the responsibility – do not dominate the discussion or leave others to do all the talking.

- Ensure that you are positive and respectful of other people's ideas, even if you may not agree with them.

Other simple contributions can be as straightforward as agreeing or nodding the head. The individual that is talking will find signals like this reassuring and will feel that their ideas are being listened to and are valuable. This will keep you active and involved in the discussion and may enable you to make a bigger contribution later.

Agreeing with people by saying 'I'd not thought about that' or 'That is a good idea' are also useful contributions. You can then go on to say why you agree or why you think something is a good idea and move the discussion on.

Offering alternative points of view is often a good way of contributing. You should not be afraid to disagree with others. By stating an alternative view you are signalling others to consider other options. Your level of involvement in a discussion will change dependent upon the content or topic. You will feel more strongly and have more to say about certain issues. It is perfectly acceptable to draw on others' experiences before making your contribution.

Try taking notes during a discussion. It will be a record of what has been said but it may also prompt you to notice something that has been missed or an issue that has only been glossed over and needs further examination.

Adapting the way that you make verbal contributions needs careful thought. It will depend on the audience, the purpose and the situation:

- How big is the audience and what is their understanding of the topic?

- How complicated is the message?

- Are you aiming to be persuasive? In other words are you trying to influence what the audience thinks or does?

- Are you aiming to get information across, such as demonstrating a process or describing an event?

- Where is the discussion taking place? Is it in a formal or informal setting?

- Are you expected to lead the discussion or just contribute to it?

● Are there set procedures about bringing up particular issues?

● What type of delivery will you be using? Will it be spontaneous or unrehearsed? Will it be a prepared presentation? Will you have to memorise it or can you use notes? Have you had sufficient time to rehearse it?

The audience, purposes and situations will also determine exactly how you use your voice:

● You will need to speak loud enough so that everyone in the room can hear – too loud and you appear aggressive, too soft and it may appear that you lack confidence.

● You will need to speak at the right speed – make sure you slow down for complex information and speed up in between.

● Pronunciation – make sure all your words are clear so your audience can understand you.

● Professionalism – avoid using slang and be careful with jargon unless you are certain that all of the audience understands it.

Gathering information

How much do you contribute to team discussions? Are there those in the meetings that tend to dominate? How do you prepare yourself for a meeting or discussion? How do you ensure that your point of view is heard? Have you received feedback regarding your involvement in discussions? Do you have to contribute to discussions with different groups of people? How does the way that you prepare and contribute differ when there are people present that you do not know very well or are senior to you in the organisation?

3.4 Describe how to use and interpret body language and
3.5 Describe how to use and interpret tone of voice

Body language is very important in face-to-face communication, more so than when speaking on the telephone, because the two people having the conversation cannot see one another on the phone. When having a face-to-face communication with people a mixture of both verbal and non-verbal communication is used. There are two considerations here:

● being able to read other people's body language

● being aware that your body language can be read by the other person.

Body language can include:

● *Facial expressions* – these are the most common form of body language and we should always be aware of what our face is telling someone else. For example:

● a smile can make a big difference when you meet someone

● our eyes can widen when we are surprised and narrow when angry

● our eyebrows move upwards when we don't believe something and lower when we are angry or confused about something

● we can look bored if our mouth is pouting.

Figure 309.4

● *Gestures* – we use our head and hands a lot when we agree or disagree with something. We can gesture to:

   ● agree with someone by nodding our heads

   ● disagree with someone by shaking our heads from side to side

   ● greet someone from a distance by waving our hands

- give someone directions by pointing with our finger

- give someone the 'thumbs up' sign to let them know everything is OK.

- *Posture* (the way we sit or stand) – can also tell us a lot about what we are thinking or how we are reacting to someone else:

  - Sitting well back in a chair with ankles crossed gives the impression of being relaxed or confident.

  - Sitting on the edge of a seat gives the impression of being nervous.

  - Standing straight with head high gives the impression of confidence.

  - Standing slumped with shoulders down gives the impression of being depressed or lacking confidence.

- *How close one gets to other people* – apart from shaking hands, we do not often get close to people we meet at work. Most people have an 'invisible circle' around them that they prefer others not to enter. This means that they may feel uncomfortable if others get too close to them. Getting too close to someone else's face can be a sign of aggression.

- Whether one is sitting or standing is also important. Someone who is seated and having a conversation with a person who is standing up can often feel 'lower' in importance than the one standing.

- *Eye contact* – having eye contact with the person one is talking to should always occur. Eye contact shows the other person that you are giving them your full attention and often helps them to understand what is being said. Sometimes it is possible to get a better idea of how someone is going to react by looking into their eyes. Be careful, though, not to 'stare' into someone's eyes as this can be a sign of aggression.

When using face-to-face communication it is possible to learn to read the other person's body language. The ability to understand and use non-verbal communication is a powerful tool. It can help you connect with others, express what you really mean, navigate challenging situations and build better relationships at work. Reading body language can:

- repeat the message the person is making verbally

- contradict a message the person is making verbally

- substitute the need to make a verbal statement

- complement what is being said verbally

- underline a verbal message.

In addition to using body language to get a message across we also communicate with our voices, even if we are not actually using words as such. Non-verbal speech is different levels of sound:

- tone

- pitch

- volume

- inflection

- rhythm

- rate.

These non-verbal speech sounds can reflect what we are truly feeling as opposed to what we are saying. For example, our tone of voice can indicate sarcasm, anger, affection, confidence. In fact our tone of voice can convey a great deal of information, from enthusiasm to disinterest. It will affect the way others respond. Showing enthusiasm, for example, involves using an animated tone of voice. This style of speaking can instill a level of enthusiasm in others.

The inflections of your voice can change the meaning of a sentence. For oral presentations this can be practised so that the delivery is natural and shows confidence. The voice can show joy, authority and energy, all of which are enhanced if the speaker is smiling as they are speaking. Breathing is important too, as an over-enthusiastic style can bombard the listener with information at a faster rate than they are able to absorb it. Taking breaks to allow the listener to comprehend what is being said can avoid this.

Gathering information

Are you aware of using body language to reinforce your verbal communications? Have you received any feedback about your facial expressions or use of gestures? What can you read from other peoples' body language? Does body language help their verbal communication and if so how? What about your voice or the voices of your colleagues? Is it obvious that someone you work with is more successful at communicating with people because of the way they speak? If so, why do you think this is so? Have you listened to your voice, for example on a voicemail message or a tape recorder?

3.6 Describe methods of active listening and 3.7 Describe the benefits of active listening

People speak at a rate of 100 to 175 words per minute. It is very easy to let your mind drift and think about other things when other people are talking. In order to cure this you will need to actively listen or listen with a purpose. If you find it difficult to concentrate, try repeating their words (in your head) to reinforce the message. Listening is an important verbal communication skill. We all listen to a number of people during a single day, but not many of us can remember what was said in these conversations. As a useful backup, it is always a good idea to try to take notes, particularly of important conversations or instructions. This will allow you to remember what has been said.

Throughout the course of any working day, most people could receive instructions from a number of different people. Being able to listen effectively is even more important if the person giving instructions is not sure of a number of things, including:

- the exact details of what they need to tell the listener

- how interested or receptive the listener is

- how knowledgeable the listener is about the subject of the instructions.

In order for the listener to understand the instructions they have to:

- hear the instructions clearly

- interpret the instructions

- evaluate their response to the instructions

- act upon the instructions and make use of the information they have heard.

If we are to make good use of our listening skills it is important to:

- concentrate on what is being said

- avoid becoming distracted

- repeat the words or phrases used in the conversation

- look at the person speaking and respond

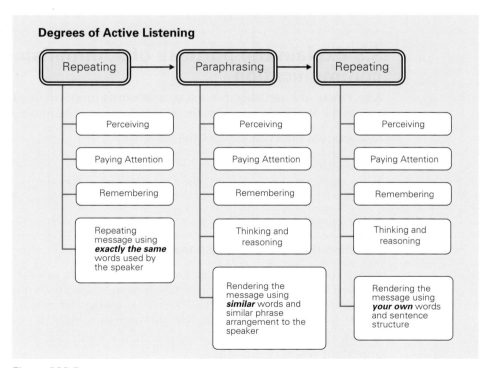

Figure 309.5

- be ready for the other person to stop speaking

- ask questions and comment on what has been said.

Active listening is more than just paying attention. Active listening means supporting the speaker by acknowledging understanding and encouraging the speaker to continue speaking and expressing their opinion. It involves responding emotionally to the speaker and showing you are absorbed in what they are saying, as opposed to just acknowledging their message.

Being a good active listener takes concentration. You should try to remind yourself and be deliberate with your listening. Try to block out other thoughts and concentrate. Ask appropriate questions and paraphrase the message for yourself in your head. Being an active listener can improve overall communication skills and productivity at work, as well as improve working relationships.

Gathering information

How effective are your active listening skills? In which types of communication situations do you find it easier to recall the content of any conversation or discussion? How much do you actually remember? You can always support your active listening by note taking. But as you take notes you are focusing on what you have already heard as opposed to what is now being said. Do you remember most of the content of team meetings? Do you have to seek clarification on points that you may have missed?

3.8 Explain the purpose of summarising verbal communication

A summary of a verbal communication is a brief rundown of what has been said during a conversation or discussion. The purpose of summarising is to:

- check the understanding of the audience

- highlight any special or important points that have been communicated

- let the audience know that the conversation or discussion is coming to an end

- restate any important points

- refresh the memory of the listener.

Being able to summarise what has been said or discussed helps avoid those involved in the meeting or conversation from leaving with questions or misunderstanding in their head. They won't be asking 'what did I say I'd do?' or 'what did I agree to?' Nobody should walk away from a meeting, discussion or any other form of verbal communication hoping that they'll remember the important points discussed.

Summarising is about:

- stating the important facts
- reinforcing
- stating any agreements made.

In summarising a brief statement is made about the longer excerpts of a meeting, discussion or conversation. It is the pulling together of the key parts of an extended communication, and restating them as accurately as possible.

Sometimes it is the speaker that summarises what he or she has said to ensure the audience has understood. At other times it is the recipient of the message that will summarise to show their understanding to the speaker.

Gathering information

Summarising verbal communication helps to clarify the meaning. Do you do this summarising verbally? Or do you find it more appropriate to note down a summary? What aspects of your job role involve you in summarising verbal communication?

4. Understand the purpose and value of feedback in developing communication skills

4.1 Describe ways of getting feedback on whether communications achieved their purpose and
4.2 Explain the purpose and benefits of using feedback to further develop communication skills

One of the main objectives of communication is to get feedback from other individuals. They can make comment on the communication and give their opinion. Feedback can come in different forms:

- It can be an immediate response, or a considered one at a later date either verbally or in writing.
- It can result in new instructions being given, or more information being provided.

An audience can provide valuable feedback, either verbally or non-verbally. This feedback will give the speaker the confidence that the audience has understood the message they have been trying to get across. Feedback can also give valuable pointers as to how communication techniques could be improved.

Even negative feedback can be valuable as it can help the speaker to restate the message in a different way, taking the feedback into consideration.

Feedback is meant to be a supportive process. It reinforces communication techniques. It also aims to correct problems and change the way things are done:

● Feedback is usually given on the basis of neutral trust rather than blame.

● Feedback, in order to be valuable, needs to be specific and also needs to be clear and concise.

● Feedback needs to be timely and refer to specific communications.

● Feedback needs to be agreed and accepted to be valuable.

● Feedback, in terms of its value, may be variable. Some may give useful feedback which is positive, while others may be negative and offer no suggestion.

● Feedback should not overwhelm.

● Feedback should not give the feeling of inadequacy.

You should ask for feedback, even if you are certain that your communication was correct. It allows you to see yourself as others see you and to adjust the

Figure 309.6

way in which you communicate. It helps you to move towards a gradual improvement across all of your communication techniques.

Positive feedback can include:

- thanking people
- commending people
- discussing progress
- praising commitment
- celebrating success.

Positive feedback can encourage people and help them through slight setbacks. It can increase confidence and prove that they are respected.

Negative feedback can include:

- constructive criticism – this should be factual, impersonal and timely
- something related to an activity or behaviour and not to a person
- a need for training rather than a statement about poor performance.

Feedback can be useful in developing communication skills. Both positive and negative feedback will have to be accepted and you should remember that not everyone is capable of giving constructive feedback, so try not to take it personally or react defensively. When receiving feedback you should:

- listen without interrupting
- wait until the end of the feedback session to make comments or discuss particular points raised
- at the end ask questions to clarify what you did or did not do and what you should attempt to do in the future
- acknowledge what has been said
- reflect on what has been said afterwards.

Feedback can help an employee to engage, it motivates and can prove to be invaluable for improvement and development.

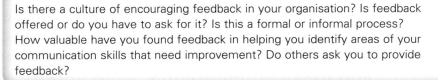

Gathering information

Is there a culture of encouraging feedback in your organisation? Is feedback offered or do you have to ask for it? Is this a formal or informal process? How valuable have you found feedback in helping you identify areas of your communication skills that need improvement? Do others ask you to provide feedback?

■ 5. Be able to plan communication

5.1 Identify the purpose of communications and the audience(s),
5.2 Select methods of communication to be used and
5.3 Confirm methods of communication, as required

Refer to 1.1 to 1.4 and then consider the following:

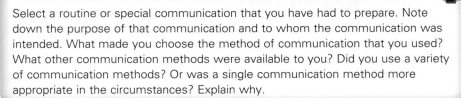

Gathering information

Select a routine or special communication that you have had to prepare. Note down the purpose of that communication and to whom the communication was intended. What made you choose the method of communication that you used? What other communication methods were available to you? Did you use a variety of communication methods? Or was a single communication method more appropriate in the circumstances? Explain why.

■ 6. Be able to communicate in writing

6.1 Find and select information that supports the purpose of written communications,
6.2 Present information using a format, layout, style and house style suited to the purpose and method of written communications,
6.3 Use language that meets the purpose of written communications and the needs of the audience,
6.4 Organise structure and present written information so that it is clear and accurate, and meets the needs of different audiences,
6.5 Use accurate grammar, spelling and punctuation, and plain English to make sure that meaning of written communication is clear and
6.6 Proofread and check written communications and make amendments, as required

Refer to 2.1 to 2.9 and then consider the following.

Gathering information

This focuses on the actual construction, look and final appearance of a written communication. If applicable you should follow any organisational guidelines as to how the written communication should be laid out in terms of format or house style. How did you ensure that the language met the needs of the audience? What steps did you take to ensure that it was clear and accurate? How did you go about checking grammar, spelling, punctuation and making sure that you used plain English? How was the document proofread and checked and what amendments did you have to make?

6.7 Confirm what is 'important' and what is 'urgent',
6.8 Produce written communications to meet agreed deadlines and
6.9 Keep a file copy of written communications sent

Refer to 2.10 to 2.11 and then consider the following.

Gathering information

Referring back to the written document that you created, how did you establish its relative importance and urgency? Did you meet the agreed deadline? If not, how did you go about renegotiating that deadline? Where are copies of the written communication kept? Are there hard copies in existence or just digital ones? Did you follow organisational procedures regarding the filing of the written communication?

■ 7. Be able to communicate verbally

7.1 Verbally present information and ideas to others clearly and accurately,
7.2 Make verbal contributions to discussion(s) that suit the audience, purpose and situation,
7.3 Use body language and tone to meet the needs of the audience, purpose and situation,
7.4 Actively listen to information given by other people, and make relevant verbal responses,
7.5 Ask relevant verbal questions to clarify own understanding, as required,
7.6 Summarise verbal communication(s) and make sure that the correct meaning has been understood

Refer to 3.1 to 3.8 and then consider the following.

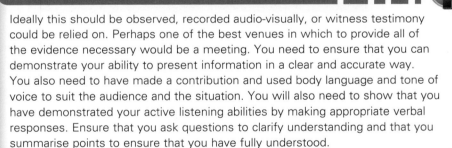

Gathering information

Ideally this should be observed, recorded audio-visually, or witness testimony could be relied on. Perhaps one of the best venues in which to provide all of the evidence necessary would be a meeting. You need to ensure that you can demonstrate your ability to present information in a clear and accurate way. You also need to have made a contribution and used body language and tone of voice to suit the audience and the situation. You will also need to show that you have demonstrated your active listening abilities by making appropriate verbal responses. Ensure that you ask questions to clarify understanding and that you summarise points to ensure that you have fully understood.

■ 8. Be able to identify and agree ways of further developing communication skills

8.1 Get feedback to confirm whether communication has achieved its purpose and
8.2 Use feedback to identify and agree ways of further developing own communication skills

Refer to 4.1 to 4.2 and then consider the following.

Gathering information

You can gather evidence for these two assessment criteria either formally or informally. One of the simplest ways will be to create a basic feedback form. This will enable you to ask for feedback from colleagues and then to annotate the feedback form, identifying areas of your own communication skills that would benefit from further development. You could use the feedback provided in the previous assessment criteria for this evidence gathering.

What is Evidence ?

A single piece of evidence can cover more than one learning outcome. Several assessment criteria can be dealt with by the one piece of evidence. You can also use the same evidence for other assessment criteria from other units. Your assessor will use a wide range of assessment methods for the learning outcomes in this unit, including:

- observing your performance
- examining work that you have produced
- questioning and discussing issues with you
- using witness testimony from work colleagues
- looking at your learner statements
- recognising your prior learning.

The range of evidence can include:

- information searches
- draft communications
- amended documents
- emails, memos, letters, reports and presentations
- minutes of meetings
- feedback on performance
- appraisals/performance reviews
- notes/minutes of one-to-one meetings
- questionnaires following a presentation
- action and development plans.

Unit 312 Design and Produce Documents in a Business Environment

■ Purpose of the unit

The purpose of this unit is to assist the learner in designing and preparing high-quality and attractive documents to agreed layouts, formats and styles.

■ Assessment requirements

There are four parts to this unit. The first two parts require the learner to understand the purpose and value of designing and producing high-quality and attractive documents and to know the resources available to do so. Part three requires the learner to understand the purpose of following procedures when designing and producing documents. The remaining part requires the learner to design and produce documents to agreed specifications. The four parts are:

1 Understand the purpose and value of designing and producing high-quality and attractive documents – different documents, different styles, different text formats and the purpose and benefits of designing and producing high-quality documents. (K)

2 Know the resources available to design and produce documents and how to use them – types of resources needed, the purpose and benefits of using different types of resources, the different types of technology available for inputting, formatting and editing text and their main features. (K)

3 Understand the purpose and value of following procedures when designing and producing documents – the value and benefits of agreeing purpose, content, style and deadlines for completion of documents, how to research and organise content, how to integrate and lay out text and non-text objects, ways of checking finished documents, the purpose and ways of storing documents safely and securely, the purpose of confidentiality and data protection, the purpose and benefits of meeting deadlines. (K)

4 Be able to design and produce documents to agreed specifications – agreeing purpose, content, style and deadlines, identifying and preparing resources, researching and organising content, making appropriate and efficient use of technology, designing, formatting and producing documents to an agreed style, integrating non-text objects into an agreed layout, checking text and objects for accuracy, editing and correcting text and objects, clarifying document requirements if necessary, storing documents safely and securely following procedures, presenting documents to the required format within agreed deadlines. (P)

■ 1. Understand the purpose and value of designing and producing high-quality and attractive documents

1.1 Describe different types of documents that may be designed and produced and the different styles that could be used and
1.2 Describe different formats in which text may be presented

Businesses communicate with their customers, with their suppliers and with one another in a number of ways, including:

- business letters
- memoranda
- reports
- emails
- agendas
- minutes of meeting
- completing forms and designing forms
- business notes
- articles
- leaflets
- advertisements
- summaries.

Business letters

An organisation's business letters should follow a specified format as laid down by the organisation's house style. They need to be on headed paper and should be neat, accurate and well presented. The order of a business letter is standardised and must always include the name and address of the person to whom the letter is being sent. It will need to be dated and at the start the person should be addressed in the correct manner, preceded by 'Dear'. It may be necessary to include a subject heading.

The bulk of the letter is paragraphs of text, which should be logically organised. It is important to match the close with the salutation. At the foot of the letter it should be signed, with the name of the person and their job title beneath. If the letter is to include anything with it, this should be indicated.

Memoranda

Memoranda are internal written communications, usually shorter than business letters and sometimes signed or simply initialled. The standard format is to have to, from, date and ref, and many businesses will use templates that employees can complete. As an alternative to memos organisations may prefer to use email for internal communications of this kind.

Report writing

Reports aim to identify problems and find solutions. Some will be progress reports, or they will focus on particular areas of activity. Reports should always have the following:

- A title page.
- Followed by what is known as terms of reference – these lay out what the report has been asked to achieve.
- A section headed 'procedure', which explains how the information was gathered.
- The main body of the report is the findings – these are what has been discovered.
- Most reports will then finish with a conclusion, which is a summary of the findings. In some cases reports will also have recommendations, which are made on the basis of the findings and conclusions.

Reports often have a series of appendices that includes all the charts, diagrams and tables that are relevant to the report.

Emails

Emails are an extremely common form of both internal and external communication. They are very flexible, allowing people to send text and pictures and attach files or images. Multiple emails can be sent out without having to write individual versions of the email, or to print out and post the communication. There are no strict conventions regarding emails, as it will very much depend on the recipient. It is generally accepted that emails should not be typed in capital letters, as this infers shouting and is considered rude. Simple, informal emails can be sent internally, while slightly more formal versions should be used for external recipients. It is important to always ensure that the email address is correct and that something relevant is put into the subject box, as effectively this is the same as the reference in a memorandum.

Agendas and minutes

Agendas and minutes of meetings are closely linked. Assuming that there has been an ongoing series of meetings, the minutes of the prior meeting are always circulated before the next meeting is called, or at the very least they are attached to the agenda of the next meeting. The minutes of the meeting are not a verbatim report of what was said at the meeting but merely a summary. The minutes pay particular attention to points that were raised by individuals and tasks that were subsequently allocated to them. An agenda summarises what will be discussed at the next meeting.

Agendas and minutes have a fairly rigid format, which must always include the date, time and venue of the meeting. There is a strict order in which agenda items are placed. Prior to the agenda being sent out, those attending the meeting will be asked whether they wish to add anything to the list for discussion. Any last-minute items can be brought up in the 'any other business' section of the meeting.

Business forms

Business forms have to be well designed, as their purpose is to ensure that the individual completes the form as accurately as possible. Confusing forms asking for unnecessary detail in an odd order can prove problematic. Forms need to be as simple as possible, leave sufficient space and, wherever possible, provide multiple options. This makes it easier for the individual completing the form and for processing the information received from them.

Business forms are used to record information. There are several key considerations when thinking about designing forms. These are:

- Make a rough copy first.
- Make sure all the necessary headings or questions have been included.
- Make sure the headings make sense and are clearly understood.
- Leave space under each heading for respondent responses.
- Get someone to check the form.
- Make sure the form looks as attractive as possible and that its layout is consistent – the headings should all look the same and the font and font size should be used consistently.

A business would want its forms to be:

- under its control
- used at the right time by employees
- used with the right procedures in place
- completed correctly
- in the right place ultimately.

The business would also want to ensure:

- the form is really needed
- the form is simple to understand and complete

- the form is the right size, regarding both the number of questions and in terms of being able to store it for future reference
- the questions are logical and asked in the correct order
- the questions are up to date
- the form is appropriate and serves the purpose for which it was produced in the first place.

Note taking

Note taking is a valuable skill to learn. Notes are taken in a variety of situations and not just at meetings, but also during conversations, as a reminder of what has been discussed. Develop your own style of note taking, perhaps using headings or underlining important parts. Notes can be kept in a book, but leave gaps for additional information if necessary. Abbreviations or initials can be used for people and notes can be typed up.

Company newsletters

Many businesses have their own company newsletters. These are used as a way of passing on information to employees, so they are designed to be read only by people who work for the business. The newsletter will contain a number of short articles, with perhaps photographs or illustrations, in order to tell employees various items of news, updates, changes in policies and procedures, or news about other employees.

One of the most useful tools in preparing articles for company newsletters is a desktop publishing program, such as Microsoft Publisher. This has the advantage of offering a number of formats, or templates, to choose from and the facility to replace the text, pictures, logos and headings on the templates with an organisation's images and text.

Preparing an article for a publication such as a company newsletter obviously involves some research and, of course, note taking. Articles can be of various lengths, but usually they are kept fairly short and to the point. Any article is always improved by a picture or a diagram or illustration. These help draw the reader's attention to the article and give them something to remember the article by.

Press releases

Although a newsletter article remains inside the business, a press release is designed to be sent out to the media or even, in some cases, customers. Businesses are very keen on having good stories about them in the press and press releases are an ideal way of making life easy for journalists. Press releases help the business maintain a good relationship with the media and are useful and easy to produce. They can be sent to appropriate people in the media before a new product or service is launched, or a new activity that the business has not been involved with before is about to launch.

A press release has a much better chance of appearing in a paper if it includes:

- embargo date – the date which is printed at the top of a press release, telling the media that the information should not be published before this date. Press releases are usually sent out ahead of something happening to give the media time to read the press release and decide whether to use it
- headlines – explaining the nature of the press release
- factual opening statement – a short paragraph at the beginning which summarises exactly what the news is
- facts – interesting true and supportable facts and figures
- quotations – adding quotations increases the chance that the media will publish the story
- closing paragraph – a summary of the press release
- photograph if possible.

Press releases have particular conventions or styles, including the following:

- If the press release goes over onto another page, the phrase 'more follows' is typed at the bottom of the first page.
- If the press release goes over onto another page, the last two or three words of the first page are repeated on the second page.
- At the end of the press release the word 'ends' is used to show that the press release is complete.
- The business's name, address, telephone number, fax number, email address and website should be placed at the end of the press release.
- A named individual from the business should be quoted as a contact.

In order to make press releases as effective as possible, the following should be considered:

- Always be factual.
- Don't be emotional.
- Be truthful.
- Be newsworthy and don't exaggerate.
- Put in a human interest element.
- Don't cram in too many facts or figures.
- Be as up to date as possible.
- Make sure there are no spelling mistakes and it looks professional.
- Include all relevant information and contacts.

Leaflets and advertisements

Leaflets and advertisements are aimed at customers or potential customers. Leaflets are often produced in large quantities and delivered by a variety of means, including hand-delivered through letterboxes, or inserted into newspapers and magazines, or distributed in the street by representatives of the business.

Leaflets are a form of advertisement. Some guidelines to producing leaflets and advertisements consider a technique known as 'AIDA', meaning:

● **A**ttention – gain the reader's attention.

● **I**nterest – get the interest of the reader and tell them something that appeals to them.

● **D**esire – make the reader of the leaflet or advertisement want to buy or contact the business.

● **A**ction – make the reader ask for more information, contact the organisation or buy the product or service.

It is important to:

● use a headline

● offer a benefit

● appeal

Figure 312.1

- say it with pictures
- use sub-headings to reduce the number of words involved
- explain so that the reader does not misunderstand your message
- help the reader by giving them all the information they need.

Summaries

Long articles or reports may need to be presented in a brief or more concise way. The original document may be long and complicated so understanding it is vital. Summaries, or précis, require all unnecessary information and detail to be removed. Some guidelines for summarising information include:

- Read through the whole document first without trying to understand everything.
- Re-read the document more thoroughly and highlight the areas of importance or cross out unnecessary information.
- List the items for inclusion in the summary.
- Compare your list with the original document to make sure that you have not forgotten anything.
- Write a draft summary.
- Once the final draft has been agreed, you can write your final summary.

In order to create an effective summary you need various skills and abilities, such as being able to:

- understand the initial information – read through it at least twice: once to get the main idea and a second time to ensure understanding and highlight areas of concern
- order the information – identify related points or topics being made in the original document. These can be put together as key points in your summary. Underline these key points and phrases in order to highlight the main points
- analyse the information – is there an argument or point of view which is being developed in the original document? Try to summarise the main argument or key points in just a few sentences
- make a judgement about the information – which points are more or less important? Try listing the points in order of their importance
- select the appropriate information – what are the most important points? These must be included in the summary. From your list of points choose the ones which must be included
- present the information in an appropriate format – choose from a series of bulleted or numbered points, a series of short paragraphs with headings, or

changing the information into a totally new format, such as a table, a chart or a flow diagram.

When reformatting a document it is never advisable to use more than four different fonts on any one page but to restrict it to two at the most. It is acceptable to use different character sizes with the same font, as well as to use **bold** or *italics* to highlight important information.

Whichever font is used, it should always be easy to read. Several handwriting-style fonts or other less common fonts are used to have a visual impact on the page.

Never change fonts within a paragraph unless it contains a single word that requires highlighting. In the designing of adverts or other promotional materials it is often a big mistake to use too many fonts – it can look messy and amateur.

Serif fonts are the most commonly used for business documents. San serif fonts are also used for some business documents as well as for emails. Many businesses have preferred fonts and formats. They will suggest the size of the font and whether bold or italics or indeed a different font is used for headings.

Making the best use of fonts is very important to produce attractive documents. The two most common fonts are Times New Roman and Arial. Times New Roman is easy to read and appears professional for most printed documents. For business letters, for example, 12 point is the ideal font size to make it easy to read. Arial is also professional looking and is ideal for emails. Although Arial can be read in small sizes, again 12 point is the recommended size.

Adapting information can be done for a number of different business documents or their formats. You may need to present information in a particular way, or it may be your decision as to which format is the most appropriate.

Once you have analysed and extracted information from a variety of sources, the choice will have to be made about the most appropriate document or format in which to present the information. Some types of business documents and formats are more or less relevant and applicable in different circumstances. Sometimes it will be obvious which type of document or format to choose, but it may be that you will have to think about how you are going to present the information, as this will affect how you adapt the information.

Converting a mass of facts and figures into a table format makes it far easier to understand and appreciate the importance of some of that information. It is not always possible to obtain information in an easy-to-read-and-understand format. In many cases information which may appear to be hidden among lots of other information will have to be extracted and adapted.

Gathering information

Do you regularly produce different types of documents in your job role? Which ones do you produce the most often? Which do you rarely become involved in producing? How do you ensure that you follow organisational procedures and conform to the organisation's house style? Do you use templates for some of your documents? Is the decision about the format in which the document is presented down to you or are there guidelines for every written communication?

1.3 Explain the purpose and benefits of organising and producing high-quality and attractive documents

The ways in which a business or organisation's documents are produced and presented have a direct impact on how people view the organisation. This means that the documents need to be easy to understand and be well presented. If this is achieved then it is possible for the document to help project a positive image of the organisation.

All business documents and different formats need to be simple to use, which means they have to be easy to read and extract information from. Headings or sub-headings help break up long lengths of text and draw the reader's eye to a new point being made. Avoid stating one particular point in a single paragraph, but break up large chunks of text into convenient-to-read and logical paragraphs.

Documents need a logical sequence – a beginning, a middle and an end:

● The beginning is an introduction and tells the reader what you are about to say and why you are saying it.

● The middle is often the largest part of any business document and contains the necessary information to support what has been mentioned in the introduction.

● The end may be a conclusion or conclusions, a series of recommendations, or a request for the reader to do something.

By adding in simple things, such as headings and sub-headings, breaking up the paragraphs and making sure that there is a logical sequence to thoughts and statements, the document is more useful.

Tone and style of writing will differ for different purposes. It is important to consider how the document will be viewed by those outside the business. Rudeness or poorly chosen words can give a bad impression of both the writer and the organisation. All written material which will be seen by other people needs to be:

● tactful

- polite
- clear
- helpful
- informative
- able to offer a solution to a problem.

Table 312.1 shows various approaches to dealing with people and the impressions they receive about the writer and the business.

Table 312.1

Discourteous	Indifferent	Courteous	Special
Confrontational	Apathetic	Polite	Very courteous
Rude	Bored	Friendly	Problem solver
Impolite	Uncaring	Positive	Adaptable
Aggressive	Avoiding	Good contact	Shows care

If written communication is handled correctly it can lead to:

- fewer customer complaints
- more time to spend on other things rather than dealing with problems
- a more positive working environment
- greater job satisfaction
- more business for the organisation.

Gathering information

Do you have to produce a large number of documents that are seen by those outside your organisation as part of your regular job role? How often do you have to present information in a variety of formats? Does this involve extracting information from a different source, or summarising information in a different format? What are the main benefits to your organisation of producing high-quality and attractive documents?

■ 2. Know the resources available to design and produce documents and how to use them

2.1 Describe the types of resources needed to design and produce high-quality and attractive documents,
2.2 Explain the purpose and benefits of using different types of resource to design and produce high-quality and attractive documents and
2.3 Describe different types of technology available for inputting, formatting and editing text, and their main features

Businesses will use a wide variety of resources to produce high-quality and attractive documents. The use of software packages can go a long way to ensuring this. However, photocopiers can be used to produce enlarged documents or very good copies of documents. Increasingly, businesses tend to use laser printers not only because they are more economic to use than other forms of printers but also because their output is a better quality. Businesses will also use laminators to protect key documents that will be referred to on a regular basis and they will bind documents together to produce booklets. It is important that good quality paper is used. This can be achieved by using high-quality recycled paper.

Many organisations use the Microsoft Office suite of programs to produce a range of documents. The basic functions of Word, which is the word-processing package, provide a good start to ensuring that high-quality documents are produced, as the package allows you to:

● edit the text

● use the help screens

● use the spellchecker and thesaurus

● use a print preview to see what the document looks like before printing

● import text, images and tables from other applications

● use the mail-merge facility, to bring in addresses from a database.

The Microsoft Office suite is a multi-purpose package, incorporating word processing, spreadsheets, databases and graphics. Effectively it allows you to do whatever you wish with a document and transfer information from one

Figure 312.2

application to another. The key advantages of using a software package such as Word are:

- text can be stored and edited later
- documents can be stored and printed
- mistakes can be edited
- documents are automatically laid out and professional-looking by the use of templates
- mistakes can be picked up before printing
- you can attach documents to emails.

Microsoft Excel is a spreadsheet package that allows number processing and the presentation of data in the form of tables, graphs, charts and other types of graphics.

Databases are also invaluable. They are like an electronic filing system – information is collected and stored in a series of records, structured into fields. The fields and the records can be searched and sorted. Reports can then be generated. The records are also valuable sources of contact details, such as addresses, which can be used for mail merging.

The Microsoft Office suite provides many of the basic functions routinely needed for producing high-quality documents. Businesses and organisations do not just use keyboards to input data as there is a variety of methods; collectively they are known as data-input devices:

- keyboard and mouse – standard input devices
- stylus – this works like a pen or a pencil and the movements appear on the screen
- touch pad – like a simple keyboard and used for graphics and design
- scanner – can read text and images, which can be imported into a Word document
- voice recognition – recognises speech and the words appear on the screen and can be edited if required
- bar code reader – found on almost every product and identifies the product and any associated information
- optical mark reader – picks up pencil marks on documents and is ideal for multiple choice questionnaires
- optical character recognition – a feature of scanners, these read the text characters and allow editing on screen.

Credit cards and loyalty cards use magnetic strips; electronic point of sale used in shops reads bar codes.

The keyboard and mouse are often the primary means of inputting, formatting and editing text and changing font style and type, moving text around, changing the line spacing or altering the alignment of the text. Headers and footers, text boxes or borders can all be inserted and edited.

Another major advantage of using application software such as Word is the ability to create templates. These can be standard versions of how particular documents should look and will already incorporate addresses and other contact details. Some of them may be forms or specialised documents. Others are simple templates that can be used for memos or agendas. These templates will usually be blank for the operator to input information and the template will format the input information into the correct style and layout.

Orientation and paper size is another consideration regarding presentation. In Britain it is standard practice to use an A4 size page, although in other countries this can be different. The size of the page determines what you can fit onto it. Print preview can be selected and the layout can be amended if it looks messy or cramped. Some forms or complicated tables may need landscape orientation. Other key issues to take into consideration include:

- column layout – the operator can determine how many columns will appear on each page, from one to several
- font – various designs and a variety of sizes can be used in combination with bold, italic or underline
- headers and footers – some of these may appear in templates, but they can be amended or deleted. They will usually have a page number, date and perhaps the title of the document

- indent – this controls the space between the page margins and the paragraphs by having large left indents, which make it easier to pick out bulleted or numbered points, quotations, important points or even separate paragraphs

- justification – businesses will have preferred views about the right-hand margin. Some prefer a justified right margin, where each line of text finishes at the same point, giving a straight right margin. This gives slightly irregular spacing. An unjustified right margin gives a more ragged look because each of the lines will end at a different place

- line spacing – template documents may already be set up for single or double line spacing, which are the two most common. This can easily be changed if required. Double line spacing makes it easier for people to read the text.

Gathering information

What resources or different types of technology are available to you in your job role? What do you use to input, format and edit text? What various features does the technology or software provide you with that enable you to present information in an attractive, high-quality document? Are you familiar with all aspects of the technology or software? Do you have any suggestions as to how or what could improve the way you prepare and present your documents?

3. Understand the purpose and value of following procedures when designing and producing documents

3.1 Explain the value and benefits of agreeing the purpose, content, style, and deadlines for the design and production of documents

In agreeing the purpose, content, style and deadline for a document the individual creating that document needs to be fully aware of the requirements of the user. This will help ensure that the document meets with the user's approval. It is very important that finished documents meet those needs, so agreement before the document is produced is essential.

It may be that clear instructions are given or that the organisation's house style has to be followed. However, there may be only a limited amount of time to produce the document, making it vital that the first attempt comes as close to perfection as possible.

Templates help ensure that the house style, or preferred appearance of documents, is followed, as well as ensuring that each document is presented and formatted in a specified way. This can include:

- paper size and orientation
- margins and spacing
- font type, style and size
- alignment of text
- use of headers, footers and page numbers
- preferred ways of formatting tables.

If templates are not provided by the organisation, a set of house style guidelines may mean:

- amending the page setup – changing the margins, page orientation and page size and applying the changes to one or all of the pages in the document
- modifying the text – changing the formatting of the text by amending the font and its size
- modifying or creating headings – some businesses will prefer them to be bold, while others require them to be underlined. The styles and formatting can be changed and set to be implemented for each new paragraph or for every heading
- adding headers or footers – different organisations prefer page numbers, dates, company names or logos or other information to appear at the top or bottom of each page. They will also state what font to use
- using lists – bulleted or numbered, but each has a different style. There may well be a preferred standard
- using the spellchecker – either English (UK) or English (US). This will determine whether the spellchecker picks up on the incorrect spelling of particular words. There are, of course, hundreds of other languages that can be set as the default language for the document
- using special symbols and characters – different symbols and characters can then be inserted into the document and some of these special symbols can be used to customise bulleted lists
- creating tables – a range of styles can be used. The organisation may have specified styles, including table column widths and the way the table headers are displayed
- using borders and gridlines – these are particularly relevant if you are designing forms, where different types of lines can be used to break up the page, either as a series of boxes or perhaps as a tear-off slip
- shading – whole documents and tables can be shaded with different colours. Again the organisation may have preferred colours and styles.

Deadline information is probably the most important aspect of the document.

This must be negotiated at the outset. If necessary, the operator should renegotiate a new deadline at the earliest possible point if it becomes obvious the job will not be completed on time. One way of avoiding missing deadlines is to listen carefully to what is being asked and to produce the best attempt of the ideal document the first time. Clarifying what is needed at the outset can go a long way to eliminating errors and wasted time in reproducing a document.

Gathering information

Is it always made clear to you at the outset what the purpose, content, style and deadline are for a particular task? Do you have to negotiate deadlines? How often have you needed to renegotiate because you were not given or did not clarify the details at the outset? How much freedom do you have in the way in which documents you produce are presented?

3.2 Describe ways of researching and organising content needed for documents and
3.3 Describe ways of integrating and laying out text and non-text

Carrying out research will depend on the type of document, its purpose and the level of detail required. In some cases it may simply be a question of referring to one or more other documents and framing a response or follow-up to that document. In other cases, the research may need to be more complex and time consuming:

- Is the information that you need in existence already within the organisation?
- Is the information accessible?
- What format is the information in?
- If the information is incomplete, what can you do to fill in the gaps?
- Where is the missing information likely to be?
- Is there an external source of information?
- Is the information available and is there a cost?
- Is there someone who can guide you to finding all of the information that you need?
- How long will it take to assemble and process the information?
- How will you be sure that you have a full set of information and that nothing is still missing?

Research needs to be systematic. Ideally you should:

- determine what you need to put in the document and where you will find that information

- review the available information and check it for completeness and accuracy
- cross check with the person who has asked for the document that you have not missed any vital pieces of information
- ask them to suggest other possible sources of information
- request information from internal and external sources
- double check that you have all the necessary information
- refer to the brief you have been given for the document and try to match your collated information with the requirements of the document
- draft the document and show it to the person who has asked for it
- research additional information if required
- complete the document and present it.

For many documents there is not an internationally accepted style, but there are some common ways to organise the content for particular types of documents. In order to give a document a professional appearance you can combine text and graphics. These can highlight key points, such as figures or facts. This is not restricted to the use of graphics or Clipart, shapes or charts; you can combine tables and diagrams into a text-based document.

Word can help combine these so that the page does not look too cluttered, while at the same time valuable space is not wasted. Document templates use this approach, as they will already have symbols, logos or names. Some will even have a lightly shaded watermark, which will appear under the text of the letter.

It is worth bearing in mind that the majority of documents are actually printed in simple black and white rather than colour. So the use of shades of grey rather than bright colours for shading is more sensible.

Other application software, such as Microsoft Publisher, provide a number of readymade templates. In these templates whole sections of text, pictures, diagrams or graphics can be inserted. Publisher is ideal for creating fliers, leaflets, newsletters and brochures.

Graphics can be positioned behind or in front of the text, in line with the text, square to the text or tight to the text. You can also text wrap, which allows the text to be placed around the whole of the graphic or diagram in whatever manner proves to appear the most effective.

Typical non-text items include:

- callouts
- WordArt
- pictures
- drawings

- diagrams
- charts, graphs and tables imported from either Excel or Access.

Gathering information

Do you import charts, tables, pictures and other graphical objects into a Word document on a regular basis? Do you use the text wrap facility? Does your organisation provide a template for this purpose? Do you have the final say as to whether or not the finished product is of a satisfactorily high quality? How do you go about researching what has to be contained within the document you are producing?

3.4 Describe ways of checking finished documents for accuracy – including spelling, grammar and punctuation – and the correctness, and the purpose of doing so

Microsoft Word automatically highlights spelling mistakes and grammatical errors. However, it is not foolproof as it will not pick up the fact that 'their' has been used instead of 'there', for instance. Word will underline incorrectly spelled words in red and underline sentences that do not make grammatical sense in green. Punctuation errors or additional spaces between words are also underlined in green.

In the majority of cases the spellcheck facility will use English (UK). Word will automatically highlight any spelling or grammatical mistakes and usually offer a series of suggestions. Choose the correct spelling from a list and click 'change'. However, if a wrong word has been used but it is still a proper word and the sentence makes grammatical sense, Word will not pick it up.

Word's spellchecker has thousands of words, but it will not have many proper names or abbreviations, although these can be added to the Word dictionary, making that word or abbreviation regularly available.

Proofreading should be done with every document onscreen before printing. Carefully check each sentence to make sure it makes sense. If it is a long and complicated document, get someone else to check it too.

The purpose of making sure that spelling, grammar and punctuation are correct is to ensure that every document created is professional-looking and reflects well on the employee, as well as the business or the organisation.

Gathering information

Do you regularly spellcheck and proofread documents at work? What is the procedure for this in your organisation? Is every document checked in the same way? What is the value of doing this to your business? Is there a different way that you could recommend that would enhance the quality of the documents produced?

3.5 Explain the purpose of storing documents safely and securely, and ways of doing so

Documents are not stored just in a paper format but also electronically. This brings with it its own problems as the documents are extremely portable and original versions can easily be lost. Documents are stored for a variety of reasons. Certain documents will have to be stored for legal purposes, such as contracts of employment or agreements with suppliers and customers. Other documents will be stored as a result of the need to refer to them from time to time. It is usual for businesses and organisations to store documents for at least five years. In some cases documents are stored for longer but the older documents are often removed and archived although not destroyed.

Archiving means storing away old files. There will be procedures in place that have to be followed, mainly because someone with authority will have to decide when a file becomes an old file. A file could be an old file if, for example:

- the information in it relates to a previous customer or business the organisation no longer deals with

- the information in it relates to an employee who has now left the business

- the information in it is out of date.

Obsolete files may be needed again in the future and need to be archived only

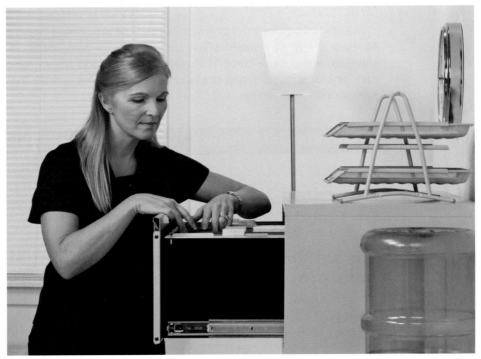

Figure 312.3

until they become current once more. Archiving can mean storing in another room, a cupboard, or perhaps a storage area or another building belonging to the business.

Computerised filing to some extent eliminates the need to archive files. The vast majority of businesses will make sure that documents are stored on hard drives in different locations. This is known as backing up and it is done to protect the documents should there be a major problem at the main site, which means that the documents could become either lost or corrupted. Copies of documents can be put onto:

- flash drives
- memory sticks
- zip disks
- CDs
- CD-ROMs.

Some businesses use these to store archived copies of documents rather than allowing them to clutter their hard drives and electronic filing systems.

Businesses will store documents for a considerable period of time in case they need to be referred to at a later date. In order to protect the documents, archived material may be write protected (read only). This means that nobody can edit the original documents.

Access to the documents will be limited to only those who have authorisation to view them. Businesses often use a series of passwords, allowing access to different levels of document storage. This restricts the number of people who can look at specific types of documents and helps ensure that the documents remain safe and secure.

Gathering information

Do you know how long your organisation keeps stored documents? Is there a reason for doing this or are they complying with legislation? Is there a set procedure for storing digital copies? Is access to these stored documents restricted in some way? For what purpose are these levels of access used?

3.6 Explain the purpose of confidentiality and data protection when preparing documents

Many business documents may contain confidential or sensitive data. Particular care needs to be exercised and any confidential or sensitive information needs to be secured while it is being used to prepare the documents. Personal information in particular needs to be kept confidential. A duty of confidentiality falls on all businesses and organisations. Under the terms of the Data Protection Act the processing and disclosure of information are important, as are the rights of access to that information. It is important to remember that data refers to anything that is either processed by a computer or recorded as part of a filing system, so this includes hard copies.

All businesses and organisations process data: they organise it, alter it, retrieve it, use it and may eventually destroy it. Each major business or organisation will have a data controller who determines the way in which information is processed.

All information held by a business or organisation should be considered to be confidential, unless stated as otherwise. A business or organisation should not pass on information about an individual or another business without permission. There are exceptions, however, when there are legal requirements to do so, such as under the Social Security Fraud Act.

For more information about confidentiality and security of information refer to Unit 303: Work in a Business Environment, Part 2.

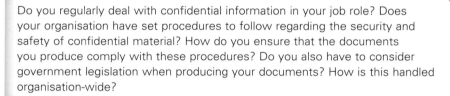

Gathering information

Do you regularly deal with confidential information in your job role? Does your organisation have set procedures to follow regarding the security and safety of confidential material? How do you ensure that the documents you produce comply with these procedures? Do you also have to consider government legislation when producing your documents? How is this handled organisation-wide?

3.7 Explain the purpose and benefits of meeting deadlines

Deadlines will invariably be set for tasks, activities or documents to be completed. For organisations, a failure to meet a deadline could mean that valuable business is lost. For the individual, meeting deadlines can mean a less stressful working environment. It can also improve self-confidence and, by meeting deadlines rather than rushing to meet them, will mean that the work produced will be of a higher quality.

All businesses and organisations rely on a number of employees being able to complete specific tasks on time. Tasks are rarely isolated but are part of a far bigger task that relies on a number of employees. It is easy to underestimate how long a task will take and it often becomes clear when the job has been started. It is always a good idea to take a close look at the task as a whole and see what is involved before agreeing a deadline.

Often more than one person is being relied on to complete part of the task or to provide vital information. If they fail to do this it may be impossible for others to complete their part of the task. It may not be their ultimate responsibility and they may have other calls on their time. Always try to agree strict deadlines when needed, so that your own deadline can be met.

Time should be built in to make revisions and corrections. It is rare for a task to be completed correctly at the first attempt. Changes or updates may be needed along the way. The task setter may be interested only in a completed task and not just a draft version of it.

Delegation is always an option if a deadline is looming. Offloading, or delegating, a task or even a small section of it to another colleague is sensible when a deadline may not be met because of pressure of work.

Some employees thrive when working to a strict deadline. Many others, however, find deadlines daunting and stressful. Deadlines are set to help employees to manage their time. An employee's work is also likely to be of a higher quality if deadlines are consistently being met, as their attention to detail can suffer if they are rushing to complete a task. Setting interim deadlines can help meet goals and breaks down the whole, what might be very large, task into more manageable sections. Tackling the most difficult work first can also help an employee's ability to meet their final deadline. This could be because an employee feels anxious about the task and tries to avoid starting on it. Starting and finishing this type of task first will help reduce the anxiety and once it is completed, the remainder of the task will seem much more straightforward.

Meeting deadlines is an important indicator for an organisation of the level of productivity of its workforce. All organisations strive for high levels of productivity because it means the workforce is working to its full potential. This can only be of benefit to organisations, as high levels of productivity means:

- they are more efficient
- they are making more profit
- they have an opportunity to grow
- they are being successful
- the staff are motivated
- there is probably less waste
- there are probably fewer complaints
- there is more efficient use of resources
- the good image is being projected and maintained.

Gathering information

How good are you at meeting deadlines? How often does your workload involve a series of tight deadlines? Are you in a position where you can delegate sections of a task when required? The ability to meet deadlines consistently comes down to good time-management skills. How good are your time-management skills? Does the fact that you meet deadlines have a benefit to your organisation? If so, in what way?

4. Be able to design and produce documents to agreed specifications

4.1 Agree the purpose, content, style and deadlines for documents,
4.2 Identify and prepare resources needed to design and produce documents,
4.3 Research and organise content required for documents,
4.4 Make appropriate and efficient use of technology, as required,
4.5 Design, format and produce documents to an agreed style,
4.6 Integrate non-text object into an agreed layout, if required,
4.7 Check texts and objects for accuracy,
4.8 Edit and correct texts and objects as required,
4.9 Clarify document requirements, if necessary,
4.10 Store documents safely and securely following organisational procedures and
4.11 Present documents to the required format, and within the agreed deadlines

Refer to 1.1 to 1.3, 2.1 to 2.3 and 3.1 to 3.7 and then consider the following.

Gathering information

You could present a series of documents that you have created to agreed specifications. Alternatively, your assessor could observe you producing and manipulating documents. Other assessors will undertake a professional discussion with you. The areas that will be focussed on will include:

● a purpose and content – e.g. information or responding to a query

● a style – which will be dependent on the recipient of the document

● a deadline – when the document had to be designed, produced and sent to the recipient

● preparation – you will have needed resources, such as information, in order to design and produce the document

● technology – you will almost certainly have used word-processing software, you may have emailed and you may have printed off copies or made duplicates using a photocopier

● design and format – you will have followed either organisational styles or a generally agreed style

● non-text objects – you may have designed, imported and resized tables, charts, diagrams or illustrations from other sources

● checking and editing – before sending the document to the recipient you will have checked for accuracy, edited the document and made necessary corrections

● last check before sending – you may have clarified with the task setter that the document met their requirements

● safe storage – you will have filed either a paper or electronic copy and you may have created additional copies for the task setter's reference

● deadlines – you will have completed all of these tasks within an agreed deadline with the task setter.

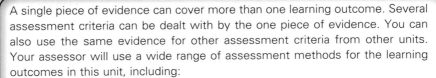

What is Evidence ?

A single piece of evidence can cover more than one learning outcome. Several assessment criteria can be dealt with by the one piece of evidence. You can also use the same evidence for other assessment criteria from other units. Your assessor will use a wide range of assessment methods for the learning outcomes in this unit, including:

- observing your performance
- examining work that you have produced
- questioning and discussing issues with you
- using witness testimony from work colleagues
- looking at your learner statements
- recognising your prior learning.

The range of evidence can include:

- work requests
- work plans, including resources and deadline details
- records of research undertaken
- draft documents
- completed documents
- screen prints
- records of times when clarification was sought.

Analyse and Report Data

■ Purpose of the unit

This unit is about analysing and reporting data to meet the aims and objectives of the research.

■ Assessment requirements

To meet all of the assessment criteria for this unit, you will need to understand how to research, organise, evaluate and report that data. There are four parts to this unit. The first two cover the essential understanding and the second two focus on you demonstrating your ability to handle data. The four parts of the unit are:

1 Understand how to organise and evaluate data that has been researched – organising data so that it can be analysed, evaluating the relevance, validity and reliability of data, ensuring that it is accurate and free from bias, the differences between primary and secondary research, the differences between quantitative and qualitative research methods and how to search for relevant data sources. (K)

2 Understand how to report data that has been researched – reporting data so that it meets agreed aims and objectives and is accurate and free from bias. (K)

3 Be able to analyse and evaluate data – organising data for analysis, selecting data to be analysed, applying analysis and evaluation techniques, reviewing data to produce accurate and unbiased results and conclusions, checking the accuracy of analysis and making necessary adjustments and obtaining feedback on data analysis. (P)

4 Be able to report data – presenting the data in an agreed format and to an agreed timescale. (P)

■ 1. Understand how to organise and evaluate data that has been researched

1.1 Describe purpose and benefits of organising data so that it can be analysed

The key to structuring collected data for analysis is how that data is captured in the first place. This means considering the following:

● The choice of analysis should be based on the question you need to answer.

● What conclusion are you trying to reach?

- What type of analysis do you need to perform in order to demonstrate that conclusion?
- What type of data do you need to perform that analysis?

In reality, it is often the case that you will spend more time organising the data into a format that you can use than the time you will take to analyse it. If you are using data from a variety of sources, this can be even more time-consuming.

Regardless of whether the data being used has already been collected or its source (e.g. sales figures or numbers of complaints, etc.), at this stage it needs to be considered to be 'raw data', in other words, unprocessed or disorganised data that needs to be categorised and collated so that it is clear how it can be used and how it can be analysed. Ideally, the nature of the data would be the same, for example a set of questionnaires with the same questions but a variety of responses. In most cases, however, the 'raw data' may come from different sources and will be organised in different ways.

The starting point should always be the questions you need to answer or the subject of the research project. What are you trying to prove, disprove, report on or comment on? Where is this information in the data that you have collected or have been presented with? Is it possible to organise that data so that you can identify the answers to key questions? In a larger organisation, a database approach to the organisation of information, such as that shown in Figure 318.1, can be useful.

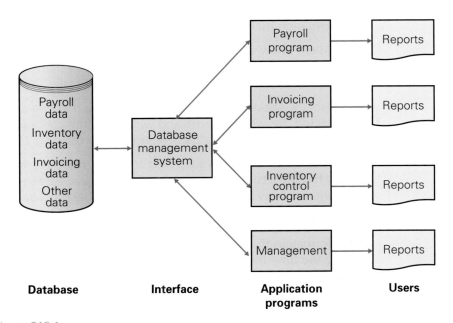

Figure 318.1

Before carrying out data analysis it is often necessary to carry out a 'data cleaning' procedure. This means:

● looking at the data and correcting any mistakes

● saving the original data (as well as saving the amended data)

● identifying inaccurate, incomplete or unreasonable data

● improving the quality through correction of detected errors and omissions.

At this stage, the data should now be ready to begin analysis, but other checks are necessary before this can take place.

Gathering information

What is the range of data types you have to work with? What is the source of this data and why was it collected? Do you use data that has been specifically collected for the research? How do you go about organising the data to make the process of analysis easier?

1.2 Explain how to evaluate the relevance, validity and reliability of data

These are three key issues which could undermine the entire research. They are all linked, but specifically they mean:

● Relevance – does the data actually relate to your research, is it key to your understanding of the research questions or purpose or is it simply additional information that is not required?

● Validity – how representative is the data that you are using? How was it collected and does it give you a true picture of the facts and figures? If not, it will undermine all of the findings that you make.

● Reliability – how much do you trust the data that you are using? How was it collected, for what purpose and what were the controls? Has the data been correctly processed? Are there noticeable errors in it? How old is the data?

In sets of data, validity is supposed to imply reliability and consistency. This means having sets of data that will ultimately give a true reflection of the facts. Relevance, validity and reliability relate to whether the data and the research will actually measure what it claims to be measuring. It is necessary to understand how the data was collected and determine whether the data actually captures the information that is needed. The data can be measured in a number of ways, but by the time the data has been analysed and the report completed, it may be too late and the results may be questioned. It is important to be confident about the reliability of the data: would similar results come from a different set of data using the same questions? This may mean you need to look at the size of the sample and the way the sample was organised.

Another consideration is to look at the way in which the data was actually gathered. Did the researchers all use the same data-gathering methods? If the data from one source is broadly similar to another, then the data is probably reliable. If it is radically different, there may be problems.

Research precision is expressed as validity and reliability. Validity represents how well a variable measures what it is supposed to measure – if the validity is poor, you may need masses of data. However, reliability will tell you how reproducible your measures would be if they were retested.

Gathering information

How much do you know about the source of the data you use? Where does it come from? Who collected it? How old is it? What guarantees are there that it is accurate, valid, reliable and relevant? What steps can you take to check it? What would you do if it proves to be inadequate?

1.3 Explain how to analyse and prepare researched data so results will be accurate and free from bias

The way in which the data can be analysed and evaluated will very much depend on how it was collected. For example, the more complex a questionnaire is, the greater the difficulty in collating, analysing and evaluating that information. Straightforward questionnaires are far easier to handle.

The complex data may need statistical data analysis and this will take time and will cost money to carry out. There are a large number of highly specialised statistical analysis methods. Some look at factors within the information, others look for trends. The process of collating, analysing and evaluating data has a series of key stages:

- To collate the information – in other words, take the information from each questionnaire and compile it into a single document.

- Basic graphic representations of each question from the questionnaire are prepared, as this will aid the checking process.

- Sample questionnaires will be checked for errors.

- The second collation process takes place after the cross checking and an initial presentation of the data will be made.

- The researchers will now look at links, trends and patterns, within individual questionnaires, across questions and across questionnaires themselves.

- The raw (original) data will now be compared with existing data, perhaps from a previous research project.

- Significant shifts, changes or errors should be highlighted.

Figure 318.2

● Final presentation of the data in the preferred form can now be made.

Bias is another consideration. This means that the data may not be a true reflection of the facts. Bias can creep into data for a variety of reasons:

● Design bias – the way in which the data was collected is flawed – it either asks the wrong kind of questions or phrases the questions so that respondents tend to give the same answer.

● Measurement bias – the way in which the data has been recorded is wrong or it fails to take into account important factors that had an influence on the data.

● Collector bias – the individual who collected the data had a bias of their own and deliberately chose to use data that reflected only what they believed to be the case.

● Sampling bias – the amount of data is simply too small to be representative or the data that was collected does not represent the true range of figures, views or opinions.

● Procedural bias – something has been missed when the data was processed.

A good way of ensuring that your analysis of researched data is accurate and free from bias is to check the reliability of the results:

● Objective results and analysis should reflect reality.

- You should provide a clear and precise description of the research methodology that you used.

Another person should be able to come to exactly the same conclusions as you did if your research was reliable.

Gathering information

What steps do you take to ensure the accuracy of the data you use? How do you check for bias? How much do you trust the sources of the data that you use? Have there been problems with the data in the past? How were these problems resolved?

1.4 Explain the differences between primary and secondary research methods

Research is one of the main ways that an organisation investigates issues. They can be problems, projects, ideas and studies regarding certain aspects of its operations. On other occasions, it may be market research where the organisation is keen to learn about its customers and the environment in which it operates.

It is possible to divide research into two main areas:

- Primary research involves the collection or collation of fresh and new information that has been collected solely for the purpose of the research project.

- Secondary research involves the use of existing data that has already been collected by another organisation, or by the organisation undertaking the research, but for another purpose or reason. It can make use of statistics and other information that can be bought in from another source or reused from an existing source.

Primary research involves searching out new information for the first time by a business commissioning a research agency, or for employees of the organisation being assigned to the project. Primary data is usually collected by field research. This means that the individuals carrying out the research are interacting with the subjects or respondents and collecting the data or information directly from them.

Primary data is not a cheap option: it can be time-consuming and easy to get wrong. Once the key objectives of the research have been set, methods need to be developed or adopted in order to collect and collate that information. Examples of primary research are given in Table 318.1.

Table 318.1

Primary research method	Description
Observation	Observation, or observational field research, is a method borrowed from the social sciences. It involves the researcher watching the behaviour of subjects. The most common form of observational research is to watch the shopping habits of customers, using the CCTV in a department store or supermarket.
Experimentation	Experimentation research involves respondents chosen because they match the target group, testing out prototype versions of products and services. The research and development of new products and services is a costly and time-consuming affair. As prototypes become available, they are routinely 'crash tested' by individuals representative of the types of customers who will later purchase them.
Surveys	Surveys are a range of methods used by organisations (including the business itself or research agencies working for a business) to collect data, responses and opinions from target groups. Surveys can be face to face, telephone, email or postal.
Focus groups and panels	Focus groups involve selecting a group of individuals representative of a larger target group. These individuals could be representative of a business's customers, distributors, potential customers or those who match a typical customer's age, gender or income level. The focus groups are organised so that discussions are encouraged regarding the group's views and experiences of a product, service or topic. Panels are a variation of a focus group. Instead of choosing individuals who match the target group, panels are made up from experts in a particular field. A business that deals with retailers, for example, would bring together a focus group or panel of retailers rather than consumers who purchase from the retailers.
Field trials	Field trials take the concept of testing new products and services one stage further. There are various ways a business could use field trials to gain valuable information about products and services before they are launched. The most basic form of field trial is an extension of the work carried out by focus groups.

Secondary research involves the collecting of existing data and manipulating it so that a summary of the findings can be used for the research project. Among the most common forms of secondary research are published statistics, including the census, or published texts, including books, magazines and newspapers. Sources of secondary research data can be broken down into internal and external types, as shown in Table 318.2.

Table 318.2

Internal sources	Description	External sources	Description
Data records	Customer records, containing information regarding the customer in terms of their name, address, purchasing habits, credit ratings and other information.	Internet	Many businesses will use the Internet to trawl for information, reactions and opinions about themselves or their competitors. That kind of information can be valuable, as can constant monitoring of competitors' websites, which can reveal information about future direction, strategy, tactics and advertising.
Loyalty schemes	Supermarkets such as Tesco run extensive loyalty schemes and programmes. They are able to match customers' purchasing habits with targeted offers to encourage them to buy more of the same or similar products.	Official statistics	The government produces an array of statistics, from the census, different industries, marketing and trade initiatives. Much of the data is well researched and collated from wide sources.
EPOS	Electronic point of sale was envisaged to link the sale of a product against the stock control system. EPOS is used in conjunction with loyalty cards to monitor customer purchases and to generate sales offers linked to popular brands.	Libraries	Businesses use dedicated business libraries, which compile data from industries by trawling magazines and newspapers, as well as the Internet, for clippings and references to specific businesses.
Website monitoring	A form of observation, it involves monitoring the number of clicks made by customers on an organisation's website, noting how long they have been on the website and which pages they have visited, to judge the activities on the website and the pages visited compared with the purchases made by the visitor.	Trade journals	Magazines or newspapers whose readership is restricted to those in the industry. Rather like newspapers and magazines, they feature articles and information about the trade, advertisements, information about special events and warnings about new legislation that may impact on the industry.

Internal sources	Description	External sources	Description
Accounts records	By monitoring the accounting records a business can see how long, on average, it takes a customer to pay an invoice and which payment method they have chosen. This is useful only when a business is dealing with regular customers, as it is possible to monitor changes in payment methods.	Agencies	Examples include Mintel, Datastream and Dun and Bradstreet, which have extensive research and information-gathering potential and produce regular reports on particular industries, countries, markets and products.
Sales figures	These should show the accurate level of sales, and peaks and troughs in demand. Businesses can more confidently predict the level of sales in a similar future period, assuming the same conditions apply.	Company reports	The structure of a company report is determined by law and requires a business to outline its profit and loss, balance sheet and use of funds.
Product information	Production figures can be seen as a mirror of sales or orders. Many manufacturers have only a small buffer stock of products and do not over-produce and store huge levels of stock in anticipation of sales. Therefore production is very much reliant on accurate sales data or accurate orders.	Universities	A major part of universities' work, beyond teaching, is research. They will routinely carry out research and may well cooperate with businesses or industry to collect and collate data.

Gathering information

Which types of research methods do you use? Are they primary or secondary? Do you tend to use one type or the other? How do you handle research when you are using both types of data? Is the majority of the data generated by your organisation or do you use data from external sources?

Figure 318.3

1.5 Explain the differences between quantitative and qualitative research methods

In many cases, there is always a choice of volume or quality: this is the key difference between qualitative or quantitative research. Qualitative research tends to be on a smaller scale, with a great deal of in-depth information gathered from a relatively small sample of respondents or sources – it is the sheer detail of the information that is important rather than the scale of the information gathering.

Quantitative research, meanwhile, looks at far larger sets of data and considers the volume of the information rather than the detail to be important. Usually, quantitative research is statistics based rather than being opinions and ideas based, which is far more likely to be the feature of qualitative research.

Table 318.3 illustrates the choices between qualitative and quantitative research and identifies the situations when they are appropriate.

Table 318.3

Method	Qualitative or quantitative?	Characteristics, benefits and drawbacks
Postal survey	Quantitative	Cost is low Response rate can be poor Answers may be incomplete Responses are coded and must be simple so people can understand them
Telephone survey	Quantitative	Cost-effective method of achieving robust sample Responses are coded Certain groups do not have access to the telephone, so may be excluded from the sample It is difficult to ask sensitive questions over the telephone Works well with employers
Face-to-face survey	Quantitative	Can include both open and coded questions Can achieve robust sample Expensive and time-consuming Ideal for gathering sensitive information or exploring complicated issues
In-depth interview	Qualitative	Rich and detailed information can be gathered Interviewers are allowed more flexibility Answers to open questions can be difficult and time-consuming to analyse Expensive and time-consuming to administrator
Focus group	Qualitative	A group discussion with around 8–12 people Usually lasts between 1 and 3 hours Capitalises on interaction between participants Participants are not representative of wider population, which does not allow for generalisation Good for gathering sensitive data Requires careful and unbiased analysis
Case study	Qualitative	Researcher gains understanding of a specific person's experience through an in-depth interview Provides good quotations and rich data Can bring alive other research, such as survey data Findings cannot be generalised to a wider population

Qualitative research aims to understand the patterns in individuals' minds that lead them to make different choices or decisions. Often these patterns are hidden and qualitative research uses cutting-edge tools to capture both verbal and non-verbal information. Qualitative research uses a mixture of exploration and evaluation through techniques including face-to-face interviews and focus groups.

Researchers ask what individuals were thinking and why they made a decision. The patterns involved in the decision are hidden from view, usually from both the researcher and the respondent, but the organisation undertaking the research wants to identify the patterns that drive the behaviour.

Qualitative research can be useful in identifying views, opinions and attitudes. The researchers can investigate respondents in-depth to understand how a decision was made. Qualitative research differs from quantitative research:

- The data gathered is usually less structured.

- The findings are more in-depth as they use open-ended questions.

- They provide detail on behaviour, attitudes and motivation.

- The research is more intensive and flexible.

- The research involves smaller sample sizes.

- The analysis of the results is more subjective.

- The researchers need to be well trained to make sure that they question the respondent correctly and log the answers given.

Many businesses use quantitative research to guide them in their decision making. Quantitative research techniques are used as a formal research method to measure, describe or forecast quantity using a range of sampling methods. Quantitative research involves measuring a subject and quantifying that measurement with data. In market research often the data required relates to:

- market size

- market share

- market penetration

- market growth rates.

The research can also be used to measure customer attitudes, satisfaction, commitment and a range of other useful market data (and these can be tracked over a given time period). Quantitative research can also be used to measure customer awareness and attitudes towards different manufacturers, retailers or suppliers and to understand overall customer behaviour in a market by taking a statistical sample of customers. For many organisations, the primary focus of quantitative research is on decision makers in businesses or major buyers and is designed to answer very specific questions. The questions would tend to focus on a particular issue.

Gathering information

Which type of data do you use? Is it quantitative or qualitative? Which is the easier to handle? Where does the data come from? How do you process the different types of data?

1.6 Describe how to search for relevant data sources

We have already seen that it is possible to use primary and secondary data and that it can be qualitative or quantitative. It is also possible to add internal and external sources into the range to provide a more comprehensive list of relevant data sources, as shown in Table 318.4.

Table 318.4

Data source	Example	Relevance
Internal primary quantitative	Sets of organisation's sales figures	Will be reliable and relevant if they cover a sufficient period of time
Internal primary qualitative	Internal customer feedback forms	Relevant if there are sufficient forms as representative sample
Internal secondary quantitative	Organisation's annual report including balance sheet	Relevant if it covers the areas being researched
Internal secondary qualitative	Employee appraisal forms	May be relevant if sections cover the research areas, but each form will be significantly different as it is personal data collected for a different reason
External primary quantitative	External agency's research on the market in which the organisation operates	Relevant if the agency has been told to collect specific data to answer specific questions
External primary qualitative	External agency interviews with customers	Relevant if the agency has been told to collect specific data to answer specific questions
External secondary quantitative	Published facts and figures on the sector in which the organisation operates	Relevant if up to date and covers areas that are the subject of the research
External secondary qualitative	Published research on views and opinions related to the organisation's market or operations	Will have been collected for purposes other than the research under way, but may provide valuable insights; age of the data is important

The process of searching for relevant data should:

- begin with internal sources of data – are there existing sets of data that can be used as the basis of the research? Is the data available? Is it up to date? Will it be a useful starting point?

- look for existing published data – has a research company carried out similar research in the recent past? Is it available to buy or to use? How old is the data? Does the research cover broadly the same areas you wish to look at?

- commission primary research – this can be carried out either by the organisation itself or by an external agency. In both cases, the researchers will have to be thoroughly briefed

- commission secondary research – this can be carried out by the organisation itself or by an external agency. Clear guidelines will need to be given to ensure validity, reliability and accuracy of the data as well the age of the data being used.

Gathering information

How do you choose relevant data sources? How do you test their relevance? Do you begin with an internal search for data or can you commission new research?

2. Understand how to report data that has been researched

2.1 Describe ways of reporting data so that it (a) meets agreed aims and objectives, (b) is accurate and free from bias

The most common way in which to report data that has been researched is to commission a report. Most people find writing reports quite difficult. However, all reports should follow a particular pattern, regardless of whatever kind you are asked to write. These basic steps are as follows:

- Make a plan.

- Discuss what should be in the report.

- Draft the report.

- Leave the report for at least a couple of days.

- Revise and edit the report.

There are different types of report, but in general they begin with an introduction, which usually describes a problem which needs to be solved and the significance of the problem itself. So, the introduction poses a question. The conclusion suggests the answer, and the rest of the report is a series of points, evidence or arguments which allows the reader of the report to understand why you have reached the conclusions that you have.

The most effective reports are written in a clear and direct style. You do not have to try to be clever and as long as the report is logical and you have mentioned all of the main points related to the problem before you have arrived at the conclusion, your suggestions are as valid as those of anyone else.

Reports are used to examine particular problems and the responsibility of writing a report is usually given either to an individual or a team that is expected to investigate the problem and receive assistance from anyone who has experience of the problem. Although the writing of the report is left to the report writers, the collection of information to help them is a joint effort.

Reports are just another form of presenting information. There are several different types of reports which you may be expected to write at some point in your career. Organisations can commission reports for many different reasons, including the following:

● to identify problems and find solutions to these problems

● to provide progress reports on particular projects

● to investigate particular areas of the business's activities

● to identify the need to change policies.

Although memo-style reports (a memo is an internal document largely replaced by internal emails) are useful for faster responses to problems, a more formal and longer form of report can also be used. There are many different ways in which these reports can be written, but generally they have the following headings included:

● Title page (which is the subject of the report).

● Terms of reference (which replaces the introduction of a memo-style report and states what you have been asked to do or research).

● Procedure (this details how you have gone about gathering the information which you have included in the report).

● Findings (which in effect replaces the information of a memo-style report and states what you have found out).

● Conclusion (this is the general statement about your findings and is similar to the first part of the conclusions in a memo-style report). Here you conclude and sum up your findings.

● Recommendations (this is the second part of the memo-style conclusion). On the basis of your findings and conclusions you make your recommendations.

● Appendices – this is the place to put related documents, charts, diagrams,

Unit 322 | Plan and Organise Meetings

■ Purpose of the unit

The purpose of this unit is to assist the learner in planning and organising meetings in order to meet the agreed purpose of the meeting.

■ Assessment requirements

This unit has four parts. The first part focuses on your understanding of the necessary arrangements and actions for planning and organising meetings. The remaining three parts provide you with opportunities to demonstrate your abilities in planning, supporting and following up meetings.

The four parts are:

1 Understand the arrangements and actions required for planning and organising meetings – the role of the person planning and organising the meeting, different types of meetings and their features, planning meetings to meet aims and objectives, agreeing briefs for meetings, identifying suitable venues, resources needed, the main points covered in agendas and meeting papers, meeting attendees' needs and special requirements, health, safety and security requirements to be considered, briefing the chair before the meeting, welcoming and providing refreshments for attendees, information, advice and support that may be needed during the meeting, problem solving during a meeting, records of meetings, how to record actions and follow-up, collecting and evaluating participant feedback, improving the organisation of future meetings. (K)

2 Be able to prepare for a meeting – agreeing and preparing a meeting brief, agreeing a budget, agenda and meeting papers, organising and confirming venues, equipment and catering requirements, inviting attendees, confirming attendance and identifying special requirements, arranging catering, equipment and lay out of the room, briefing the chair. (P)

3 Be able to support running a meeting – welcoming attendees and offering refreshment, distributing papers, nominating someone to take minutes, providing information, advice and support. (P)

4 How to follow up a meeting – producing a record, seeking approval for the meeting record and making any amendments, following up actions, evaluating meeting arrangements, evaluating participant feedback, identifying improvements that can be made to future meeting arrangements and support. (P)

1. Understand the arrangements and actions required for planning and organising meetings

1.1 Explain the role of the person planning and organising a meeting

The level of formality and the type of meeting involved will determine the degree of planning and organising that is required. It is normally the role of an administrator to arrange meetings and to liaise with attendees regarding the dates and times convenient to all involved.

Organisation and efficiency in planning are essential. One way of ensuring this level of organisation is to compile a checklist in advance of the meeting. The same checklist could be used for a series of similar type meetings, or reused for others with slight amendment. Table 322.1 identifies possible planning requirements for a meeting that involves visiting participants requiring overnight accommodation before the meeting.

Table 322.1

Stage of the planning process	Role of the planner
2 weeks before the meeting	• Check the date of the meeting – this is often included as the last item in the minutes of the previous meeting – and ensure it is diarised • Contact all expected participants to ensure the date is convenient and diarised by them • Request any agenda items they wish to include • Book the meeting room or venue • Order refreshments for the meeting • Book overnight accommodation for visiting participants
1 week before the meeting	• Confirm the arrangements that have been made regarding overnight accommodation • Prepare and distribute the agenda • Prepare and distribute associated meeting paperwork • Prepare a chairperson's agenda and send • Book car parking if required for participants
The day before the meeting	• Prepare all meeting paperwork • List those who have sent their apologies for absence • Collect writing paper, pens, notebooks, etc. • Prepare an attendance sheet for signature

Stage of the planning process	Role of the planner
The day of the meeting	• Confirm parking arrangements • Notify reception of expected visitors • Arrange for calls to be re-routed for participants • Ensure the meeting room is ready – check heating, lighting and ventilation and ensure adequate seating • Place paperwork and writing paper, pens, etc. • Provide glasses and jugs of water • Place a 'meeting in progress' notice on the door/outside the room • Place a chairperson's agenda, list of apologies for absence and minutes of previous meeting • Have additional agenda, minutes, etc. in case someone has forgotten theirs

Effective planning before the meeting can establish the groundwork for successful meeting results. You have to know what the meeting is hoping to accomplish and have goals for the meeting. This will establish the framework for an effective meeting. The purpose of the meeting will determine its focus, the agenda and those needed to participate.

Gathering information

Do you have to plan meetings? Do those meetings involve all or some of the items listed in Table 322.1? How often do you have to do this? If you do not do this alone, how often do you plan a meeting as part of a team?

1.2 Describe the different types of meetings and their main features

There are basically two main types of meeting: informal or formal. Informal meetings include those that have no procedural rules. They might be called for a number of reasons, such as to report progress or to discuss a particular project. Informal meetings are not always documented, although someone may be responsible for providing a short resumé of the proceedings rather than formal minutes. Types of informal meeting can include:

● team meetings

● departmental meetings

● section meetings

● management meetings

● briefing meetings.

The purpose of all meetings, whether formal or informal, is to make decisions and plans of action, or to deal with problems. Meetings are held to allow verbal communication to take place for any of the following reasons:

- to share information
- to collect new ideas
- to discuss new proposals
- to vote
- to allow employees to become involved
- to gain assistance
- to report
- to coordinate
- to problem solve.

Formal meetings are often governed by the constitution of the organisation regarding the procedures involved. The chairperson of a formal meeting will need to have a sound knowledge of the procedures. Formal meetings include the following:

- Annual general meeting (AGM) – held annually and used to assess the trading or affairs of the organisation over the previous year. Officers, such as the chairperson, secretary and treasurer, are elected at the AGM for the coming year. These formal meetings are open to all shareholders of an organisation. At least 21 days' notice must be given in many circumstances to make the meeting constitutionally correct.

- Extraordinary general meeting (EGM) – these meetings are called at the request of at least 10 per cent of the shareholders. The meeting might be called if it were necessary to discuss some special business considered to be of concern to the shareholders.

- Board meetings – the directors of an organisation attend board meetings, which are chaired by the chairperson of the board of directors. They are not always run in a formal way – their level of formality will depend on the type and size of the organisation.

- Statutory meetings – these are called so that the directors and shareholders of an organisation can communicate. These meetings are governed by legislation, particularly in the case of local government committees.

Meetings can also be both internal and external. An internal meeting is one which is attended solely by individuals from within the organisation, at the premises of the organisation. An external meeting is held at alternative premises and may be attended by individuals who are not employed by the organisation, such as shareholders. External meetings tend to be more formal than internal ones.

Figure 322.1

A committee is a good example of an informal internal meeting. Committees can take the following forms:

- Executive committees – which carry out the management of the organisation. Power and responsibility are held by the committee and its members have the right to act on their own initiative on behalf of the organisation. A board of directors is a good example of an executive committee.

- Standing committees – which are more concerned with detail than with the general running of the organisation. A standing committee might be formed to deal with only one issue, such as finance. This type of committee works on its own initiative but is responsible to an executive committee.

- Advisory committee – which again is responsible to an executive committee. It is often formed from those with particular expertise to advise the executive committee in a particular area.

- Ad hoc committee – which is set up for one particular purpose, such as the planning of a special event or project. This will not be longstanding and may exist for only a matter of weeks.

- Joint consultative committee – which is usually formed with a view to improving communications and to inform the workforce on policy and management decisions. Many organisations form joint consultative committees to give employees the opportunity to become involved in decision making. They would meet regularly and relay decisions, negotiate and discuss options. These types of committees can take the form of an advisory body, a consultative body or a negotiating body.

- Sub-committee – which a committee may elect to research and discuss certain issues. It has no power to take action and will have to report back to the committee that formed it.

Gathering information

Does your organisation hold meetings such as those listed in this section? Are you involved in either planning, organising or attending any of them? What does your planning involve? Is this a large part of your job role or something that you share with someone else?

1.3 Explain how to plan meetings that meet agreed aims and objectives and
1.4 Explain the purpose of agreeing a brief for the meeting

Meetings can be very time consuming for employees, especially if the organisation has a culture for holding meetings frequently. Actions beforehand that can help make meetings successful are important to ensure that aims and objectives are met. All attendees will wish to have a positive and constructive outcome to the meeting.

Effective meetings produce results. The meeting has to have an aim or more than one aim. It is important, then, that the right attendees are available. Without crucial members of staff in attendance it could be that nobody has the authority to make decisions.

Distributing documentation in advance of a meeting can also assist effectiveness. Participants will have had the opportunity to read the documentation prior to the meeting. This will save meeting time, but will also mean they are better prepared to pass opinion during the meeting.

The meeting should always have a clear purpose. The issues for inclusion and their relative importance and urgency should be prioritised in the agenda. Urgent matters should be discussed first. The agenda could also have the desired outcome included. This is important as attendees will wish to know what is expected of them. It will make each item of the agenda have its own aim at the outset and result in a more productive meeting. Typical types of aim or objective include:

- make a decision

- have a discussion

- provide information

- arrange a workshop session or training

- generate ideas

- provide feedback
- find a solution
- agree a target
- agree a budget.

If the agenda contains controversial issues, these could be discussed later in the meeting. The important or urgent issues should be dealt with first. It is also worth considering that what could be seen as boring items could become more interesting if participants have the opportunity to become involved, for example by presenting or debating, so that they are active rather than just listening.

It will be the chairperson who controls the meeting. Effective meetings need control and planned times for each item could be added to the chairperson's agenda. In this way the chairperson can help to eliminate unnecessary discussion and move the meeting on to the next agenda item effectively. The participants will expect the chairperson to control the timekeeping and will respect his or her decision to close a discussion for the purpose of efficiency and deadlines.

For a meeting to meet its main aims and objectives, the following have to be addressed:

- The meeting has a stated goal.
- All participants are clear about the goal.
- There is a standard by which success or failure is measured.
- Only those capable of accomplishing the goal should be in attendance.
- Limit the number of issues related to the goal.
- The meeting should be in an environment that reflects the goal, for example the style, location, room size and seating arrangements.
- Documentation should have been circulated in advance.
- The agenda should be in a logical sequence, have clear outcomes and time limits.
- The chairperson should control the meeting.

Gathering information

Do you have to chair meetings? Or does someone else do it? If so, how good are they at controlling the meeting? Do the briefs and documentation for meetings you attend have to be sent out in advance of the meeting to give participants time to form their contribution? How do you ensure that the meeting is planned to give the best possible opportunity to meet the aims and objectives being discussed?

1.5 Explain how to identify suitable venues for different types of meetings and
1.6 Describe the types of resources needed for different types of meetings

Many meetings are informal and are held in an organisation's meeting room. They do not warrant the expense of an outside venue as the participants will all be familiar with the location and layout of the room. In contrast to this, important, formal, off-site venues are unfamiliar to many participants and this means that the planning process is even more important. Venue choice becomes critical during the planning stages. Major considerations include:

- size of the room
- equipment and services available
- table and seating layout
- availability of resources for demonstration items, paperwork, handouts
- electrical sockets and cable extensions
- heating and lighting
- equipment positioning, such as projectors, flip charts, whiteboards
- backup equipment availability
- toilets
- the venue's emergency exits and procedures
- reception and catering arrangements.

Every meeting will have its own set of resource and venue requirements. It is not sufficient to consider somewhere that has been used in the past. A personal visit to the venue has to be carried out to ascertain the availability of all of the above. Bookings should always be confirmed and checked a few days before the meeting is to take place.

For some meetings the positioning of seating and tables may be an important factor. The layout of the venue has to be appropriate for the meeting, for instance:

- Are formal presentations being made to a large group of people?
- Do the participants need to be sitting with tables or in rows?
- Can the venue provide a horseshoe-shaped table or are they restricted to a boardroom-style rectangular table with the chairperson sitting at one end?
- Does the meeting have to be a relaxed one, with lounge chairs and coffee tables?
- Will everyone be able to see screens and flip charts?

- Will one screen be sufficient? If not, is there a white wall that can be used?

- Are there health and safety issues with trailing cables?

- Does the venue provide laptops, flip charts and other resources or will they have to be taken in advance of the meeting?

- Are the staff at the venue friendly and helpful and will they be available on the day?

Figure 322.2

Gathering information

Are the meetings you attend large or small affairs? Are they held onsite or at an outside venue? What resources have you found are required at the majority of the meetings you attend? Have you been responsible for booking an outside venue and had to consider the options available for the meeting regarding the seating arrangements and resources available? If so, how did you go about this and how did you document your inspection? What factors affected your decision to choose the venue or otherwise?

1.7 Outline the main points that should be covered by an agenda and meeting papers

The meeting agenda is the tool with which the chairperson controls the meeting. It must include all the relevant information and be circulated in advance. Additional items can be submitted for consideration and if this is done it limits the final agenda item of 'any other business'.

Formal meeting agenda, for example for board meetings and committees, will have a fixed format. This format will apply to all meetings of this kind and contains the following:

- the date, time and venue of the meeting
- apologies for absence
- minutes of the last meeting
- matters arising from previous meeting
- a list of specific items to be discussed
- any other business
- the date of the next meeting.

For informal meetings, such as team, project and departmental meetings, an agenda may be produced, but sometimes a notice of meeting is sent out. This summons all those who are expected or entitled to attend to the meeting. A notice of meeting can be:

- emailed or posted in advance
- a verbal notification
- a notice board notification.

A notice of meeting will contain:

- the date of the notice
- the type of meeting
- the name of the person calling the meeting
- the venue
- the day, date and time
- details of any special business to be discussed.

Meeting papers include the agenda, chairperson's agenda and minutes of the previous meeting. The chairperson's agenda will contain more information than the meeting agenda. Space is left on the right-hand side of the page so that the chairperson can make notes during the meeting. The chairperson may also have indicated on their agenda the time each of the agenda items has been allocated.

The minutes of the previous meeting will have been circulated to those who attended. They will have been read before the meeting on most occasions and the chairperson will ask the attendees to accept them as being a true record of what was discussed, what was voted on and what actions were determined at the meeting. Usually in a formal meeting they will be signed by the chairperson as being a true and accurate record.

Other types of meeting papers will depend on the nature of the meeting and the topics to be discussed or voted on. They, too, may have been sent to participants in advance of the meeting so that they could familiarise themselves with the content. Meeting papers can include reports, feedback and review notes or research into a particular topic to be discussed.

Meeting notes are essential for managing meeting actions and outcomes. They also cement agreements and clarify confusions.

Gathering information

How involved are you in producing meeting documentation? Do you do this on a regular basis? Is this involvement for formal or informal meetings? Are documents tabled (laid out during the meeting) or are they distributed to participants ahead of the meeting?

1.8 Explain the purpose of meeting attendees' needs and special requirements, and providing them with information required for meetings, 1.9 Describe the health, safety and security requirements that need to be considered when organising meetings and 1.10 Explain the purpose and benefits of briefing the chair before a meeting

A successful meeting is all about a constructive and well-controlled discussion. It is about reaching an amicable solution to problems and finding a way to address targets, aims or objectives. This means that the ideal environment for a meeting is a comfortable and safe one that is being led by a well-informed and in-control chairperson. The attendees need to be well informed prior to the meeting and attend armed with all the information they need to make a decision or put forward their point of view.

Visiting participants are like guests of the business and as such they need to be treated as visitors. They may:

- be unfamiliar with the surroundings
- be unfamiliar with the other participants
- have English as their second language
- need wheelchair access
- be tired after travelling
- need to take medication

- need duplicate copies of documentation as they have forgotten their copies
- need to make telephone calls to their office
- need to be on a certain train or plane at the end of the meeting
- need directions to a hotel or other organisation.

The list could be endless, as each meeting may bring forth a whole new set of requirements from participants.

Meeting protocol means following the correct procedures for holding and attending a meeting. This also involves ensuring that the participants all have what they need, when they need it. Their needs may include:

- information in advance
- an introduction to the other participants
- assistance of some kind, possibly to make them feel more relaxed
- refreshments
- toilets
- an explanation about procedures
- an explanation about what is expected of them.

If the meeting is to be a success then all participants must be focused on what is being discussed. If this is not the case because one or more participants have not been offered a coffee, or have no idea who is sitting next to them, they will not be able to concentrate and contribute effectively.

From a health and safety point of view, the normal office considerations have to be taken into account. The organiser may need to do a risk assessment if the venue is an external one. The requirements included in the Health and Safety at Work Act apply to all workplace environments, however large or small. The act applies to anyone who is on the premises, including employees, managers, customers, visitors and even contractors who are involved in maintenance or temporary work.

The act states that:

A. All employers must ensure the health, safety and welfare at work of all their employees as far 'as is reasonably practicable'. Specifically this includes:

- All entry and exit routes must be safe.
- There must be a safe working environment and adequate facilities for the welfare of staff (somewhere to make a drink, toilet facilities, a quiet area).
- Safe and well-maintained equipment.
- Safe transportation and storage of all articles and substances.
- The provision of protective clothing.

- Clear information, instruction and training on health and safety, with adequate supervision of issues to do with health and safety.

B. Where the business has five or more employees there should be a written statement on health and safety policy for the business. The statement should be written by the employer and continually updated to include any changes. This document must be circulated to all employees and is often wall mounted in a reception area.

C. The business should allow a trade union to appoint safety representatives who must be allowed to investigate accidents or potential hazards, follow up employee complaints. Safety representatives should be given time off to carry out their duties. All employees must:

a) Take responsibility for their health and safety.

b) Take responsibility for the health and safety of others who may be affected by their activities or actions.

c) Co-operate with their employer to meet health and safety requirements.

Because your employer is paying you to represent the business in the best possible way, it is both your responsibility and in your own interests to assist in ensuring that the organisation is providing a healthy and safe environment for:

- all employees, whatever their job role within the business

- any visiting workers (such as those repairing, servicing or maintaining machinery or equipment)

- all the customers of the business

- any visitors or representatives from other organisations

- the general public.

It is important to remember that the health and safety regulations do not just apply to the business premises themselves but also relate to any work undertaken by the business in other locations. This means that representatives of the business who may be carrying out repair work in another organisation also have to comply with the legislation. In this case, perhaps also extra ones, depending on where the work is being carried out. Maintenance workers carrying out repairs on a building site, for example, would have to wear hard hats and comply with legislation relating to construction sites.

Briefing the chair usually takes place at a special meeting before the main meeting begins. It is important that the chair be made aware of any issues and is brought up to date with developments and topics that will be discussed at the meeting. This is essential in order to ensure that:

- all topics are covered in sufficient detail

- the chair is made aware of any potential problems

- the chair appreciates the relative importance of different topics that will be discussed

- the chair understands what might be necessary to ensure that the meeting runs smoothly

- the chair is able to direct the meeting in an efficient manner so that all participants get the most out of the meeting.

Gathering information

Are participants involved in the meetings you have to attend provided with information in advance of the meeting? Do the meetings involve those from outside the organisation, perhaps who have never visited before? How are they informed about the facilities available? Who does this? What about the chairperson – are they informed in advance and provided with a chairperson's agenda before the meeting? Who provides this?

1.11 Explain the purpose of welcoming and providing suitable refreshments to attendees, if required and
1.12 Describe the types of information, advice and support that may need to be provided during a meeting

Greeting visitors who have arrived to attend a meeting is one example of protocol. This reception may last only a few minutes, but it will give the visitor the opportunity to freshen up if they have been travelling and also to have some refreshment. The purpose of doing this is not just consideration for the participant in the meeting but also to ensure that they are capable of participating fully and to their best standard. Tired, hungry, uncomfortable participants cannot concentrate on either what is being said or what they are expected to contribute.

During the meeting consideration should be given to those who may have travelled. Regular refreshment breaks can be built into lengthy meetings, as can lunch breaks. Unless people are participating and fully involved, their concentration can drop after approximately 45 minutes. Breaks need not be lengthy ones and include refreshments, but could be five-minute breaks to stretch the legs, get some air or visit the toilet. If lunch is being provided, a buffet is less time-consuming than a sit-down meal and is much more relaxed, giving people the opportunity to talk to different participants rather than just those seated beside or opposite them.

Despite the fact that briefing papers and documents will have been circulated to participants prior to the meeting, issues may arise or discussions extend to areas that require more information. Even if this information is ready to hand, time may have to be allocated for the participants to read and understand that information. This means having a facility to print and copy should the need arise. A short break may be necessary for participants to read and discuss the new information and its relevance.

Equally, some discussions on agenda items may require specialist advice or guidance. It may be necessary to call in the assistance of a specialist, such as

Figure 322.3

a representative in health and safety or finance, or perhaps a management representative who can advise about the implications of a decision. It may be as important to ensure that any decisions made at the meeting do not conflict with the overall aims and objectives of the organisation.

Reference to previous minutes may be necessary to check on a technicality.

On a more general level, administrative support may be necessary for some meetings to provide additional copies, make telephone calls or find paperwork.

Gathering information

Backup information, advice and support may be dependent on the type of meeting and the needs of the participants. When you organise meetings, do you anticipate having to provide backup services? How do you go about planning this and how often are additional services required?

1.13 Describe the types of problems that may occur during a meeting and how to solve them

There is a wide range of problems that could occur during a meeting. Many of these problems can be avoided by having a prepared agenda, or at least establishing one at the outset of the meeting. This means reviewing the agenda with the participants at the beginning. It is also valuable to set aside a short time at the end to evaluate the meeting process.

The common problems and possible solutions are outlined in Table 322.2.

Table 322.2

Problem	Solution
Lack of focus	If participants fail to stay on topic, perhaps the key topic could be broken down so that different aspects of it can be discussed in order.
Repetition	Summarise or paraphrase what is being said and highlight the fact that certain things have already been covered.
Competition	Try to combine ideas so that one individual is not constantly competing to come up with the best solution.
People talking too long	Gently interrupt. If this does not work, be more forceful. Perhaps set time limits.
Shyness	Encourage quieter people to make a presentation.
Rambling	Encourage people to look at related ideas from outside the context of the meeting.
Lack of information	Contact someone from outside for the needed information and then return to the issue once the information has arrived.
Deadlock	Perhaps make a temporary or partial decision.

Problem	Solution
Avoidance	Set aside additional time to discuss difficult problems.
Trivial issues	Ask the participants to agree on the issue and quickly move on.
Rushed atmosphere	Ensure that the participants have not got other commitments and allocate more time to meetings.
Poor response to assigned tasks	If participants have been asked to do something between meetings, then to ensure that they know what is necessary review all tasks at the end of the meeting to remind people of their responsibilities.
Contradictory positions	If there are two opposing groups, get the groups to meet outside the meeting to discuss the issue and bring it up again at the next meeting.
Dominant individuals	Ask quieter participants specifically to add to the discussion.
Off-topic conversations	Encourage people to publicly state what they are saying rather than talking among themselves.
Boring meetings	Add breaks and perhaps meet less often.
Uneasy silences	Move on to the agenda item or adjourn the meeting.
Poor attendance	Make the meetings shorter and more focused.

Other common problems can include:

- interruptions – participants being called out of the meeting or having to answer calls. A 'meeting in progress' sign and diverted telephone should help avoid this

- overruns – having timed agenda items and a controlling chairperson can help to avoid this.

Gathering information

What are the common problems that you encounter during a meeting? Have you developed strategies to solve them?

1.14 Explain what should be included in a record of a meeting and the purpose of ensuring the record is accurate and approved and
1.15 Explain how to record actions and follow up, if required

The basic information that should be recorded in a meeting is:

- date and time of the meeting

- purpose of the meeting

- meeting lead or chair's name

- assigned action items

- decisions made

- record of attendance and apologies.

Before the meeting, gather as much information as you can. Ask for a list of attendees, as well as some information on the purpose of the meeting. To make the task of recording the proceedings of a meeting easier:

- Make sure that all the essential elements are noted. This includes the type of meeting, the date and time, name of the chair, main topics and time the meeting ended.

- Prepare an outline based on the agenda before the meeting begins. Make sure that you leave room for notes.

- Prepare a list of expected attendees (you can mark the names as they enter the room or pass around an attendance sheet that can be signed by everyone before the meeting begins).

- To assist you in making sure that you know who has contributed, make a simple seating map to help you identify each participant.

- Do not record every word that has been said, simply the main points. The minutes are a record of what happened at the meeting, not what was said.

- Use any aid that you find will help you record the proceedings, from a notepad to a recording device.

- Be aware of the issues that will be discussed beforehand – this will help you understand your notes.

- Type up the minutes as soon as possible and make sure that the chair approves them before you distribute them to participants and others.

Someone may have to take the role of recording the events of the meeting. These are known as minutes. They are supposed to be a short, objective summary of the key points of any discussion and the result of any decisions that were made at the meeting. Ideally, the notes should be typed and circulated immediately, directly after the meeting, with copies going to all attendees. They should include the date of the next meeting, if applicable. Additional copies should go to anyone else who needs to see the record of the meeting.

Minutes should be brief, precise and clear. They should include any agreed actions. Individuals who were declared responsible for certain actions to be taken should be named along with agreed deadlines. The minutes should:

- be written in the third person and the past tense

- briefly state what was said and what decisions were made

- provide only an outline of discussions, not be verbatim.

The minutes of the previous meeting are always the second item on the agenda of the following meeting. Participants confirm that they have read the minutes and that they consider them to be a true record of that meeting. If there are problems with the minutes, adjustments can be made and then the participants agree that they are a true record.

Not only are minutes valuable in terms of providing a record of the meeting, they also identify agreed actions and responsibilities. These require people to respond or perform or carry out duties, so that they can report their progress at the next meeting.

Decisions made at a meeting normally require a show of hands. This means that each participant votes either to approve or to reject a particular course of action or decision. The minutes should include the results of each vote. If each participant agrees then it is sufficient to state 'unanimous'. Otherwise the numbers of participants voting in favour, voting against or choosing not to cast a vote (abstention) is noted and the outcome of the vote is stated in the minutes.

It may also be the meeting organiser's responsibility to check that any individual who was required to carry out an action before the next meeting has done so. This may require information, documents or simple confirmation verbally.

Gathering information

Generally, who is responsible for taking a record of meetings? Does this responsibility always fall on one individual or do the participants take it in turns to produce the minutes? What process do you use in order to ensure that it is an accurate and approved record of the meeting? Have you had any difficulties with individuals challenging the accuracy of events?

1.16 Explain the purpose of collecting and evaluating participant feedback from the meeting and
1.17 Describe how to agree learning points to improve the organisation of future meetings

Many participants of meetings will state that meetings were a waste of time, but they will say this only after the meeting. It is possible to get feedback during the meeting, so that the processes can be improved straight away. A quick satisfaction check, asking each participant to indicate how the meeting is going, is a good way of achieving this.

At the end of the meeting it is also possible to evaluate. Each participant should explain how they felt the meeting went and what had been achieved. This can be formalised by asking each participant to make a personal evaluation of the meeting. They can indicate their feelings on a scale of 1 to 5, as in Table 322.3, for example.

Table 322.3

Meeting was interesting	1, 2, 3, 4, 5	Meeting was boring
I understood everything that was said	1, 2, 3, 4, 5	I understood very little
People listened to what I had to say	1, 2, 3, 4, 5	No one listened to what I said
The meeting was well prepared	1, 2, 3, 4, 5	The meeting was badly prepared
It was easy to trust one another	1, 2, 3, 4, 5	It was difficult to trust others
Decisions were reached in a satisfactory way	1, 2, 3, 4, 5	I felt unhappy about the way decisions were made
I felt we achieved a great deal in the meeting	1, 2, 3, 4, 5	Little was achieved

In this way the following areas of the meeting can be evaluated:

- interest
- understanding
- contribution
- preparation
- honesty
- processes
- tasks.

This type of evaluation form can be used straight after the meeting. The information can be used to see what was right and what was wrong about the meeting and how the process, style and organisation of the meeting could be improved.

Some people can spend an enormous amount of time in meetings. It is therefore important that these meetings are valuable. Simple evaluation, leading to ways in which to improve the organisation of future meetings, can pose the following questions:

● Did the meeting start on time?

● Did it end on time?

● Did participants stay on topic?

● Did everyone involve themselves in discussion and decision making?

● Were the most important issues covered?

● Were decisions that were made followed through?

These will all give indications as to the organisation and effectiveness of the meeting. If there is a negative response on any of these questions, solutions need to be sought. This can be achieved by asking participants to suggest ways to make the meetings more effective. Again, simple evaluation forms can be of great value.

Each meeting should have clear aims and objectives. These help clarify the purpose of the meeting. Some organisations recommend using action words for each agenda item, such as 'decide', 'discuss', 'review' or 'select'. Other organisations break down what they see to be the four key roles in any meeting:

● Leader – convenes the meeting and leads discussions.

● Facilitator – keeps the discussions and decisions moving along.

● Recorder – takes notes on paper, laptop or flip charts.

● Timekeeper – reminds the leader when the time is almost up on an agenda item.

Gathering information

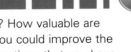

What evaluation methods do you use for your meetings? How valuable are these evaluation methods in identifying ways in which you could improve the organisation of meetings in the future? How have the meetings that you have organised changed as a result of evaluation?

■ 2. Be able to prepare for a meeting

2.1 Agree and prepare the meeting brief, checking with others, if required,
2.2 Agree a budget for the meeting, if required,
2.3 Prepare and agree an agenda and meeting papers,
2.4 Organise and confirm venue, equipment and catering requirements, when necessary,
2.5 Invite attendees, confirm attendance and identify any special requirements,
2.6 Arrange catering, if required,
2.7 Arrange the equipment and layout of the room, if required and
2.8 Make sure the chair receives appropriate briefing

Refer to 1.1 to 1.10 and then consider the following.

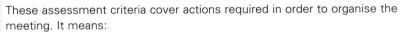

Gathering information

These assessment criteria cover actions required in order to organise the meeting. It means:

- agreeing and preparing the meeting brief
- budget considerations
- agenda and meeting papers
- venue, equipment and catering requirements
- invitations, confirmations and special requirements
- equipment and layout of the room
- briefing the chair.

Evidence can best be collected either by observation or by witness testimony supported by documentation. The same meeting should ideally be covered across this learning outcome and the remaining two learning outcomes.

■ 3. Be able to support running a meeting

3.1 Welcome attendees and offer suitable refreshments (if required),
3.2 Make sure attendees have a full set of papers,
3.3 Make sure a person has been nominated to take minutes, if required and
3.4 Provide information, advice and support when required

Refer to 1.11 to 1.13 and then consider the following.

Gathering information

This learning outcome covers events during the meeting and can be best evidenced through observation or by witness testimony supported by appropriate documents. It needs to cover:

● welcoming attendees and providing refreshments
● distributing full sets of meeting papers
● nominating someone to take minutes
● providing information, advice and support during the meeting.

■ 4. How to follow up a meeting

4.1 Produce a record of the meeting,
4.2 Seek approval for the meeting record, amend as required,
4.3 Respond to requests for amendments and arrange recirculation of a revised meeting record,
4.4 Follow up action points, if required,
4.5 Evaluate meeting arrangements, and external services where used,
4.6 Evaluate participant feedback from the meeting and share results with relevant people, where used and
4.7 Summarise learning points and use these to identify improvements that can be made to future meeting arrangements and support

Refer to 1.14 to 1.17 and then consider the following

Gathering information

These seven assessment criteria cover the post-meeting actions. Again, they are best evidenced either through observation or by the use of witness testimony supported by appropriate documentation. Evidence needs to include:

- a record of the meeting
- steps taken to approve the record and the making of amendments, if necessary
- recirculating revised meeting records
- following up action points
- meeting evaluation
- evaluating feedback and sharing results
- summarising ways in which to make improvements to future meeting arrangements and support.

What is Evidence ?

A single piece of evidence can cover more than one learning outcome. Several assessment criteria can be dealt with by the one piece of evidence. You can also use the same evidence for other assessment criteria from other units. Your assessor will use a wide range of assessment methods for the learning outcomes in this unit, including:

- observing your performance
- examining work that you have produced
- questioning and discussing issues with you
- using witness testimony from work colleagues
- looking at your learner statements
- recognising your prior learning.

The range of evidence can include:

- meeting briefs and venue and budget requirements
- planning records
- resources list
- venue searches
- agenda and meeting papers and minutes of previous meetings
- correspondence relating to booking and confirmation of venue, including equipment and catering
- invitation letters and emails
- special requirement requests
- confirmation of attendees
- room preparation notes

stationery. Alternatively, this can be the purchase of equipment or other physical items that may be needed by the department, such as office furniture or production line machinery.

Gathering information

What is the range of products and services that you provide to internal customers? How broad is the range and how significant a part of your work is it? How has it affected the overall balance of your workload?

3. Understand how to deliver customer service that meets or exceeds internal customer expectations

3.1 Explain the purpose and value of identifying internal customer needs and expectations

Internal customer needs and expectations are as important as those of external customers. The following example explains why this is the case:

- The health service exists to meet the health needs of patients (clients or customers).

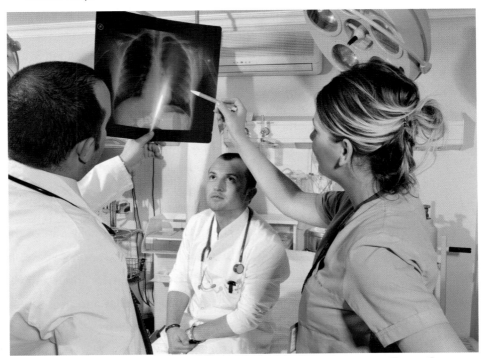

Figure 328.1

- The health service aims to meet the needs and expectations of its clients by providing high-quality care.

- A focus on clients by the health service should include all those who receive a service, including all those employees involved in the delivery of the care for external clients.

- Internal customers will include doctors, nurses, administrative workers and cleaners. All of these groups are involved in delivering the output of the health service, which is healthcare.

- If these internal customers receive high-quality customer service from the healthcare system itself, then they will be in a position to perform their jobs more effectively and as a result better meet the needs of the external customers.

Good internal customer service should share many of the same qualities as external customer service, including:

- timeliness

- courtesy

- consultation with the customer.

A prime example would be the standards of service by telephone or dealing with correspondence. An organisation may well adopt exactly the same standards of service that it applies to external customers, such as:

- all calls answered within 20 seconds

- all correspondence (including emails) acknowledged within three working days of receipt and definitive replies given within 20 working days.

The approach to internal customers may be clearly defined by the organisation in order to identify the precise needs of these customers and to give them a clear indication of the service that they will receive:

- A promise that all colleagues (internal customers) will be treated in the way that the service provider would like to be treated themselves.

- A guarantee that any dealings will incorporate courtesy, professionalism, friendliness, mutual respect and approachability.

- A clear message that all employees are essentially part of the same team.

- A service that takes into account openness, respect and duty of care.

- Acknowledgement that the internal customers' input and views are valuable.

- A fair application of any organisational rules and procedures.

- An equal opportunities and rights approach.

- A commitment from the service provider that the internal customer will receive 'best practice treatment' in all respects.

Gathering information

How do you establish the needs and expectations of internal customers? Is there a set procedure that allows them to specify their needs and expectations? Does your organisation have a minimum set of standards which lays out what they can expect in terms of service?

3.2 Explain why customer service must meet or exceed internal customer expectations and 3.3 Explain the value of meeting or exceeding internal customer expectations

Good external customer service relies on effective internal customer service, which in turn means that the organisation benefits from the effort. Although internal customer service is invisible to external customers, working together towards a common goal of excellence in all collaborative work means that the organisation is able to deliver high-quality products and services to customers.

Providing high-quality internal customer service begins by setting clear guidelines about what internal customers can reasonably expect. In some cases, an organisation will set up service level agreements (SLAs). This is particularly true of larger organisations (especially those in the public sector). They will define exactly what to expect in terms of internal customer service. Even without these SLAs internal customer service can exceed the expectations of the internal customer if the levels of expectation have been set out in advance. There will always be problems with levels of service, but these can be avoided. An internal customer should always try to define exactly what they are expecting (in regard to timeline and quality, for instance). Any last-minute requests could be problematic and unreasonable requests need to be dealt with on a case-by-case basis. The internal customer needs to be realistic about their demands and not expect the unachievable.

In order to meet expectations, the internal service provider needs to clarify what is needed from the customer in terms of deadlines, quality and any special requirements. This means cooperation and sufficient lead time as well as providing sufficient information so that the service provider can deliver exactly what is expected. This can often be simply phrased as 'we need to know this from you in order to make sure that we meet your requirements'.

Internal customers need to understand how their requests will fit into the overall work of the internal service provider. This will ensure that the internal customer does not always think that they are the only priority. The situation is never helped when the internal customer insists that their needs are urgent and should have the highest priority. A clear communication between internal customers and service providers is essential.

In terms of balancing the demands of the internal customer and the ability of the service provider to give excellent customer service, Table 328.1 outlines the key considerations.

Table 328.1

Internal service provider	Internal customer
Know the customers' expectations and ensure that you are part of their expectation setting	Discuss your expectations with the service provider
Explain how they can be good customers by telling them what to expect and negotiate delivery dates and quality levels	Think ahead and give the service provider sufficient time to deliver on your request
Always keep the customer informed about progress	Provide all the information they need in your original request and be prepared to provide additional information if requested
Talk to the customer so that they understand the pressures you may be under	Always be professional and try to understand their workflow, priorities and processes
Try to develop a broader view of how the organisation works and how your contribution fits in with that of the internal customers	Remember that they are part of the same organisation and they are not deliberately working against you

Gathering information

Why is it important to establish the expectations of internal customers? What policies and procedures are in place to ensure this? Why is it vital to exceed their expectations? What are the benefits to you, to the internal customer and to the organisation?

3.4 Explain the purpose and value of building positive working relationships

The ability to build strong and positive working relationships with others is based on:

- commonalities – shared experiences, ideas, interests and values
- connectivity – developing a bond with others
- communication – speaking in simple terms and using active listening
- collaboration – being able to share problems and help each other succeed.

The primary purpose of building these relationships is to ensure that different parts of the organisation are able to understand each other and appreciate one another's role in the organisation. It also reduces stress in the working environment. All working relationships can have either a positive or negative impact on the individual and can affect your ability to develop and progress. By focusing on building positive relationships, you can feel more comfortable with your interactions with others. It will help to prevent you from feeling demoralised when things do not go according to plan, and you will have a closer connection with those to whom you provide services and products on a regular basis.

Building the relationships is not an easy task, particularly as many working environments are competitive and there are numerous other challenges and demands on your time. Unfortunately, many people do not take the time or the effort to try to build relationships.

If there are positive broader working relationships within a business, the workforce tends to be happier and more productive. A good working relationship across departments and teams facilitates working together towards the achievement of both individual and shared objectives. Poor working relationships can have a serious impact on the overall performance of the business. In developing a good relationship with another person, it is possible to have secured an ally should any problems arise. You should also be prepared to provide them with support and assistance they may require in return. Positive relationships can help to build trust across the organisation, ensuring that people feel comfortable with airing their concerns or issues without having to raise the matter with a more senior member of staff.

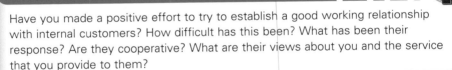

Gathering information

Have you made a positive effort to try to establish a good working relationship with internal customers? How difficult has this been? What has been their response? Are they cooperative? What are their views about you and the service that you provide to them?

4. Understand the purpose of quality standards and timescales for delivering customer service

4.1 Identify quality standards for own organisation and work and
4.2 Explain the value of agreeing quality standards and timescales

ISO 9000 is a family of standards on good quality management practices. It is a set of standards and guidelines that relates to quality management systems. The latest is ISO 9001:2008, which covers all types of organisations regardless of their size, what they do or whether they are a private- or public-sector organisation.

The first principle of the ISO 9000 is customer focus. It states:

> 'Organizations depend on their customers and therefore should understand current and future customer needs, should meet customer requirements and strive to exceed customer expectations.'

It is important to note that the standard does not define a customer; this means that internal customers should be treated in exactly the same way as external customers. This sets a benchmark for organisations. In practical terms, SLAs are often used to identify the following:

- the customer's expectation of quality, performance and value
- the minimum acceptable standards of the service and the customer requirements
- the performance measure of what is being provided
- an agreement between the customer and the service provider for providing a range of services.

In effect, this is a contract between the service provider and the internal customer. Quality assurance systems underpin the whole approach to ensuring minimum standards. Quality assurance systems will usually be a policy statement supported by a manual. The policy statement will outline the organisation's commitment to quality assurance, covering all customer service, including internal customers. The manual will provide a detailed interpretation of the way in which each of the quality standards is to be met. It will include the procedures that will need to be followed in order to ensure that work complies with the quality assurance system.

In setting quality standards it is important to remember the impact if you fail to do so – see Table 328.2.

Table 328.2

Tangible effects of not setting quality standards	Intangible effects of not setting quality standards
Increased rejection/rework	Loss of goodwill
Less production/productivity	Conflicts between different areas of the organisation
Higher number of customer complaints	Loss of employee morale

Setting customer service quality standards and ensuring that timescales are met requires you to consider all aspects of the interactions you have with internal customers. This means establishing a series of promises or minimum standards that you undertake to follow. Typically, this will mean looking at the following areas and making a statement of your minimum standards (or sets of promises). It is important to remember that every organisation has different sets of standards and these may have been developed over a period of time to reflect the nature of the organisation itself.

General standards:

- Anticipate the needs of customers by identifying expectations and working toward meeting those needs.

- Exceed expectations of all customer groups.

- Hold yourself accountable for service commitments.

- Be aware of communication style and communicate professionally.

- Be sensitive to eye contact and tone of voice.

- Turn off mobile phones during meetings.

General customer commitments:

- Listen to customer requests and take immediate action to assist them.

- Keep customers informed of any delays.

- Greet all customers in a professional and courteous manner.

- Inform customers what to expect and normal delivery times.

- Respond to requests and questions by the end of the business day.

- End all interactions with customers in a professional and courteous manner.

Internal customers:

- Inform customers of typical process time and any delays that may arise.

- Interact in a professional and courteous manner.

- Communicate with internal customers by email or phone daily with updates in the process.

- Work to resolve internal issues with other departments and colleagues by addressing problems and working toward solutions.

- Show respect for each other and behave in an appropriate manner.

Telephone etiquette:

- Answer the phone within three rings.

- Identify yourself when answering the phone.

- Listen to callers' requests and help to answer questions or resolve issues.

- Ask for caller's permission before putting them on hold.

- Offer to take a message if someone is not available to speak to them.

Voice mail etiquette:

- Update voicemail greeting when out of the office.

- Inform callers of anticipated return and contact person for questions.
- Respond to all voicemail messages by the end of the business day.

Email etiquette:

- Update email 'out-of-office' notification when out of the office.
- Give name of contact person and expected return date.
- Respond to emails before the end of the business day.

Gathering information

Do you have quality standards and timescales for customer service delivery in place? How do you ensure that you stick to the standards? How complex are the standards and how often do they need to be updated?

5. Understand how to deal with internal customer service problems

5.1 Describe the types of problems that internal customers may have and
5.2 Explain ways of dealing with problems

Colleagues, other departments or branches are just as important as external customers and they deserve to have their problems and complaints taken seriously. External customers can sense that there is a good working atmosphere and a coordinated approach to customer service. Internal customers may know different and they can see through poor excuses and attempts to shift blame to others.

Lack of communication is often the key problem for internal customers and can lead to poor working relationships. Even the most efficient communication systems break down if people do not read their emails, look at notice boards, log on to their computers, check their voicemails or attend meetings. Simply getting someone to sign a document proves only that they have had the document; they may not have read it.

The most typical reasons for problems and complaints are:

- broken promises
- missed deadlines
- poor quality products or services
- lack of communication
- rudeness and unreasonable behaviour.

Figure 328.2

First, it is important to know the difference between problems that you can deal with yourself and those that you need to refer to others. You may face anger, for instance. The internal customer may not necessarily be angry with you but complaining about the product or service provided. Whoever is dealing with the problem is simply a representative and has now become the frontline individual responsible for solving the problem. The main priority is to listen and then decide on a course of action.

When there is a problem or complaint you should:

● let the customer have their say and take notes

● ask questions in order to clarify points

● summarise the problem

● tell them what you propose to do

● give them a timescale

● promise and follow through with the promise that you will keep them informed.

Many organisations will have established complaints policies and procedures, which will probably incorporate the majority of the points. But they may be more detailed. It is vital that you keep track of problems – this will ensure that each problem is dealt with in the correct manner, but it will also highlight other issues. If there are recurring problems or complaints about particular products or services, then the quality of these will need to be examined in more detail. There may well be an underlying problem.

Complaints usually fall into three distinct categories:

1 Quality issues – the actual quality of the product or service that was expected by the customer is not up to the standard that they anticipated or were promised.

2 Organisational issues – these are usually failures in processes and procedures. Something has simply been forgotten, missed out or ignored, which should normally be part of the internal customer service process.

3 Personnel issues – these are problems with specific individuals, such as a service provider showing lack of commitment, rudeness, arrogance, or failing to communicate with the internal customer.

It is valuable to keep details of problems or complaints that you deal with. These can be straightforward logs using basic headings, including:

- date
- complainant
- details of the problem or complaint
- action taken and by whom
- costs involved in resolving the problem.

Gathering information

What are the typical problems that your internal customers bring to you? Can you categorise them as being largely one-off problems or is there a pattern? Does your organisation have set procedures or policies in dealing with problems? How appropriate are they to the majority of situations?

5.3 Explain the purpose and value of a complaints procedure, if applicable

The main purpose of a complaints procedure is to ensure that all complaints are dealt with in a fast and efficient manner. It also acts as a guarantee that all complaints are treated seriously, that the organisation acts in a courteous and professional manner, and that anyone who does complain is given sympathy and understanding. Complaints procedures also act as a means by which the organisation can learn from its mistakes.

For many organisations the internal customer complaints procedure will be exactly the same as the one used for external customers. The complaints can be resolved either informally or formally. Informal resolution can be achieved by swift action by the service provider, which should be to the satisfaction of the internal customer. Formal complaints may need to be referred to more senior management and may have to be put in writing.

Ideally, a complaints procedure should have the following features:

- a definition of what constitutes a complaint
- confirmation of who is assigned to deal with complaints and how they are passed on to them
- confirmation that complaints will not be handled solely by the individual against whom the complaint was made
- a summary of key steps to investigate the complaint
- confirmation that the response to complaints will fall in line with agreed rules and deadlines
- whether a written acknowledgement will be given
- when any final response must be completed
- outline procedures for logging complaints by date, nature and name
- confirmation about who the complaint handler needs to report the complaint to internally
- how recommendations for revised working practices can be made.

The main purpose of a complaints procedure is to:

- focus on putting matters right whenever possible
- ensure that anyone involved in the problem is made aware of it at the earliest possible stage
- identify lessons that can be learned from the situation to avoid the same problem or issue in the future
- issue an apology, if appropriate to the situation.

The complaints procedure should always ensure:

- proper handling of complaints
- complaints are acknowledged within a reasonable time
- an invitation to confirm an oral complaint in writing
- that complaints will be dealt with by individuals with sufficient experience
- that any appropriate remedial action will be taken immediately
- that where complaints are not dealt with in a prompt way they can be referred to more senior members of staff.

■ 6. Understand how to monitor and evaluate internal customer service and the benefits of this

6.1 Explain the purpose and benefits of monitoring internal customer satisfaction and how to do so and
6.2 Describe techniques for collecting and evaluating customer feedback

Monitoring internal customer satisfaction is as important as monitoring external customer satisfaction. It is a measure of how the service provider is perceived by the rest of the organisation. It allows the service provider to identify areas that are problematic and those that need to be reviewed or radically changed. It gives them the opportunity to look at the service that they provide in an objective way and to draw conclusions from the monitoring and evaluation process. However, the whole process is valuable only if the service provider intends to follow up on problems that have been highlighted.

A well-designed internal customer survey programme gives employees an opportunity to share ideas and opinions. The process can ultimately help to:

● reduce any frustration

● eliminate procedures or practices that are causing problems

● identify any training needs

● improve overall service and responsiveness

● cut costs by eliminating mistakes and lost time.

Internal customer satisfaction questionnaires (ICSQs) aim to measure how satisfied internal customers are with a department or a team. They are a measurement of perceptions of service in three key areas:

● communication – the ability to communicate and listen effectively

● productivity – the ability to maintain high levels of efficiency, reliability and quality

- responsiveness – the ability to respond effectively to customer need.

An ICSQ focuses on impressions rather than actual performance as it is clear that how internal customers view customer service is more important than the reality of the service that they actually receive. The way that the questions are phrased incorporates the expectations of the internal customer. They are asked to indicate how satisfied or dissatisfied they are with the service that they receive. The survey summarises three key areas:

- strengths
- weaknesses
- areas for improvement.

The ICSQ uses a five-point system:

- 0 = can't answer
- 1 = very dissatisfied
- 2 = dissatisfied
- 3 = satisfied
- 4 = very satisfied.

Typical questions could include the following:

1 Keep me appropriately informed.
2 Handle my requests efficiently.
3 Operate smoothly and efficiently.
4 Listen effectively to my needs.
5 Handle problems skilfully.
6 Answer my questions efficiently.
7 Make it easy to work with them.
8 Communicate effectively.
9 Respond to problems quickly.
10 Be well organised.
11 Respond promptly to my requests.
12 Find out what I need.
13 Treat me as a valued customer.
14 Build cooperation.
15 Show consideration and respect.
16 Provide a valuable service.

17 Follow through well on their commitments.

18 Meet my expectations.

19 Be courteous.

20 Look for ways to improve their service.

21 Handle details well.

22 Maintain high standards.

These types of questions will provide valuable numerical data, but you can also ask questions that require more information. Examples can include:

- What would you like us to do more of?

- What would you like us to do less of?

- What would you like us to do better?

- What do you like most about us?

Gathering information

Do you routinely monitor internal customer satisfaction? How is this achieved? Does your organisation have a policy of requesting internal customer feedback? What is done with this data?

6.3 Explain the benefits of continuous improvement

An essential part of achieving quality systems across the whole of the organisation is to strive for continuous improvement. This means setting a series of targets in terms of performance and efficiency. Once these have been achieved, new targets are then set.

It is not sufficient to have achieved a certain level of performance or efficiency. In order to continually improve the service offered to internal customers, new ways must always be sought to streamline processes, ensure high quality and succeed in having the highest levels of customer satisfaction, both internal and external.

Continuous improvement was a concept brought in that originally focused on manufacturing. It aimed to improve products, services and processes. The efforts can either be incremental, in other words small improvements over a period of time, or breakthrough improvements, which could mean radically changing the whole way in which a service is delivered.

Continuous improvement actually comes from a Japanese word, kaizen. This literally means 'change is good'. The key principles behind it are:

- looking at the processes through feedback

Figure 328.3

- eliminating any parts of the process that are unnecessary, thus being more efficient
- emphasising continuous improvement steps, rather like evolution.

Improvements are based on a number of small changes. Many of the ideas for improvements will come from either the service providers themselves or from internal customers. Each small improvement does not radically change everything and neither does it mean that the improvement will cost a lot to implement.

The fact that ideas for improvements come from existing employees, who are actually involved, means that each change is relevant and valuable. Continuous improvement means encouraging anyone involved in a process to look at what they do and to try to improve their performance. Above all, it encourages people to take ownership of their work.

Some businesses achieve continuous improvement by a gradual and natural streamlining of processes. In effect they learn how to do things better from experience. Others look towards the best practices in other businesses and seek to copy the way that they carry out processes. This is known as bench-marking, or best practice benchmarking. Adopting this way forward can often mean that systems need to be radically changed. This may not always be the ideal situation, as there will always be a period of confusion during the changeover.

Gathering information

Where do ideas for improvements come from in your organisation? If an internal customer suggests a better way of doing something, is this followed up? How is the suggestion logged and where is it discussed? Can you identify any small changes that you could make in the processes or the way in which you deliver internal customer service? How would you go about suggesting these ideas? How likely is it that they will be taken up?

■ 7. Be able to build positive working relationships with internal customers

7.1 Identify internal customers,
7.2 Confirm internal customer needs in terms of products and services,
7.3 Confirm internal customer needs in terms of quality standards and timescales and
7.4 Agree procedures to be followed if internal customer needs are not met

Refer to 1.1, 2.1 and 3.1 to 3.4 and then consider the following.

Gathering information

For this learning outcome you will have to begin by identifying your internal customers. Are they individuals, teams, departments or whole divisions of your organisation? What kind of products and services do you provide to them? How do you establish their requirements in terms of quality standards and timescales? Do they specify these or do you tell them what to expect? What procedures are involved if the needs of internal customers are not met? How are these problems resolved?

8. Be able to deliver customer services to agreed quality standards and timescales

8.1 Provide customer service(s) to agreed quality standards,
8.2 Provide customer service(s) to agreed timescales and
8.3 Check internal customer needs and expectations have been met

Refer to 4.1 to 4.3 and then consider the following.

Gathering information

Is there a written policy with regard to quality standards and timescales in your organisation? If not, how are these agreed at the point at which the internal customer makes a request to you? What checks are in place in order to ensure that their needs and expectations have been met? At what point do you check that they have been met? How do you make this check?

9. Be able to deal with internal customer service problems and complaints

9.1 Follow procedures, within agreed timescale, to (a) process problems and complaints, (b) resolve problems and complaints, (c) refer problems and complaints, where necessary

Refer to 5.1 to 5.3 and then consider the following.

Gathering information

Assuming your organisation has a set procedure to deal with internal customer service problems and complaints, you will need to retrieve this documentation relating to a problem or complaint. It needs to show that you have followed procedures within the agreed timescale. The procedure needs to also show how you processed it, resolved it or referred it if necessary. If your organisation does not have a set procedure you will need to explain how you process and resolve problems and complaints from internal customers.

10. Be able to monitor and evaluate customer services for internal customers

10.1 Obtain and record internal customer feedback,
10.2 Analyse and evaluate internal customer feedback and
10.3 Take action that will lead to improvement in customer service(s) to internal customers

Refer to 6.1 to 6.3 and then consider the following.

Gathering information

This learning outcome focuses on how you collect, record, analyse, evaluate and take action on feedback from internal customers. Your organisation may have a procedure in order to do this and you will need to demonstrate that you have followed this process and that it has led to an improvement in internal customer service. This learning outcome is more problematic if a process is not in place, as it may require you to request customer feedback and then to analyse, evaluate and act upon it.

What is Evidence ?

A single piece of evidence can cover more than one learning outcome. Several assessment criteria can be dealt with by the one piece of evidence. You can also use the same evidence for other assessment criteria from other units. Your assessor will use a wide range of assessment methods for the learning outcomes in this unit, including:

- observing your performance
- examining work that you have produced
- questioning and discussing issues with you
- using witness testimony from work colleagues
- looking at your learner statements
- recognising your prior learning.

The range of evidence can include:

- annotated procedures relating to customer service
- records of communications with colleagues and internal customers
- records of complaints
- internal customer complaints logs
- monitoring records
- internal customer feedback logs and surveys
- communications relating to complaints
- problems referred to others
- written notes in response to complaints dealt with
- suggestions
- minutes of meetings
- evaluation of provision of customer services to internal customers
- evaluation reports
- development plans.

Unit 329 Deliver, Monitor and Evaluate Customer Services to External Customers

■ Purpose of the unit

The unit looks at providing and continuously improving customer services to external customers.

■ Assessment requirements

There are ten parts to this unit. The first six parts consider all aspects of the external customer. The remaining four parts look at your ability to deal with external customers. The ten parts of the unit are:

1   Understand the meaning of external customer – describing what is meant by an external customer. (K)

2   Know the types of products and services relevant to external customers – the range of different products and services that your organisation offers to external customers. (K)

3   Understand how to deliver customer service that meets or exceeds external customer expectations – the purpose and value of identifying external customer needs and expectations, the need to meet or exceed them, the value of doing so and the purpose and value of building positive working relationships with external customers. (K)

4   Understand the purpose of quality standards and timescales for delivering customer service – identifying quality standards, agreeing quality standards and timescales and how to set and meet quality standards and timescales with external customers. (K)

5   Understand how to deal with customer service problems for external customers – types of problems that external customers may have, consequences of not meeting their expectations, ways of dealing with external customer services problems and the purpose and value of a complaints procedure. (K)

6   Understand how to monitor and evaluate external customer service and the benefits of this – the purpose, benefits and ways of monitoring external customer satisfaction, the techniques used to collect and evaluate customer feedback and the benefits of continuous improvement. (K)

7   Be able to build positive working relationships with external customers – identifying external customers, confirming their needs, confirming their

256

needs in terms of products and services, quality standards and timescales and agreeing procedures if their needs are not met. (P)

8   Be able to deliver customer services to agreed quality standards and timescales – providing customer services to agreed quality standards and timescales, checking that internal customer needs and expectations have been met. (P)

9   Be able to deal with customer service problems and complaints for external customers – following procedures within agreed timescales in relation to process, resolve or refer problems and complaints. (P)

10 Be able to monitor and evaluate customer services to external customers – obtaining and recording feedback, analysing and evaluating feedback and taking action leading to improvements to external customer services. (P)

1. Understand the meaning of external customers

1.1 Describe what is meant by external customers

In many organisations, there is a wide variety of customer types. When we talk about customer types, the following list shows you those that could be considered to be external customers; in other words, those who do not work inside the organisation:

- individual customers
- groups of customers
- customers from different age groups
- customers from different cultures – this means people from different backgrounds or from different countries
- non-English-speaking customers
- customers with specific needs, for example those who are sight or hearing impaired, those in wheelchairs, or young children
- other businesses, for example suppliers of the business's raw materials.

Normally the term 'customer' can refer to an individual or a business. It is usual for a customer to be actually paying for the products and services in the normal way. Many businesses refer to other organisations as customers rather than individuals.

Consumers are usually individual customers, such as customers who purchase products from a supermarket. You will often hear the phrase 'the consumer

Figure 329.1

market' and this refers to individual members of the public as customers, rather than other businesses.

The term 'client' is also used to describe customers. It has several different meanings, for example, a professional, such as an accountant or solicitor, would refer to their customers as clients whether they are other businesses or individuals. The term client is also often used by the public services. Dentists, doctors, social services and opticians often refer to their customers as clients rather than customers. Hairdressers, beauticians and cosmetic surgeons also prefer to use the term client rather than customer or consumer.

In identifying the type of customer, the business seeks to match both its products and services to its expectations, as well as designing its advertising and publicity to suit its particular set of customers.

Gathering information

What types of external customers are dealt with by your organisation? Are they individuals, groups or other businesses? How often do you deal with them?

2. Know the types of products and services relevant to external customers

2.1 Describe the products and services offered by an organisation to external customers

The first major way of categorising what an organisation offers to its customers is to distinguish between products and services. Broadly speaking, a product is a tangible item, something that you can touch, such as a photocopier or a car. A service is an intangible item; you cannot touch it, such as insurance or banking.

These categories can be broken down even further if you consider:

- perishable – a product or service that will last for only a limited period of time. Food is a perishable product and travel insurance is a perishable service as it covers a limited period of time

- non-perishable – a product or a service that has a long or indefinite lifespan. A car could be considered to be a non-perishable product or a rolling contract to supply accountancy or legal advice for a client a non-perishable service.

Both products and services have to be delivered. However, while a product will have to be physically delivered, a service is also delivered by providing that service in accordance with the timescale required by the customer.

There is a vast range of products and services that can be supplied to customers. Business organisations will tend to:

- manufacture their own products and sell them to customers (or other businesses)

- use distributors who will handle products from other businesses and sell them on to customers or other businesses

- use retailers who will receive products from other businesses and sell them to customers

- provide services using their expertise and sell these services to customers and other businesses.

All of these types of transaction aim to make a profit. In other words, the manufacturer sells their products for more than the cost of manufacture. The retailer sells products to customers at a higher price than they paid their supplier. A service-based business sells services to customers at a higher price than the cost of the expertise (employees) used to work on that service.

Other organisations do not seek a profit as such to provide products and services to customers. Nonetheless, they work within cash restraints and need to provide those products and services to customers within the budget they have been given. For example, a hospital will have a budget to provide medical services to the local population. A charity will provide services to clients based on their ability to raise funds.

External customers are consumers of the products and services of businesses and other organisations. The external customers will usually have a choice of which business or organisation to use. For businesses in particular, it is vital to establish a reputation for quality of products and services and customer service is an important part of the relationship they try to create with the customers.

Gathering information

What is the range of products and services that you provide to external customers? How broad is the range and how significant a part of your work is it? How has it affected the overall balance of your workload?

◼ 3. Understand how to deliver customer service that meets or exceeds external customer expectations

3.1 Explain the purpose and value of identifying customer needs and expectations

In identifying the customer's needs and expectations it is possible for the organisation to ensure that these are matched and ideally exceeded. Regardless of the type of organisation, steps always need to be taken to try to ensure that customers are satisfied (some suggest they should be delighted or surprised) by the level of service that they receive from the organisation.

The organisation may have set ways in which it wants its employees to deal with customers. These set ways are known as procedures and the employees have to be made aware of these when they start their job. Sometimes organisations issue booklets to all employees and these contain the procedures for dealing with customers. The procedures will be about all aspects of customer care.

If all employees are working with a good knowledge of these procedures, then they will all be doing the same thing. This will help to make sure that the customers are being treated in the same way by all members of staff. It will help the organisation to give all existing customers, and those who might become customers, a more professional and efficient image of the facility. If a business is to provide an efficient and effective customer service, the trained and experienced staff will have to carry out a variety of tasks to a high standard.

Customer service is all about effectiveness, efficiency and reliability. Often an organisation will make a commitment to its customers by producing a charter. This makes promises about the standard of service a customer can expect from the organisation. Anyone helping an organisation to provide a good customer service would carry out the following jobs on a regular basis.

- providing information, assistance and advice to customers

- receiving and passing on messages from customers

- keeping accurate and up-to-date customer records

- dealing with customer complaints.

Many businesses have customer service departments that routinely contact customers who have made purchases and ask them how the product has performed and whether they are happy. Sometimes businesses may make a telephone call to do this. Alternatively, they may email the customer or send them a questionnaire by post. By finding out customers' views and whether or not they are satisfied, a business may be able to avoid mistakes or problems in the future.

An organisation that is concerned with improving its customer service will carefully check all the complaints it receives. It will want to know how often different customers complain about the same thing. If it finds that complaints about the same subject are occurring regularly, it will attempt to improve the situation. Often there will be a special form that customers need to complete. Reading these forms will help the organisation's managers to decide whether the service can be improved or whether extra services can be added to help the customer remain satisfied.

If part of your job involves handling complaints from customers, you should remember to:

- listen carefully to what the customer is saying

- apologise for the inconvenience they have been caused

- let them know that the matter will be investigated
- let them know that the organisation wants the matter to be put right
- let them know that you understand and can see the problem from their point of view
- keep calm and never argue with the customer
- try to find a solution to their problem while they are there with you. If this is not possible, promise them that you will come back to them with a solution
- ask the right questions to make sure you have got all the information you need
- agree the solution with the customer
- make sure that what you promised to do for the customer actually gets done.

Gathering information

How do you establish the needs and expectations of customers? Is there a set procedure that allows them to specify their needs and expectations? Does your organisation have a minimum set of standards which lays out what they can expect in terms of service?

3.2 Explain why customer service must meet or exceed customer expectations

Meeting or exceeding customer expectations is crucial to the success of any organisation. Many organisations do not even know what their customers expect from them. Understanding their expectations can be vital:

- a fast and efficient service
- quality products and services at competitive prices
- well-trained staff
- being treated with politeness and respect
- answering the phone promptly and professionally
- responding to other communications within a reasonable timescale
- keeping promises
- having a clear and fair complaints procedure.

Poor customer service is a bad news story that can travel very fast as customers tell others about their experiences and dissuade others from having anything to do with the organisation. Good customer service does pay in the longer term – not only are existing customers satisfied with the service, but they will tell others about the good experience that they have had with the organisation.

Prompt attention and a quick response to customers are important in an organisation. The necessity to greet visitors politely, promptly and courteously helps to give the right impression and the same applies when dealing with telephone calls. Some organisations have a policy of answering the telephone after only three rings and guaranteeing the customer that their request will be dealt with in a certain amount of time. Organisations have realised that prompt response is possibly one factor in a customer's decision to purchase something from them. This reputation of efficiency may well then be passed on to business contacts, friends and relatives.

Regular customers are vital to any organisation. A great deal of hard work, not to mention advertising and other costs, have been incurred in making a buyer a regular customer. It is, therefore, essential to build and maintain good relationships. Try to remember the following when you are greeting a visitor to your organisation, or talking to them on the telephone:

- Introduce yourself.

- Try to use the customer's name during the conversation.

- Try to remember something about the customer, their business or their family.

- Tell customers the truth.

- Inform regular customers about special offers.

- Inform regular customers about any changes to products or services (for example, if an item they regularly buy is about to go out of stock).

Providing high-quality internal customer service begins by setting clear guidelines about what external customers can reasonably expect. In some cases, an organisation will set up service level agreements (SLAs). This is particularly true of larger organisations (especially those in the public sector). They will define exactly what to expect in terms of customer service. Even without these SLAs internal customer service can exceed the expectations of the customer if the levels of expectation have been set out in advance. There will always be problems with levels of service, but this can be avoided. An external customer should always try to define exactly what they are expecting (in regard to timeline and quality, for instance). Any last-minute requests could be problematic and unreasonable requests need to be dealt with on a case-by-case basis. The customer needs to be realistic about their demands and not expect the unachievable.

- In order to meet expectations, the organisation needs to clarify what is needed from the customer in terms of deadlines, quality and any special requirements. This means cooperation and sufficient lead time as well as providing sufficient information so that the organisation can deliver exactly what is expected. This can often be simply phrased as 'we need to know this from you in order to make sure that we meet your requirements'.

263

● Customers need to understand how their requests will fit into the overall work of the organisation. This will ensure that the customer does not always think that they are the only priority, although the customer will invariably think this and the organisation needs to take this into account. The situation is never helped when the customer insists that their needs are urgent and should have the highest priority. Clear communication between customers and the organisation is essential.

Gathering information

Why is it important to establish the expectations of customers? What policies and procedures are in place to ensure this? Why is it vital to exceed their expectations? What are the benefits to you, the customer and the organisation?

3.3 Explain the value of meeting or exceeding customer expectations and
3.4 Explain the purpose and value of building positive working relationships

Meeting or exceeding the expectations of the customer is vital to the long-term relationship between the customer and the organisation. The customer's expectations and the opportunity to build a positive working relationship will often begin with the way in which you communicate with that customer. Communicating effectively with customers relies on many things, which include:

● dealing with a customer promptly

● the tone or manner in which you deal with the customer

● the messages which you give them

● your non-verbal (body language) signals

● your listening skills

● your ability to understand their body language

● your ability to deal with problems as they arise.

Just as each employee is different, so is each customer, and while there is no foolproof way of dealing with every customer, the following list suggests some of the more usual ways of using your verbal and non-verbal communication skills to the best effect:

● Always approach a customer with either a smile or a greeting, depending on whether it is face-to-face or on the telephone.

● Try to build a good relationship with a customer from the beginning, either by looking at their body language or listening to them.

- Make sure you have listened and remembered what they have said.
- When you give them information, be confident and accurate.
- Do not make promises which you cannot keep.
- Be aware that the customer is sizing you up by your voice and body language.
- Find out what the customer actually wants rather than assuming you already know what they want.
- If you need to take more time than usual in dealing with a customer, this is acceptable as the customer needs to be satisfied.

Body language can send various messages to the customer. To repeat some of what we have already said, you should always remember the following:

- Turn your whole body towards the customer and not just your head when you are speaking to them. This shows you are interested in what they are saying.
- Do not stand too close to a customer as they may feel intimidated.
- Make eye contact with the customer – it shows that you are interested and honest.
- Do not show signs that you are frustrated or bored, by fiddling with a pen or tapping your feet.

Figure 329.2

- If you are standing or sitting up straight, it shows that you are confident.

- Nod your head at appropriate points when the customer is talking to show that you are concentrating on what they are saying.

Building positive working relationships with customers is all part of customer service, or customer relations. Organisations have always known that a high-quality customer service means that customers will inevitably come back to them for future purchases. There is a saying that suggests that 80 per cent of all of a business's profits come from its most loyal 20 per cent of customers. In effect, a business is always interested in customers who can provide them with the greatest level of profit.

Customer needs and expectations are constantly changing. Awareness of new technology, consumer legislation and what competitors have to offer creates new demands. It is vital for a business to be able to constantly improve its range of products and services and the ways they are supported and sold in order to satisfy customer needs and wants.

Customer needs include reliable products and services that they can trust, at the price they want to pay and for these to be available when and where they want them. These are the basic customer demands, but they require far more and the business needs to be aware of this. Customer expectations revolve around what is known as customer satisfaction. This means that the business needs to be aware of a customer's needs and expectations and provide products and services in such a way as to meet these demands.

Gathering information

Have you made a positive effort to try to establish a good working relationship with customers? How difficult has this been? What has been their response? Are they cooperative? What are their views about you and the service that you provide to them?

4. Understand the purpose of quality standards and timescales for customer service to external customers

4.1 Identify quality standards for own organisation and work and
4.2 Explain the value of agreeing quality standards and timescales

Setting quality standards means ensuring that products, services and delivery meet defined requirements. Quality is also about customer satisfaction, which means meeting customers' expectations. Quality standards are a key feature of all successful organisations. Many of the quality initiatives came from Japan and over time they have become recognised standards. The approaches outlined in Table 329.1 are all valuable ways of setting quality standards.

Table 329.1

Quality standard	Explanation
ISO 9000/9001/9004	Based on nine principles: • customer focus • leadership • involvement of people • process approach • system approach to management • continuous improvement • factual approach to decision making • mutually beneficial • supplier relationships. The whole delivery service is documented to ensure that the quality of products and services meets the needs of the customer and that all aspects of the delivery conform to predetermined standards.
The European Foundation for Quality Management's Excellence Model, European Quality Award and RADAR Model	The Excellence Model is particularly useful as it covers: • self-assessment • benchmarking with other organisations • identifying areas for improvement • common vocabulary and ways of thinking.
Total Quality Management (TQM)	A widely used approach to improve quality, which includes: • encouraging continuous and sustained improvement of all processes and systems • encouraging a comprehensive, consistent, integrated, organisation-wide approach which includes all activities • being customer-focused, to meet customers' expressed and implied requirements.
Five S	A Japanese approach which focuses on high efficiency: • Seiri or organisation – focusing on necessary activities only • Seiton or neatness – quickly finding what you need to do a task • Seiso or cleanliness – clear desks • Seiketsu or standardisation – having straightforward systems • Shitsuke or discipline – having good habits at work.

4.3 Explain how to set and meet quality standards and timescales with external customers

Setting customer service quality standards and ensuring that timescales are adhered to requires you to consider all aspects of the interactions you have with customers. This means establishing a series of promises or minimum standards that you undertake to follow. Typically, this will mean looking at the following areas and making a statement of your minimum standards (or sets of promises). It is important to remember that every organisation has different sets of standards and these may have been developed over a period of time to reflect the nature of the organisation itself.

General standards:

- Anticipate the needs of customers by identifying expectations and working towards meeting those needs.
- Exceed expectations of all customer groups.
- Hold yourself accountable for service commitments.
- Be aware of communication style and communicate professionally.
- Be sensitive to eye contact and tone of voice.
- Turn off mobile phones during meetings.

General customer commitments:

- Listen to customer requests and take immediate action to assist them.
- Keep customers informed of any delays.
- Greet all customers in a professional and courteous manner.
- Inform customers what to expect and normal delivery times.
- Respond to requests and questions by the end of the business day.
- End all interactions with customers in a professional and courteous manner.

Telephone etiquette:

- Answer the phone within three rings.
- Identify yourself when answering the phone.

- Listen to callers' requests and help to answer questions or resolve issues.
- Ask for the caller's permission before putting them on hold.
- Offer to take a message if someone is not available to speak to them.

Voice mail etiquette:

- Update voice mail greeting when out of the office.
- Inform callers of anticipated return and contact person for questions.
- Respond to all voice mail messages by the end of the business day.

Email etiquette:

- Update email 'out-of-office' notification when out of the office.
- Give name of contact person and expected return date.
- Respond to emails before the end of the business day.

Gathering information

How would you go about setting and meeting quality standards and timescales for your customers? Do you have a set of procedures, promises or a charter? Where would you begin if you do not have one? Who would need to be involved in creating one?

5. Understand how to deal with customer service problems for external customers

5.1 Describe the types of problems that external customers may have

There are a number of reasons why problems can occur with external customers, most of which arise when communication fails to be effective. Some of them will not be obvious until a problem occurs. Some of the problems are avoidable if the communication methods are thought through properly. In other cases the problem will remain until something dramatic is done to improve it. Barriers to communication mean problems between the sender and the receiver of the information; in other words, a block of some sort exists which stops the message getting through or stops it getting through in the intended way. Some common barriers to communication are as follows:

- Lack of training – if employees are not trained to use the different ways of communicating then they will either make mistakes or not be able to use that form of communication at all. Training in the use of equipment and the ways in which communications should be written or spoken is essential. These forms of training and ways of doing things will often be part of organisational procedures.

- Lack of information – one of the most common barriers to communication is not having all the information that you need to make a decision or to help someone make a decision. If, for example, a customer called a business and asked for the price and availability of a product and was told that it was out of stock, a sale would be lost. If the employee who had taken the call had known that the warehouse had just received a delivery of that product, then the sale would have been made.

- Personal relationships – one of the most common reasons why communications are ineffective within an organisation is that individuals either do not like one another or do not understand one another. Personal likes or dislikes may mean that employees will avoid one another, even if this means that information is not passed on between them and has a bad effect on both their own work and the business itself. This is a very difficult barrier to deal with, but may be solved by either getting to the root of the problem between the two individuals or changing the job role of one of them so that they do not have direct contact so often. An alternative to this is for the business to attempt to help them to get along better by giving them some team-building training.

- Faulty systems –there may be a problem with the organisational procedures and something in the process has been forgotten which causes a barrier. Perhaps one part of the whole process of dealing with an order has not been considered and this causes a blockage in the customer receiving the product or service.

Barriers to good communication with customers might include:

- writing something down incorrectly

- not hearing the customer's request correctly

- losing important notes or documents

- not telling the right person about a problem

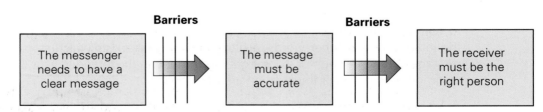

Figure 329.3

- having too many other things to do
- not realising the importance of the query.

The most typical reasons for problems and complaints are:

- broken promises
- missed deadlines
- poor quality products or services
- lack of communication
- rudeness and unreasonable behaviour.

First, it is important to know the difference between problems that you can deal with yourself and those that you need to refer to others. You may face anger. The customer may not necessarily be angry with you but complaining about the product or service provided. Whoever is dealing with the problem is simply a representative and has now become the frontline individual responsible for solving the problem. The main priority is to listen and then decide on a course of action.

When there is a problem or complaint you should:

- let the customer have their say and take notes
- ask questions in order to clarify points
- summarise the problem
- tell them what you propose to do
- give them a timescale
- promise and follow through with the promise that you will keep them informed.

Many organisations will have established complaints policies and procedures, which will probably incorporate the majority of the points. But they may be more detailed. It is vital that you keep track of problems; this will ensure that each problem is dealt with in the correct manner, but it will also highlight other issues. If there are recurring problems or complaints about particular products or services then the quality of these will need to be examined in more detail. There may well be an underlying problem.

Complaints usually fall into three distinct categories:

1 Quality issues – the actual quality of the product or service that was expected by the customer is not up to the standard that they anticipated or were promised.

2 Organisational issues – these are usually failures in processes and procedures. Something has simply been forgotten, missed out or ignored, which should normally be part of the internal customer service process.

3 Personnel issues – these are problems with specific individuals, such as a service provider showing lack of commitment, rudeness, arrogance or failing to communicate with the internal customer.

It is valuable to keep details of problems or complaints that you deal with. These can be straightforward logs using basic headings, including:

- date
- complainant
- details of the problem or complaint
- action taken and by whom
- costs involved in resolving the problem.

Gathering information

What are the most typical problems you have to deal with from external customers? How common are the problems? Are there established ways of dealing with them, such as an organisational policy?

5.2 Explain the consequences of not meeting external customer needs and expectations

The most important consequence of not meeting a customer's needs and expectations is that the customer will not be satisfied. They may not necessarily complain to the organisation, but it is certain that they will complain to others and pass on the information. They will also be less likely to be a customer in the future.

It is rare to receive any thanks from customers, but sometimes you may be surprised that they will show their satisfaction about the service they have received. In order to make sure that customers are satisfied with the service they have received, you should:

- make sure that you agree what you have offered to provide in the first place
- ensure that whatever you have offered meets with their approval and needs
- if possible, do better than their needs and surprise them
- if you have agreed to sort out a problem by a particular date, or deliver something by a particular time, ensure that this is done and they are not disappointed
- ensure that the quality of what you give the customer would be acceptable to you at the very least.

It is very important to ensure that any dealings, particularly complaints or problems, are recorded and reported. Many businesses have forms which are specifically designed to provide employees with an opportunity to briefly summarise the situation and to enter onto that form, when appropriate, actions which have been taken in order to deal with the customer's requirement. In this way a form, which not only summarises the situation, confirms that the requirements have been met and notes any decisions which have been made relating to the meeting of those requirements.

Gathering information

How do you monitor customer satisfaction or otherwise? What are the first steps that need to be taken if there is a problem with customer service? Is there a procedure to follow?

5.3 Explain ways of dealing with external customer services problems and
5.4 Explain the purpose and value of a complaints procedure

Many businesses actually consider that customer complaints and problems are useful as they alert the business to potential difficulties which they have not considered. In dealing with particular complaints or difficulties the business is able to change or amend its policies or procedures and, perhaps, improve its products or services. This helps the business and helps ensure that customers do not encounter these difficulties in the future.

Written records will be stored by staff who are specifically dealing with customer service issues and may require the different departments which have contact with customers, and have dealt with complaints, to forward records of the problem to them for analysis.

As with any record, it is important that all of the details of the customer complaint or problem are accurate. In many businesses, although you may receive the customer complaint, perhaps face to face or on the telephone, you will not be the individual dealing with the customer's difficulty. In order to give the individual who is dealing with the complaint the best opportunity to deal with it efficiently and effectively, they need to have all the correct information. It would not project a very good image of either yourself or the business as a whole if vital customer details or information about the nature of the complaint were incorrect.

Figure 329.4

Unless you can deal with a customer difficulty immediately, you will need to refer back to the customer and contact them at a later date. You should promise to keep the customer informed and you may be able to obtain guidance on the procedures involved in contacting customers related to your own business's policies.

You should always ensure that if you have promised to contact the customer, this is done when it has been promised. The customer should not have to continually pester you to keep them informed.

Many businesses now use computer software to enter customer queries and complaints. The system alerts the user that update contact should be made at specific times, in line with the organisation's procedures.

For many organisations the complaints can be resolved either informally or formally. Informal resolution can be achieved by swift action by the service provider, which should be to the satisfaction of the customer. Formal complaints may need to be referred to more senior management and may have to be put in writing.

The main purpose of a complaints procedure is to ensure that all complaints are dealt with in a fast and efficient manner. It also acts as a guarantee that all complaints are treated seriously, that the organisation acts in a courteous and professional manner, and that anyone who does complain is given sympathy and understanding. Complaints procedures also act as a means by which the organisation can learn from its mistakes.

Ideally, a complaints procedure should have the following features:

- a definition of what constitutes a complaint
- confirmation of who is assigned to deal with complaints and how they are passed on to them
- confirmation that complaints will not be handled solely by the individual against whom the complaint was made
- a summary of key steps to investigate the complaint
- confirmation that the response to complaints will fall in line with agreed rules and deadlines
- whether a written acknowledgement will be given
- when any final response must be completed
- outline procedures for logging complaints by date, nature and name
- confirmation about who the complaint handler needs to report the complaint to internally
- how recommendations for revised working practices can be made.

A complaints procedure should:

- focus on putting matters right whenever possible
- ensure that anyone involved in the problem is made aware of it at the earliest possible stage
- identify lessons that can be learned from the situation to avoid the same problem or issue in the future
- ensure the issuing of an apology, if appropriate to the situation.

The complaints procedure should always ensure:

- proper handling of complaints
- that complaints are acknowledged within a reasonable time
- an invitation to confirm an oral complaint in writing
- that complaints will be dealt with by individuals with sufficient experience
- that any appropriate remedial action will be taken immediately
- that where complaints are not dealt with in a prompt way they can be referred to more senior members of staff.

Gathering information

Does your organisation have a complaints procedure that is applied to customer service problems? If so, how effective is the complaints procedure? If your organisation does not have a complaints procedure, what would be the value in creating one?

■ 6. Understand how to monitor and evaluate external customer service and the benefits of this

6.1 Explain the purpose and benefits of monitoring external customer satisfaction and how to do so and
6.2 Describe techniques for collecting and evaluating external customer feedback

Many organisations set up their customer service provision as a direct result of experiences they have had with customers. They can only base their systems on what they know and cater for the most common problems that customers may present to them. They also need to make sure that the customer service provision not only maintains its high standards but also is adaptable and can be improved on a number of different levels as and when required.

The first aspect in ensuring that customer service remains efficient and effective is to set up monitoring systems. The purpose of the monitoring systems is to pick up problems, as well as customer perceptions of the customer service provision. The first and perhaps least efficient way of doing this is to rely on informal customer feedback. This means taking note of comments that customers make in relation to the customer service they receive. This is not a terribly good way of obtaining objective information about the customer service, as only the most vocal customers will make comment.

A more structured way of collecting information is the use of customer questionnaires and comment cards. These are now widely used and certain customer service questions are even included on guarantees and warranties. They will ask customers various questions concerning customer services, such as the politeness of staff, their helpfulness and whether a situation was resolved to their satisfaction. The only problem with these types of questionnaires and comment cards is the number of them completed by customers. They will also need to be looked at in some detail and the results collated to be of any particular use to the business.

Staff can also provide useful feedback for monitoring and evaluating customer service. They can identify problem areas and most common complaints from customers. If taken together with customer feedback, questionnaires or comment cards, this can provide a good indication of how the customer service provision is working in practice.

Some businesses use 'mystery customers'. These are individuals unknown to the business and its employees. They will test the customer service provision by pretending to be a customer with a specific customer service problem. They will provide a report on how they were treated and whether they were satisfied with the level of help they received. This can prove to be a useful double check for the business, particularly if it has just changed the way in which it carries out customer services.

The final way of monitoring and evaluating customer service is to examine the number and nature of complaints or compliments received, either verbally or in writing from customers. Many businesses pin up their compliment letters, but are at pains to hide those that contain complaints.

The complaints or compliments will probably contain detailed information about the transaction and use of customer service. How these were responded to can provide the business with useful case study material with which to train its staff.

There are several different ways in which a business can evaluate its customer service provision. These are in addition to the regular feedback, comments and other information gained from actually carrying out customer service. A business would evaluate its customer service using some of the following methods:

- Level of sales – a steady or increasing level of sales would indicate that customers are happy overall with the customer service they are receiving from the business. Businesses would also take account of the number of products that have been returned faulty compared with the number of those products sold.

- Repeat customers – as we have already seen in this unit, repeat customers are of enormous importance to a business. Loyal customers provide the bulk of the profits for the business and keeping these customers increases not only sales but also profitability.

- New customers – there are a number of ways in which new customers could come to the organisation. Perhaps they are responding to advertising, but many purchase from the business for the first time as a result of recommendations. Once these customers have made their first purchase the business will want to ensure that they become repeat customers.

- Level of complaints/compliments – businesses want to minimise the number of complaints while increasing the number of compliments. It is rare for businesses to receive many written complaints or compliments, so for the most part these are not a great way of evaluating customer service.

- Staff turnover – experienced and reliable staff are of great importance to any business. Continued problems with customers can force employees to look for work elsewhere. Employees become tired and frustrated if they are constantly dealing with complaints and problems from customers.

By continually monitoring and evaluating customer service, a business will hope to make steady improvements. A business will try to ensure that its levels of service, products and services remain good value for money and that its overall package provides a reliable service to its customers. If it can achieve this then there are a number of key improvements that can be made to the business overall:

- By improving customer service it will retain existing customers.

- By improving customer service it will retain its experienced and most valued members of staff.

- As its customer service excellence becomes known it will attract new customers.

- This means that the business will sell more products and services, increasing its turnover.

- The result of this is that the business will probably become more profitable and will almost certainly employ more staff.

- If the business is doing well then it will be able to quickly respond to its legal obligations and exceed the requirements of law.

- Finally, as the numbers of customers increase, staff increases and turnover increases, profitability increases and so the opportunity to continually improve is higher.

6.3 Explain the benefits of continuous improvement

Research shows that a 5 per cent increase in customer loyalty can boost profits by 25–85 per cent. Research has also revealed satisfied clients lead to greater profitability and growth. To excel in today's competitive marketplace, organisations must create positive experiences for customers with each and every interaction.

There is a general acceptance in today's business environment that customer service and customer satisfaction are key elements for success. Customers are promised great service by advertising campaigns, so expectations are high. Customer satisfaction has many key advantages, both to the business and to the customers. If a business can establish a reputation for high levels of customer service then it can hope to ensure that customers are not merely satisfied but delighted and amazed at the level of service they receive from the business.

A business will always strive to exceed its customers' expectations of it, such as having a no-quibble refund policy (such as Marks and Spencer) or trying to source Fairtrade products from developing countries as standard (such as the Co-Op).

Although providing high levels of customer service is important, it is always expensive. Employees have to be taken on to carry out roles in customer service and are not actively selling products and services (although they may indirectly if the customer is pleased with the way they have been treated). This all adds costs to the business at a time when customers are demanding ever increasing value for money.

The FAIRTRADE Certification Mark appears on products to show that the producers have received a fair and stable price for their crops

Figure 329.5 The FAIRTRADE Mark

Businesses now realise that they need a major and recognisable reason for not charging the same or less than their competitors. Great customer service can be one of these reasons, but for the most part, customers will tend to buy from an organisation that offers products and services at the lowest possible cost or is at least competitive in terms of price with other suppliers.

As a business builds up its customer base, the hope is that it will begin to achieve a reputation for high-quality products, services, staff and customer service. A business stands and falls on its reputation and the last thing that it wants is to be associated with poor quality service. The worst examples of poor service can be seen on BBC Watchdog, but daily customers have problems with organisations and report them to local Trading Standards (run by the local government to investigate customer complaints). As far as a business is concerned, good news travels fast, but bad news travels faster. They cannot afford for it to be known that they provide poor quality service; if they fail to sort out a problem, then their reputation will suffer.

One of the greatest problems in providing customer service is to measure its effectiveness and gauge the impact it has on the profitability of the business. One of the first things that a business will do when setting up a customer service provision is to establish a series of targets in dealing with customer complaints and problems. For instance, it will have a recommended, maximum waiting time for customers; it may have clear instructions to its staff about the exchange of products or the refund of money paid.

With businesses increasingly using customer loyalty cards or store debit cards, organisations are able to see whether a customer problem has led to a decrease in that customer's spending with the business. This would infer that they were not happy with the customer service. Or the organisation could detect whether the customer was happy with the provision and continued to shop with the business.

Although there is legislation to protect customers from hazards when they visit a business's premises, many businesses in fact take this far further than is legally required. Customers cannot be exposed to dangers and simple hazards, such as slippery floors, fumes, trailing wires and a host of other potential problems, so these are monitored and dealt with by health and safety represent-atives in the business. Above all, customers want a safe and secure shopping environment, and cameras, security staff and special training for shop floor staff are all designed to assist this, in addition to stopping shoplifting and theft.

Businesses want to respond to customer needs. They also want to encourage new customers. It is vital that a business has a good image as far as existing customers and potential customers are concerned. Obviously, though, businesses do not have customer services just for the benefits of their customers – they know that good customer service will benefit them. The first key benefit to good customer service is increased sales. They need to generate enough money to pay their staff (which is obviously a benefit to the employees), buy equipment and stock (which will be a benefit to the business, employees and customers) and make a profit, which will benefit the owners of the organisation.

Another key benefit to an organisation of having effective customer service provision is that customers will be happy. If they are happy they will continue to use the business and buy products and services from it. This is known as repeat business. The organisation wants the customers to keep coming back and to recommend it to their friends and family.

Many businesses spend a huge amount of money on advertising in order to not only tell customers about their products and services but also put across a positive and strong public image. They want customers to believe that their products and services are reliable, are value for money, and are safe, healthy and a host of other features. Every business is in competition with hundreds, thousands, or tens of thousands of other organisations. As we have seen, having a good level of customer service can give the business an advantage over the competition. This means that the business has to build up and then maintain a reputation for having excellent customer service. A business knows that a dissatisfied customer is a lost customer and that that customer, now lost, will tell others of their bad experience.

7. Be able to build positive working relationships with external customers

7.1 Identify external customers,
7.2 Confirm external customer needs in terms of products and services,
7.3 Confirm external customer needs in terms of quality standards and timescales and
7.4 Agree procedures to be followed if external customer needs are not met

Refer to 1.1, 2.1 and 3.1 to 3.4 and then consider the following.

Gathering information

For this learning outcome you will have to begin by identifying your external customers. Are they individuals, groups, other businesses or overseas buyers? What kind of products and services do you provide to them? How do you establish their requirements in terms of quality standards and timescales? Do they specify these or do you tell them what to expect? What procedures are involved if the needs of external customers are not met? How are these problems resolved?

8. Be able to deliver external customer services to agreed quality standards and timescales

8.1 Provide external customer service(s) to agreed quality standards,
8.2 Provide external customer service(s) to agreed timescales and
8.3 Check external customer needs and expectations have been met

Refer to 4.1 to 4.3 and then consider the following.

Gathering information

Is there a written policy with regard to quality standards and timescales in your organisation? If not, how are these agreed at the point at which the external customer makes a request to you? What checks are in place in order to ensure that their needs and expectations have been met? At what point do you check that they have been met? How do you make this check?

9. Be able to deal with customer service problems and complaints for external customers

9.1 Follow procedures, within agreed timescales, to (a) process problems and complaints, (b) resolve problems and complaints, (c) refer problems and complaints, where necessary

Refer to 5.1 to 5.4 and then consider the following.

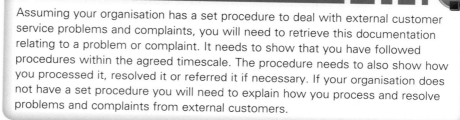

Gathering information

Assuming your organisation has a set procedure to deal with external customer service problems and complaints, you will need to retrieve this documentation relating to a problem or complaint. It needs to show that you have followed procedures within the agreed timescale. The procedure needs to also show how you processed it, resolved it or referred it if necessary. If your organisation does not have a set procedure you will need to explain how you process and resolve problems and complaints from external customers.

10. Be able to monitor and evaluate services to external customers

10.1 Obtain and record external customer feedback,
10.2 Analyse and evaluate external customer feedback and
10.3 Take actions that will lead to improvement in service(s) to external customers

Refer to 6.1 to 6.3 and then consider the following.

Gathering information

This learning outcome focuses on how you collect, record, analyse, evaluate and take action on feedback from external customers. Your organisation may have a procedure in order to do this and you will need to demonstrate that you have followed this process and that it has led to an improvement in external customer service. This learning outcome is more problematic if a process is not in place, as it may require you to request customer feedback and then to analyse, evaluate and act upon it.

What is Evidence ?

A single piece of evidence can cover more than one learning outcome. Several assessment criteria can be dealt with by the one piece of evidence. You can also use the same evidence for other assessment criteria from other units. Your assessor will use a wide range of assessment methods for the learning outcomes in this unit, including:

- observing your performance
- examining work that you have produced
- questioning and discussing issues with you
- using witness testimony from work colleagues
- looking at your learner statements
- recognising your prior learning.

The range of evidence can include:

- annotated procedures relating to customer service
- records of complaints
- customer complaints log
- records of communication with customers/colleagues/suppliers
- communications relating to complaints/problems referred to others
- written notes in response to complaints dealt with
- monitoring records
- customer feedback questionnaires
- external customer feedback logs/surveys
- customer Happy Calls log
- suggestions
- minutes of one-to-one meetings
- evaluation of provision of customer service to external customers
- evaluation reports
- development plans.

Index